# The State
## against the Peasantry

# The State against the Peasantry

## RURAL STRUGGLES IN COLONIAL AND POSTCOLONIAL MOZAMBIQUE

Merle L. Bowen

**University Press of Virginia**

Charlottesville and London

The University Press of Virginia
© 2000 by the Rector and Visitors of the University of Virginia
Printed in the United States of America
*First published in 2000*

Frontispiece: Mozambican peasant woman in front of the CAIL state farm
machinery park in Chokwe, Gaza Province, 1987

♾ The paper used in this publication meets the minimum requirements of the
American National Standard for Information Sciences—Permanence of Paper
for Printed Library Materials, ANSI Z39.48-1984.

Library of Congress Cataloging-in-Publication Data

Bowen, Merle L., 1953–
   The state against the peasantry : rural struggles in colonial and
postcolonial Mozambique / Merle L. Bowen.
      p.     cm.
   Includes bibliographical references (p.     ) and index.
   ISBN  0-8139-1910-X (alk. paper). — ISBN 0-8139-1917-7 (pbk.)
   1. Peasantry—Government policy—Mozambique.  I. Title.
HD1538.M6B69 2000
305.5'633'09679—dc21                                        99-40175
                                                                 CIP

To Firmino and Tahar
and in memory of my parents
Balbina Emilia Reno and James Charles Bowen

# Contents

# Illustrations

## Maps

## Tables

# Acknowledgments

**A**n incredibly diverse group of people in Mozambique, Portugal, Canada, and the United States assisted and encouraged me in a variety of ways throughout this project. To all I express my deepest gratitude. I regret that because of the war in Mozambique many did not live to see the final product.

I would first like to thank the Mozambicans who so willingly shared with me their knowledge and insights. This book records some of the turbulent transitions through which they have lived—I hope that it expresses their concerns, and that they will recognize in it their voices. On Ilha Josina Machel, I would have accomplished little without the contributions of the late Josef Tlemo and Jacinto Alexandre Cossa, my interpreters, colleagues, and friends. But above all, I owe thanks to the peasant cooperative members and farmers who shared their understanding of their history with me. Although I cannot list them individually, I have tried to relate their accounts as accurately as possible. Among those interviewed whose assistance was particularly helpful were Albino Bila, José Binto, Rita Chauque, Fernando Chavango, the late Fernando Cossa, Cecilia Fulana, Carlos Majonane, Talita Mucavete, the late Pedro Novela, the late Jeremias Nguenha, Lucia Nuvunga, João Nwendzana, the late Sebastião Sitoe, Vasco Juma Sumbana, the late Joaquim Tembe and the late Eduardo Timana. I am indebted to all of them. My research was facilitated by fellow workers of Project CO-1, especially João de Azevedo, Américo Manhiça, Camilo Mortágua and the late Angelo Raul. I would especially like to thank the technicians of the Ilha Josina brigade: Alberto Azarias, Domingo Ceia, Alípio de Freitas, Domingo Guambe, Elias Mula, Ricardo Pedro and Mussá Rachyd. I learned a great deal from them about animal husbandry and agricultural management systems.

In Chokwe, many others were helpful as well. I can name only a few, but I hope others will find here an expression of my gratitude. My work was made possible by the support I received from the then head of the agricultural set-up in the area, João Mosca and his staff, notably Ernesto Maússe and Francisco

Tivane. Especially important were those who worked with me for varying lengths of time. Silva Baloi, Pedro Bambo, the late Dinis Chivurre, Eugenio Cossa, and Ruth Muchanga introduced me to the community. They persevered through much of the work. I shared many enjoyable and enlightening conversations with Cristina Amaral, Maya de Bragança, Maria do Carmo Carrilho, and Kenneth Hermele.

I owe special thanks to the Government of Mozambique for allowing me to carry out research there. João Carrilho, Alfredo Gamito, Sergio Vieira, and Paulo Zucula made my visits not only possible, but also productive. The faculty and staff of the Centro de Estudos Africanos (CEA) at the Universidade Eduardo Mondlane offered a great deal of assistance. Kurt Habermeier, Judith Head, Helena Dolny, Alpheus Manghezi, and Bridget O'Laughlin reaffirmed the project's importance. Their interest in my work and personal friendship often sustained me through the difficult periods. Both the late Aquino de Bragança, the director, and the late Ruth First, the director of research, were extremely helpful in the initial stages of the project and also allowed me the use of many facilities of the CEA. Maria Inês Nogueira da Costa, the director of the Arquivo Histórico de Moçambique and her staff helped me to locate some valuable materials from the colonial period.

Research in Mozambique would have been impossible without the hospitality and intellectual stimulation that I received from Hans Abrahamsson, Sam Barnes, Carlos Cardoso, Julie Cliff, Paul Fauvet, Polly Gaster, Joseph Hanlon, Susanne Hedman, Fernando Lima, Judith Marshall, and Kok Nam. I was extremely lucky to have Denise Khoury, Don Kossick, Linzi Manicom, Colin McCord, Susan McCord, George Povey, the late Rebecca Reiss, Patricia Saul, and Heather Spears in Maputo. They always ensured that my short visits from the countryside to the city were enjoyable and comfortable. I also would like to thank my extended family in Mozambique. In particular the late Suzana de Sousa Pinto offered her home to me and made my stay as relaxed as possible under very difficult circumstances. Her son, Paulo, has been a part of this project from Maputo to Champaign.

In Portugal, Isaú Santos, the director of the Arquivo Histórico Ultramarino, Alexandre Marques Pereira, the archivist at the library of the Sociedade de Geografia de Lisboa, and their respective staffs assured that I had access to materials in their collections. I also extend my thanks to Eduardo de Sousa Ferreira, the director of CEDEP at the Instituto Superior de Economia, and the faculty who were friendly and helpful.

Numerous other people have offered assistance over the years. At the University of Toronto, the comments and advice of Professors Jonathan Barker, Ian Parker, Richard Sandbrook, and John Saul have been very helpful. I thank

Jonathan Barker particularly for stimulating my interest in agrarian politics, for his enthusiastic support during the fieldwork, and for astute comments on early drafts of the manuscript. For their suggestions and comments on later versions of the manuscript I am grateful to Kenneth Coleman, Kandioura Dramé, Jonathan Hartlyn, Timothy McKeown, Catharine Newbury, David Newbury, Julius Nyang'oro, and the late Otto Roesch. Jacques Depelchin, John Higginson, Mahmood Mamdani, William Martin, William Minter, and Michael West read the entire book and offered particularly valuable advice. I also wish to thank Allen Isaacman, Edmond Keller, Michael Lofchie, and Richard Sklar for their interest in this study and my work. Joye Bowman and I have helped one another negotiate the trials and tribulations of graduate school, fieldwork, manuscripts, teaching careers, and family life for twenty years. I could not ask for a better friend.

I received financial support for this study from a number of sources. Archival research and fieldwork were funded by grants from the Social Sciences and Humanities Research Council of Canada, the Fundação Calouste Gulbenkian in Portugal, and the John D. and Catherine T. MacArthur Foundation. Supplementary support came from the Campus Research Board, the Center for African Studies, the International Programs and Studies, and the Office of the Vice Chancellor for Academic Affairs at the University of Illinois at Urbana-Champaign (UIUC). Assistance for writing and additional library research was provided by postdoctoral fellowships from the Frederick Douglass Institute for African and African American Studies at the University of Rochester and the University of North Carolina at Chapel Hill, as well as by the Center for Advanced Study at UIUC. I am grateful to all these institutions for their support; the opinions and interpretations expressed here, of course, are my own.

Richard Holway, the editor of History and Social Sciences at the University Press of Virginia, has given excellent editorial guidance, bringing the book to publication with patience and adeptness. Patricia H. Neumann of the Department of Geography, University of North Carolina at Chapel Hill, skillfully drew the maps. All uncredited photographs are from my personal collection.

My immediate family has provided support and understanding over the long haul. I thank my parents, the late Balbina Emilia Reno and the late James Charles Bowen for encouraging me to believe in myself and to continue my education. My sister, Heather Lord, has always been there for me. I especially thank my husband, Firmino da Mata de Sousa Pinto, who never let me forget that this study needed to be written. Both he and our son, Tahar, gracefully tolerated the long absences it required. It is to Firmino, Tahar, and my parents that I affectionately dedicate this book.

# Abbreviations

| | |
|---|---|
| ANC | African National Congress |
| ASDI | Swedish International Development Agency |
| CADECO | Centro de Apoio ao Desenvolvimento Cooperativo (Projecto CO-1) |
| CAIL | Complexo Agro-Industrial do Limpopo |
| CIM | Companhia Industrial da Matola |
| CRED | Centro Regional de Experimentação e Desenvolvimento (Projecto CO-2) |
| DDA | Direcção Distrital da Agricultura |
| DINECA | Direcção Nacional de Economia e Comercialização Agrária |
| DINOPROC | Direcção Nacional da Organização da Produção Colectiva |
| DNDR | Direcção Nacional de Desenvolvimento Rural |
| DNEA | Direcção Nacional de Educação de Adultos |
| DNH | Direcção Nacional de Habitação |
| DPA | Direcção Provincial de Agricultura |
| EC | Equipe Central |
| FAO | Food and Agriculture Organization |
| Frelimo | Frente de Libertação de Moçambique |
| GAPECOM | Empresa de Comercialização de Gado e Peles |
| GDs | Grupos Dinamizadores |
| GEs | Grupos Especiais |
| GODCA | Gabinete de Organização e Desenvolvimento das Cooperativas Agrárias |
| IAM | Instituto de Algodão de Moçambique |
| ICM | Instituto dos Cereais de Moçambique |
| IFAD | International Fund for Agricultural Development |
| IMF | International Monetary Fund |
| INC | Instituto Nacional do Cinema |
| INIA | Instituto Nacional de Investigação Agronómica |
| JEAC | Junta de Exportação de Algodão Colonial |
| JEC | Junta de Exportação dos Cereais |
| JVCs | Joint Venture Companies |

| | |
|---|---|
| Lomaco | Lonhro Mozambique Agro-Industrial Company |
| MA | Ministério da Agricultura |
| MANU | Makonde African National Union |
| MAP | Ministério da Agricultura e Pescas |
| Mecanagro | National company of agricultural machinery |
| MONAP | Mozambique Nordic Agricultural Program |
| NGOs | Non-government Organizations |
| OJM | Organização da Juventude Moçambicana |
| OMM | Organização das Mulheres Moçambicanas |
| PEC | Plano Estatal Central |
| PIDE | Polícia Internacional e de Defesa do Estado |
| PPI | Plano Prospectivo Indicativo |
| PRE | Programa de Reabilitação Económica |
| PRES | Programa de Reabilitação Económica e Social |
| Projecto CO-1 | Projecto de Apoio ao Desenvolvimento Cooperativo |
| Projecto CRED | Projecto de Apoio ao Centro Regional de Experimentação e Desenvolvimento |
| Renamo | Resistência Nacional Moçambicana |
| RTI | Regulamento do Trabalho dos Indígenas |
| SADCC | Southern African Development Coordination Conference |
| SERLI | Secretaria de Estado para a Região Limpopo-Incomati |
| SODAN | Sociedade de Desenvolvimento Algodoeiro de Namialo |
| UDENAMO | União Democrática Nacional de Moçambique |
| UN | United Nations |
| UNAMI | União Africana de Moçambique Independente |
| UNCTAD | United Nations Conference on Trade and Development |
| UNDP | United Nations Development Program |
| WENELA | Witwatersrand Native Labour Association |
| WFLC | World Federation of Lutheran Churches |
| WFP | World Food Program |
| ZANU | Zimbabwe African National Union |

# The State
# against the Peasantry

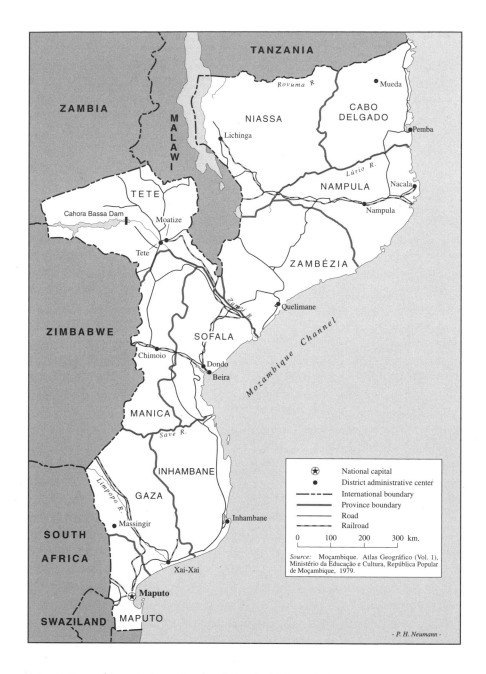

Map 1. Mozambique: International and Provincial Boundaries

# Introduction

In 1975, the Front for the Liberation of Mozambique (Frelimo) led the country to independence after a ten-year guerrilla war against Portuguese colonial rule. Peasants had been critical to its success; without them it is unlikely that the liberation movement could have overthrown Portuguese colonialism. This peasantry included poor peasants, who objected to colonial forced labor and forced cultivation practices, and middle peasants, who resented the privileges conferred upon the European settlers. Yet once in power Frelimo evolved from a popular and victorious liberation movement into a bureaucratic, antipeasant, one-party state. Despite regime changes both the colonial and postcolonial Mozambican state pursued policies inimical to the peasantry. While their reasons were different, the results were the same: increased peasant dissatisfaction and alienation from the state. Although focused on Mozambique, this book has wider significance to the study of the changing relations between the state and the peasantry in Africa.

The agendas of the colonial and postcolonial Mozambican state were varied. In the colonial period, the Portuguese government supported European settler farms and foreign-owned plantations to the detriment of African agriculture. For the poor peasants the colonial objective was to prevent them from making an independent livelihood from agriculture. Poor peasants were small-scale farmers who generally did not own plows and oxen, relied on family labor to work their half- to two-hectare landholdings, and consumed most of their agricultural production. Middle peasants were rural producers with three to twenty hectares who owned plows and oxen, relied on family labor and sometimes hired seasonal workers, and regularly marketed a small proportion of their crops; the colonial state wanted to regulate their capital accumulation. As in other African settler colonies, the Portuguese wanted to control the development of an African agrarian capitalist class that would compete with settler farms and plantations for land and labor. In this context, the colonial state's

1

concession to European farmers and plantation owners was to provide them with subsidies and ensure that they had a sufficient labor supply.

In spite of Portugal's commitment to European agriculture, the colonial state also promoted an indigenous class of capitalist farmers. Beginning in the late 1940s with cotton production, Portugal was forced to make concessions in Mozambique, fostering a process of commodification and differentiation among African producers. The reasons for shifts in state policy were both economic and political, ranging from the declining competitiveness of colonial exports to emerging African nationalism. By providing assistance to an upper stratum of peasants, the colonial authorities hoped to contain any popular movement for independence among the rural population. Although it contradicted the "logic" of the racist agenda, this reformist policy, combined with labor migration to South Africa, created a vibrant but controlled economy in many areas, including Ilha Josina Machel, my case study. Nevertheless, in spite of their successes, African producers remained frustrated by discriminatory policies that hindered their opportunities to accumulate capital.

With independence, the Frelimo state neglected peasants because it imagined them to be self-sufficient and believed that rural transformation would be most rapidly effected through the public sector. It also sanctioned policies that were antithetical to peasant farming. By concentrating investment in public-sector enterprises that aimed for an extremely high growth rate, Frelimo's socialist development strategy of rapid accumulation resulted in a shortage of goods in the countryside and unfavorable terms of trade for the peasantry. According to Frelimo, poor peasants were to be wage workers on poorly run state farms or join underfinanced cooperatives. Middle peasants were to renounce their own status by handing over their cattle, plows, tractors, and other resources to cooperatives. In essence, Frelimo's agricultural strategy completely negated what independence meant to the peasantry.

In the early 1980s, the government finally made some concessions to the peasantry. But these concessions came only after the war against the South African–backed rebel group, the Mozambican National Resistance (Renamo), escalated and the economy plummeted. The government offered more assistance to middle peasants and private farmers (i.e., capitalist producers who owned their own means of production, often tractors and other mechanized equipment; employed full-time wage labor to work their large-scale farms; and marketed a significant proportion of their agricultural production). But the changes were not sufficient and came too late. Given its desperate economic situation, Frelimo adopted an International Monetary Fund (IMF)–approved structural adjustment program in 1987. Since then, the Mozambican regime has continued to follow policies antagonistic to peasant farmers in the name of

capitalism and with the approval of international financial capital. It is unlikely that the IMF and the World Bank–dictated policies will, at least in the
short- to medium term, improve the lives of ordinary peasants.

This study focuses on the politics of agricultural change in Mozambique
from 1950 to 1993. It covers national policy and local ramifications over a period of extraordinary change. Agricultural policy turned from colonial intervention and restriction of peasant farming to state control and promotion of
rural socialism and, finally, to open markets and private farming. The colonial
state intervened in all aspects of agricultural production (e.g., distribution of
inputs, credit, transport, marketing facilities, and labor supply) to ensure that
settler farms and plantations were economic successes. The only Mozambican
agricultural producers who received state assistance were: (1) those few *assimilados* who qualified for a specially designed second-class Portuguese citizen-
ship, (2) traditional chiefs and *régulos* who were appointed functionaries of
the colonial administration in rural communities, and (3) wealthier peasants
who owned draft animals, plows, tractors, and other mechanized equipment
and hired seasonal workers. Subsequently, the Frelimo state continued to control agriculture in its efforts to promote socialism in the countryside. It established large state farms and producer cooperatives, set agricultural prices,
dominated the marketing systems and networks, and contained the growth of
private farmers. In the mid-1980s, Frelimo turned from socialist to capitalist
agriculture, allocating land to private investors and liberalizing commercial activity. The impact of these changes at the local level is examined in the context
of disorder and insurrection. Except for the first decade, most of these changes
took place in a context of war—first a war of national liberation and then a
war of destabilization.

Unlike such relatively well-documented countries as Ghana, Kenya, and
Zimbabwe, Mozambique does not have a rich tradition of scholarship to illuminate its policies, programs, and economic trends. Until very recently most of
the Mozambican literature on the state and the peasantry was historical in nature.[1] Furthermore, the early scholarship on the postindependence period emphasized Frelimo's development, internal fissures, and political and ideological
struggles over time.[2] An implicit assumption was that the issues and contradictions pertinent to Frelimo were the same ones that concerned Mozambican
civil society as a whole. Typically the analysis was heavily informed by senior
party and government authorities, and the research method was largely dependent on official speeches and sources. As a result, more attention was given
to the intentions of the central government than to events on the ground and
the interplay of social forces. Most analyses focused directly on the state without examining local politics and their relations to the state, leaving a great need

for empirically grounded studies to strengthen our theoretical understanding of agricultural changes in both Mozambique and the African continent.

The analysis here adopts a local-level perspective. By eliciting peasant view-points—with attention given to participants' gender, class, and age—the study provides a stronger basis on which to evaluate what policy-makers said they were doing and the effects of government action or inaction as well as popular responses. It presents a nuanced analysis of struggles and contradictions within civil society as well as between state and society and examines the often-competing agendas between the central and the local state functionaries, in contrast to the theoretical tendency to treat the state as an all-powerful, mono-lithic structure. It shows, for example, that local state officials frequently ac-commodated peasant interests, even when they conflicted with central state directives.

The colonial and postcolonial Mozambican state enforced policies inimical to the peasantry. While their reasons differed, the effect was the same—to in-hibit an independent and prosperous peasantry. Under Portuguese colonial-ism, especially during the reign of António Salazar, the Portuguese dictator who set up the Estado Novo or New State (1928–1962), the state supported set-tler farms and plantations at the expense of the peasantry. It subsidized and consolidated settler farming by providing cheap credit, building the trans-portation infrastructure, coordinating marketing facilities, and maintaining extension services. In contrast, laws were imposed that limited the amount of land Mozambican farmers could have and that prohibited their employment of labor in order to check African accumulation. State intervention and assis-tance enabled the settlers to successfully overcome African competitors. Simi-larly, the Portuguese government aided the plantation companies. The state intervened in the labor market, through the creation of labor codes and inter-nal migrant labor, to ensure that plantation owners, like settlers, had a suffi-cient labor supply.[3]

This convergence of interests between the colonial state and the settler farmers did not mean that they had no conflicts. Indeed, the settlers resented the shortages of African labor due to migration. Given Portugal's own eco-nomic underdevelopment, the colonial state came to depend on the revenues it derived from the outward flow of migrant labor, especially mining labor to South Africa. Yet a continuation of migrant labor was not possible without some kind of "peasant economy." Unlike settlers who had eyes on both the land and labor of peasants, the major consumers of migrant labor—the mines—did not. Mining capital was concerned primarily with the production and repro-duction of a cheap peasant-worker labor force. Studies have shown that it was more profitable for mining capital if African workers still had a base in the countryside.[4] Because families in the rural areas bore the responsibility for the subsistence and reproduction of the workers, it was not economically feasible for mining interests to totally deprive Africans of their land. In contrast, settler farmers wanted to dispossess Africans of their land and remove them as competitors from the internal markets. They also wanted a cheap African labor force to work on their farms.

The challenge for the colonial state was to resolve the tensions and contradictions between mining capital and settlers, which it tried to do with forced labor. Throughout the countryside, peasants were subjected to forced labor and to expropriation from their fertile land by the colonial regime on behalf of settler agriculture. But in the south, the three provinces were made into labor reserves for South African mining capital, and a series of agreements between Portugal and South Africa ensured a regular and cheap supply of African labor to the mines. In return the South African government pledged a guaranteed tonnage of goods to and from South Africa through the Maputo port. Settler farmers, unable to compete with mining wages for African labor, came to depend on forced labor recruitment. In the center, huge plantations of sugar, coconuts, sisal, and tea also faced severe labor shortages during the Salazar era. This was due to the large-scale recruitment of men for the mines and farms of southern Africa and other labor demands on the peasantry such as forced cultivation of cotton. Consequently, they, too, came to depend on a brutal system of forced labor that survived in one form or another until decolonization.

In the 1950s and 1960s, economic and political contradictions forced Portugal, as well as other colonial powers in the southern African region, to reconsider agrarian policies. The colonial state actively fostered the development of specialized peasant commodity production in some areas, accelerating economic differentiation among Africans. This new colonial political strategy enabled the middle peasantry to strengthen its position in a variety of ways. For example, in Gaza's Limpopo Colonato (settlement), some peasants were incorporated alongside Portuguese settlers, albeit usually on probation.[5] In the District of Alto Molocué in Zambézia, the richer peasantry managed to acquire the status of *agricultor* (farmer) alongside Portuguese farmers and were exempted from forced labor and allowed to employ labor.[6] In the District of Angonia in Tete, many wealthier peasants developed their agricultural base by buying seeds, fertilizers, pesticides, and other inputs from colonial settlers.[7] In the central and northern cotton-producing areas, African producers with high output and hectarage were given access to credit, tools, and insecticides.[8] Throughout the countryside, an increasing number of middle-peasant farmers improved their socioeconomic status toward the end of colonialism. Nevertheless, they remained frustrated because the Portuguese administration continued to favor settler agriculture. Contrary to the political aims of the state, this colonial policy toward middle peasants, which favored their economic advancement while simultaneously controlling their growth, made them receptive to the advancement of the liberation movement.

Repressive colonial policies drove a large number of peasants to support the liberation movement. In particular, the middle peasants, whose ranks were both increased and frustrated by the Portuguese, backed Frelimo on the assumption that an independent Mozambican state would eliminate the constraints that the colonial administration had erected against their own economic growth. As Kenneth Hermele has argued for the middle peasantry in the Lower Limpopo Valley, many of these rural producers were perturbed by restricted marketing practices.[9] They supported the independence struggle, hoping that Frelimo would return their confiscated land and enable them to participate equally in the market once the war was won. Frelimo in general had strong support among the peasantry in areas in which its guerrilla forces operated, and it made relatively little use of coercion.[10]

By the end of the colonial period, the socioeconomic structure was highly differentiated in rural Mozambique. Peasant households depended on a complex mixture of agricultural production, wage labor, and, more broadly, off-farm employment for their livelihood and reproduction. Even in the center and north of the country, where peasant production of marketed surpluses was much stronger than in the south, many agricultural households relied on wage employment. With independence, Frelimo should have considered alternative policies toward a regionally diverse and differentiated rural society.

But once in power, Frelimo discouraged a debate on agrarian transformation and remained predisposed to socialism in the countryside. The new leaders recognized that there were different social classes, but they underestimated the extent of peasant differentiation and the diversity of rural livelihoods. In their view, the middle and private farmers were economically weak and would eventually disappear with the exodus of the Portuguese. Furthermore, by withholding state investment, Frelimo would squeeze these wealthier peasants, the group it had come to distrust during the war of national liberation, leaving a homogeneous group of peasants. In planning their development strategy, the new leaders embraced a simplistic vision of agrarian class structure based on a dualist model of a traditional subsistence-oriented peasantry opposed to a modern large-scale commercial sector. Frelimo's strategy of agrarian transformation was not merely misinformed by dualism, as Bridget O'Laughlin has argued.[11] Rather, Frelimo tried to ensure that its vision of rural class structure became reality by not investing in peasant agriculture and letting peasants rely on their own resources.

The roots of Frelimo's anti–middle-peasant line can be traced back to the armed struggle for independence. From the days of Lazaro Nkavandame and the so-called new exploiters in the mid-1960s, Frelimo had grown suspicious of prosperous peasants. According to official propaganda and other writings on the Mozambican revolution, Nkavandame, Frelimo's party secretary in Cabo Delgado and director of the Department of Commerce, exploited peasant laborers on his private farm as well as on cooperatives for his own personal use.[12] He eventually was stripped of his official responsibilities and ousted from the movement in 1969.

Some scholars have portrayed Nkavandame and his followers as unique to Cabo Delgado.[13] Contrary to this commonly held view, new scholarship, including this study, show that the economic interests of the Nkavandame group in the northern provinces were the same as those of wealthier peasants in the central and southern provinces. These wealthier peasants included the *agricultores* in the District of Alto Molocué in Zambézia, the *machambeiros* in the District of Angonia in Tete, the *colonos* in the Colonato do Limpopo in Gaza, and the cooperative members in the District of Zavala in Inhambane, as well as those of Ilha Josina Machel in the District of Manhiça in Maputo. All these rural producers aspired to become small capitalist farmers unfettered by the colonial government.

But during the war for independence, ideological differentiation sharpened within Frelimo, and two groups emerged led by Samora Machel and Lazaro Nkavandame, respectively. According to official accounts, the Nkavandame group struggled to stir the movement toward a narrow nationalistic course — the achievement of national independence and the replacement of Portuguese by Mozambicans.[14] In contrast, the Machel group sought not only to gain independence but also to transform socioeconomic relations that went beyond the mere passing of power from the whites to the blacks. In the end, Machel won and Nkavandame was cast out.

Machel and his group opposed supporting a rural smallholder elite. Familiar with Stalinist antikulak ideas in Russia, they came to see all well-off and middle peasants as "protokulak" farmers and took a hard line against these wealthier peasants. Many of these Frelimo militants who had studied abroad in communist countries (Soviet Union, China, and Eastern Europe) or who had strong ties with communist parties in Western Europe (Portugal and France) were influenced by the prevailing orthodoxies. Based on borrowed experiences, they sought to eliminate future "Nkavandames" and other well-off farmers. Indeed, Nkavandame may have been a scoundrel, but Frelimo used him and his legacy to repress the wider social base that he was supposed to represent. In the aim of destroying his legacy, they exaggerated the threat of a

Mozambican kulak class and categorized wealthier peasants and capitalist farmers as enemies of the revolution. Unlike other scholarship that dates Frelimo's antipeasant line after independence, my work suggests that Frelimo began to turn against the middle peasantry and other prosperous farmers after the Machel and Nkavandame split in the late 1960s.[15]

In 1974, new members who joined the movement reinforced this anti–middle-peasant line. After the Gordian Knot Operation ended in the military defeat of the Portuguese in Cabo Delgado, Mozambicans understood that the colonizers were not going to win the war, and many people joined Frelimo. Junior civil servants and other non-Frelimo activists joined the liberation movement because they wanted to be on the victorious side, not because they held the same political and ideological objectives as Machel and his supporters. In addition, Frelimo started to recruit people for technical reasons, and many of these individuals came to occupy key positions within the postindependence party and state. These technocrats were usually recruited from among the educated sons and daughters of the bourgeoisie (often settler in origin), and they had little experience with the rural population. Yet following independence, Frelimo came to depend on the skills and advice of these bureaucratic "modernizers" (as well as foreign experts) and placed more emphasis on technocratic solutions to develop the country. The leadership no longer trusted its own experiences from the liberation zones when it was closer to the peasantry, when Frelimo had depended on the peasant surpluses to sustain the guerrillas, and its scale of operations was much smaller.

Frelimo relied on its own history of having crushed people such as Nkavandame. But the leadership should have realized that while socialism or some form of social redistribution would benefit its social base (poor peasants), the best way to keep generating a surplus would be to find a middle course with the upper peasantry who fought for independence. The same ideological liberalism that Frelimo practiced in filling its bureaucratic ranks should have been extended to agricultural producers in the postindependence period. This would have meant a rural strategy that included compromises with the middle peasantry.

Overconfident of its support from the masses, Frelimo proceeded to implement policies that were antagonistic to the peasantry. Over time it became a "left-wing developmental dictatorship."[16] As Mozambique's only party, Frelimo became indistinguishable from the state, thus creating the one-party state. As both party and state, it was able to pursue its radical development policies. The leadership adopted a socialist strategy in both industry and agriculture, aimed at a rapid and total transformation of Mozambican society. In the countryside, family agriculture was to be rapidly collectivized and peasant farmers were to be employed on state farms or producer cooperatives. The

rural population was to live in communal villages, settlements where basic social services would be available. This strategy clearly clashed with the aspira-
tions of the prosperous peasant farmers who wanted to recuperate the land
that the Portuguese had taken away from them.

Contradictions soon appeared in Frelimo's ideology and strategy. According
to official discourse, the middle peasants would pool their resources with poor
peasants and collectivize their individual farms to work together. Collectivization of peasant farms would require little investment because of economies of
scale. Frelimo believed that merely getting the dispersed peasantry to farm together in larger collective units would result in immediate increases in productivity. Peasants would voluntarily join cooperatives because production would
be higher in the collective fields than on their family farms.

Yet, as early as 1977, scholars from the Universidade Eduardo Mondlane observed that middle peasants were the most apprehensive and antagonistic
about the government's policy of collectivization and *aldeia comunais* (communal villages): "The middle peasant's property consciousness leads him to
fear forms of collective production, since he interprets these as an attempt to
confiscate his cattle, his trees, his chickens, his plow, etc. Specifically, the adoption of a 'poor peasant line' may lead to antagonizing the middle peasant and
thus fail to mobilize an important section of the peasantry."[17] Frelimo never attempted to mobilize middle peasants or to take into account their specific ideological outlooks and material positions. Instead its response was to advise the
middle peasantry to commit class suicide—to give up their means of production to collectives.[18] Furthermore, Frelimo only made the middle peasantry
nervous by espousing a "poor peasant line," which peasants feared would undermine their living standards.

Following Frelimo's decision to "socialize and modernize the countryside"
in 1977, contradictions between the state and different peasant strata developed
at the grassroots level. By officially restricting cooperative membership to poor
peasants—and those middle peasants prepared to hand over their oxen and
plows to the collective unit—the government indicated that the middle peasants did not have a significant role to play in the new rural society. But while
continuing to advocate the political supremacy of poor peasants, Frelimo
found itself organizationally allied to middle peasants and unwilling to help
poor peasants, who could not afford to take advantage of cooperatives without
resources and material input from the state. With little agricultural investment
in the cooperative sector, Frelimo became dependent on wealthier peasants—
with their means of production and skills—for cooperatives to work.

Over time other contradictions emerged that undermined Frelimo's plan to
collectivize peasant agriculture. These contradictions stemmed from the diverse ways that the rural population responded to and shaped government

policies in practice. In most cooperatives, middle peasants took over the leadership and management. Even when poor peasants were the numerical majority in cooperatives, middle peasants, mostly men, held the leadership
positions. Without state investment, middle peasants gradually abandoned
collective production, knowing that cooperatives would be less efficient and
productive than their own family farms. Eventually this group came to compete with cooperatives for poor peasant labor and other resources. Thus, significant discrepancies arose between what senior bureaucrats at the Ministry
of Agriculture declared and what occurred in rural communities like Ilha
Josina Machel. Consequently, Frelimo was forced to retreat from this aspect of
its program.

For a rural development strategy that placed production foremost, the middle peasantry certainly could have played an important role. At independence,
despite being a numerical minority, they were the backbone of agricultural
production in the peasant economy. Together with the upper peasants they
made up only 25 percent of the total peasantry, but they were responsible for
most of the marketed production. Many of them were excellent agricultural-
ists, and they worked extremely hard on the land. In terms of national development, Frelimo should have supported and invested in a prosperous, market-
oriented peasantry from the start.

In the 1980s, the economy worsened as the war against Renamo accelerated.
Frelimo responded with more repressive measures, including a return to
forced cultivation of crops. In 1986, a presidential order was put into practice
in Nampula Province prohibiting the free movement of peasants unless their
cotton fields and cashew trees were tended properly.[19] As far as the peasants
were concerned, this decree signaled both a very sharp break with the preindependence policies of Frelimo in the liberated zones and a return to the colonial
era. In practice, the policy led only to the further alienation of the peasantry
from the state and failed to arrest the country's economic decline. One year
later, a desperate Mozambique adopted an IMF-sponsored structural adjustment program. The country's membership in the World Bank and the IMF
resulted in a marked reorientation of internal class relations, with the dominant internal force changing from the modernizing state bureaucracy to the
private sector dependent upon the resources made available by the World
Bank, the IMF, multinational corporations, and nongovernmental organizations (NGOs). The bankrupt state aligned with international capital, private
capital, and large capitalist farmers.

While a minority of Mozambicans benefited from the opening of the market, favoring of the private sector, and other features of the country's economic
recovery program, the majority of peasant farmers were affected negatively by
the program. In the countryside, peasant farmers did not gain from price lib-

eralization because of continuing poor terms of trade, rising inflation, and declining purchasing power. The main beneficiaries of large state-farm and industrial divestiture were British, Portuguese, and South African investors. Frelimo gave large concessions with long-term leases to Lonhro (a British-owned company), João Ferreira dos Santos (a Portuguese company), and large-scale private farmers, mostly from South Africa. In addition, Frelimo allocated land and agribusiness to government officials, ministers, Frelimo veterans, and ex-state-farm managers. Thus, the state guaranteed that some Mozambicans profited from the transition to capitalism.

Many explanations have been given for the failure of Frelimo's socialist rural development strategy. Initially, scholars placed emphasis on external factors and foreign intervention, especially South African destabilization. The works of John S. Saul and Joseph Hanlon provide notable examples of this scholarship.[20] They argue that given Frelimo's inheritance—a bankrupt and backward country, technical constraints (e.g., few trained or experienced Mozambicans), and an exaggerated economic dependence on apartheid South Africa—the transition to socialism was bound to be difficult; after South Africa took over the sponsorship of Renamo, development became impossible.

For Saul and Hanlon, Frelimo's errors—including the failure to promote democracy, economic mistakes, and a rapid modernization strategy—were merely the "holes through which the enemy [Renamo] entered." Hanlon, who devotes an entire section in his first book to rural socialism, criticizes the Frelimo state for abandoning the family and cooperative sectors in favor of large-scale state farms. Rural producers were left without marketing structures, inputs, incentives, and support. According to his analysis, the greatest mistakes of the state came not so much from what they did as from what they failed to do. After the Portuguese left, for example, Frelimo failed to rebuild the marketing and transport networks and to provide other services critical to rural commercialization. Hanlon concludes that the peasant sector suffered primarily from systematic neglect rather than from imposition of collective agricultural production.

However, Frelimo's errors amounted to more than just benign neglect. As my study shows, interventionist state policies, unpopular with the peasantry, were among the causes of rural alienation from Frelimo. But the mixture of these factors—neglect and active measures against the peasantry—varied at different times and in different areas. Neglect, for example, was far more important a consideration outside the south. The government, based in the capital city of Maputo, which is at the southern tip of the country, had easier access to southern Mozambique than to other parts of the country. But neglect was not simply a question of capability; neglect as well as intervention reflected class and bureaucratic interests of those who controlled the state.

Although this work is concerned primarily with state policies, it does not ignore the impact of external factors. It analyzes those exogenous factors that were responsible for much of the instability and chaos in Mozambique in the immediate postindependence years. But these factors did not foreclose domestic policy choices. State policy also accounts for the collapse of Mozambique's socialist experiment and ensuing peasant alienation. Even if there had been no war of destabilization, the government's strategy was fraught with inherent contradictions that heralded political difficulties. Much greater attention needs to be paid to internal factors and especially to Frelimo's policies and institutional character in assessing the causes for the failure of Mozambique's socialist project.

Recent research has concentrated on internal factors, in particular the contradictions and struggles between the state and rural society. Some of these internal factors were the failure to reconstitute the rural trade network, forced villagization, and restrictive measures placed on the middle peasantry. Otto Roesch's work on communal villages in Gaza, for example, shows that Frelimo's rural collectivization policies negatively affected peasants.[21] Their access to migrant wages in South Africa, however, minimized the impact of these policies. Gaza had one of the highest rates of villagization anywhere in the country, second only to Cabo Delgado, a Frelimo stronghold. The majority of these communal villages were created in the wake of floods, which devastated the Limpopo Valley in early 1977, after which Frelimo settled hundreds of thousands of people into villages on the higher ground above the floodplain of the Limpopo and its tributaries. Few new villages were created after 1980, and those that were created were the result of government efforts to resettle drought-affected populations in the interior of the province. Others were forced settlements by the Mozambican armed forces in the wake of Renamo activities in southern Mozambique.

Roesch argues that collectivization was a less conflictual process in Gaza than it was in other areas because of the southern region's historic dependency on migrant wage labor. Although most rural dwellers considered resettlement into communal villages to be economically and culturally onerous, it was not the direct threat to subsistence security and peasant production that it was for the largely cash-cropping peasants of the north.

Roesch qualifies this general observation in "Renamo and the Peasantry in Southern Mozambique," distinguishing between those peasants who practiced agriculture in the Limpopo Valley and those who practiced agriculture in the hinterland. For the former, who are the majority of the province's population, villagization represented a continuation with colonial economic and settlement patterns. The valley peasants had experienced a process of demographic concentration and economic and residential transformation with colonial

forced cash-cropping schemes, which made villagization a less onerous adjustment than for the peasants in the hinterland. For the latter, who remained
more dependent on traditional extensive agricultural techniques and decentralized patterns of territorial occupation, villagization represented a far more
threatening economic and cultural adjustment. Thus, peasant resistance to villagization and opposition to Frelimo were more pronounced in the remote
areas of the province. Given the region's socioeconomic history, Renamo succeeded in establishing its major bases and areas of operation in the hinterland,
where the peasantry's offended sense of moral economy and opposition to the
state probably ran deepest. The bulk of the province's communal villages, however, were created among valley cultivators, making the question of villagization
less of a target for peasant discontent in the rural hinterland of Gaza than it was
in other parts of the country. Thus, Renamo was unable to use villagization as
an issue around which to mobilize support among the southern Mozambican
peasantry.

Another study in Gaza has shown that Frelimo's collectivization policies had
a different effect on rural communities. In his monograph on land struggles in
Chokwe, Hermele compares and contrasts the colonial and postcolonial state
policies on the peasantry, arguing that in both cases the state pursued policies
that deprived peasant farmers of their land.[22] In the colonial era, Chokwe was
the site of a huge Portuguese settlement scheme and the home of the largest
agro-industrial complex in postindependent Mozambique. The colonial government ousted peasants from their land and gave it to Portuguese settler
farmers who had preferential access to labor and other resources provided by
the state.

After independence, the Frelimo government nationalized the land and
transformed the Chokwe settler scheme into a large agro-industrial enterprise,
the Limpopo Agro-Industrial Complex (CAIL). Peasants were resettled in
communal villages and transformed into laborers on the state farms and cooperatives. The impact of these policies on the peasantry was negative.[23] Since the
CAIL state farm practiced rice monoculture, it required only seasonal labor,
which meant that state-farm employment could not guarantee subsistence and
reproduction for the peasant families of the communal villages supplying
labor to it. Furthermore, peasants did not have much incentive to sell their
labor because there were few basic consumer goods in the countryside to be
bought with the wages earned. Peasants thus neglected state-farm production
and cooperative farms, giving priority to their own farms as well as other economic activities.

Hermele's work shows that state farms failed because they created serious
contradictions between the peasantry and the state. Peasants were bitter at not
receiving land in the old irrigation scheme after independence. They were not

prepared to be agricultural workers on state farmland that they had originally occupied and then were expelled from, first by the colonial government and later by Frelimo. Hence, peasants resisted the government's collectivization efforts by neglecting agricultural tasks and by destroying costly imported equipment.

These studies by Roesch and Hermele illustrate the ways in which state policies affected different areas in southern Mozambique, a region of intense state intervention in agriculture. Because of its proximity to Maputo and its agricultural importance, the south became the focus of concerted government development efforts in the postindependence period.

Studies of peasant responses to state policies in northern Mozambique reveal a different dynamic from those in the southern region. Christian Geffray and Mögens Pedersen noted the possibility of widespread support for Renamo by peasants in Nampula disaffected by Frelimo's rural policies.[24] Their research shows how the government's villagization policies, especially the forced resettlement of the rural population into communal villages after 1984, created serious contradictions between different lineage groups. Given specific social and cultural-historical conditions, Renamo was successful in exploiting popular disenchantment with Frelimo to win support among some fractions of the peasantry.

In his book Geffray argues that Frelimo alienated significant sections of the rural population by excluding traditional authorities from power, giving authority to nontraditional village officials, and ultimately forcing peasants to leave their land and regroup in villages.[25] In Nampula's Erati District, villagization forced different lineage groups to reside together and gave the Erati people power over the Macuane people. Once Renamo soldiers arrived in the villages, they were able to win the support of all peasants who shared a common sense of injury wrought by Frelimo. Geffray acknowledges that the pre-1984 alienation of traditional authorities and peasants by government policies almost certainly would not have developed into armed warfare without Renamo's arrival. Although his research is based on Erati District, he hypothesizes that this pattern probably applied to other parts of Nampula and Mozambique. Other writers argue that Renamo successfully exploited widespread rural disenchantment with Frelimo's agrarian policies to fuel one of the most brutal wars in Africa.[26]

Geffray makes no explicit distinction between villagization imposed for ideological or military motives. But his description clarifies that military actions precipitated the alliance of some chiefs with Renamo. The population of remote areas in the Erati District was forcibly regrouped for defense against Renamo in early 1984, in response to rumors that Renamo soldiers were nearing the district. By the mid-1980s, the Mozambican armed forces were using forced villagization in Nampula to keep Renamo and civilians separate—the same kind of "protected village" scheme that the Portuguese used against Frelimo during the war of liberation.[27] This situation contrasted sharply with the period before the war—when the creation of communal villages in Nampula was voluntary. The major exception was forced resettlement in Gaza after the Limpopo floods in 1977. After the mid-1980s, most forced relocation to communal villages in Nampula and in central Mozambique took place for military reasons and not for development reasons. But not all the rural populations antagonized by the villagizing state entered into dissidence. Peasant-state antagonisms only developed into warfare with the militarization of the preexisting tensions.[28]

Geffray assumes that in Nampula a homogeneous peasantry lives within a traditional world dominated by traditional cults, rules, and practices. He portrays peasants as the recalcitrant objects of oppressive state policies imposed from above, and by focusing only on the mid-1980s period, he ignores the available evidence for the early postindependence period that describes a much more politically engaged rural population, genuinely committed to a transformation of its communities and the inherited colonial order. As Roesch reminds us, in the immediate postindependence years, large sectors of the peasantry in many parts of the country confronted and questioned their "traditions."[29] They saw in Frelimo a respected interlocutor and source of leadership.

In Geffray's view chiefs and other local authorities were protectors of peasant traditional values who want recognition and respect by the government. He believes that Frelimo wrongly stereotyped chiefs and other local authorities as discredited collaborators with colonial rule. Given their marginal treatment at the hands of Frelimo, traditional authorities came to resent the state, and some effectively mobilized the rural population in support of Renamo forces. Geffray applies his argument even in Zambézia, where very few communal villages were ever built. Indeed, his critique of Frelimo's socialist strategy goes beyond a denunciation for creating communal villages to an attack for imposing new political institutions to replace the *regulado* system in the countryside. This point is often overlooked in the commentaries against Frelimo's collectivization strategy. Geffray's argument, then, applies to rural communities like Ilha Josina Machel that did not build communal villages but established government and party structures.

In contrast to his positive image of the peasantry and traditional authorities, Geffray portrays the state as a rigidly modernizing institution imposed from the outside, in disregard of local cultural traditions, religious practices, and traditional authority structures. Frelimo's construction of communal villages, in his opinion, was not a strategy of development but a strategy to impose the new state apparatus in the countryside and to displace the population

from their ancestral lands. Frelimo's conception of nation-building and socialization of the countryside was politically and economically alien to rural
Mozambicans. Summing up the policies in the countryside, he asserts that the
Frelimo state, with its collectivization policy, antitraditionalism, and technocratic and urban bias, was more authoritarian than the colonial state.

My study challenges many of Geffray's assumptions about the peasantry, the
state, and agrarian policy. It shows that the integration of the peasantry into
the money economy, on terms regulated by the colonial state, did not leave
peasants as a traditional mass of agricultural producers. Rather, there was a
differentiated peasantry that organized its livelihood in diverse ways. Moreover, these peasants were not simply objects of Frelimo's repressive policies.
Peasants did not passively do what state officials told them but shaped Frelimo's policies on the ground. This book also offers a more nuanced analysis of
the state's interaction with the rural population, rather than an emphasis on
the state as solely an alien and authoritarian force. The state was less in control
of its territory and frequently unable to enforce its policies. Frelimo often
backed down when its policies were not implemented in the countryside as it
envisioned. The state, consisting of many different forces and interests, did not
always act as a coherent institution. State officials in rural areas often relied on
diverse alliances and practice, which reflected the exigencies of survival and
control, even when they contradicted official state policy.[30] As a result, there
were discrepancies between the central state's directives and policy implementation in rural communities.

Finally, Geffray's overemphasis on the importance of traditional chiefs as a
cultural and political institution in rural life misses the central question confronting the new regime: namely, how to organize the local political system.
According to Frelimo, the *regulado* system was undemocratic and inequitable.
The new leaders decided to get rid of the system that gave traditional authorities control over the rural population and to replace it with a unitary system of
government. My study examines how Frelimo's restructuring of local power
and governance affected different classes, gender, and generations differently.

Geffray's book initiated an international debate on how to characterize
Mozambique's postindependence socialist experiment and the war.[31] On the
one hand are those who are highly critical of Frelimo's socialist project and
who readily accept Geffray's research results as applicable to the entire country.[32] On the other hand, there are some who are skeptical of these writers' attempts to generalize the findings of Geffray for Nampula to the whole of the
country.[33] Geffray's study along with new research illustrates patterns of interaction between the state and local rural society that vary significantly by geo-
graphical area and time period.[34] This book, an analysis of the impact of
colonial and postcolonial government policies upon the peasantry in Maputo

Province, is part of the ongoing research on local communities. A comprehensive evaluation of Frelimo's socialist and postsocialist experiences must include the diversity of local contexts.

This new literature on state and peasant relations carries policy implications. It illustrates how government policy formulated entirely "from above" can retard agricultural development and alienate the peasantry. Although this study will show that the Mozambican state has consistently taken an antipeasantry posture, it is not antistatist. Contrary to popular orthodoxy, it does not call for the withdrawal of the state from the economy and its replacement by the "free market." Rather, it acknowledges that the state still must intervene in the economy to promote development. After all, the state played an important role in all modern societies that have achieved successful agricultural economies. In the United States, Canada, and Western Europe, for example, governmental intervention (e.g., regulation of producer prices and the provision of vital inputs such as research, pest control, and systems of irrigation) is absolutely critical in sustaining high levels of productivity. The problem is not the extent of state intervention, but the nature and quality of such intervention.

The material on which this book is based was collected over a period longer than ten years. Field investigation was carried out in rural communities in 1981–1983 and then under very difficult war conditions in 1986–1987, 1989, and 1991. A short visit in 1993 enabled me to complete this study. The research methods rely on close- and long-term participant observation of rural areas, supplemented by data in the form of statistics, government documents, and case studies.

As a graduate student at the University of Toronto, I became interested in the liberation movements in southern Africa. In 1981 I went to Mozambique with the support of a fellowship from the Social Science and Humanities Research Council of Canada. I was a visiting research fellow at the Universidade Eduardo Mondlane in the Center for African Studies, which worked closely with government ministries in determining research priorities and approving projects. Foreign researchers were required to make a practical contribution to Mozambique's development. With a recommendation from the center, I was employed by Project CO-1 at the Ministry of Agriculture from 1981 to 1983. While there were many different views within the ministry concerning the proper direction of agricultural development, my immediate supervisors and the project sponsors agreed that empirical research was an indispensable component of long-term development success.

I returned for subsequent field research in 1986, as a postdoctoral fellow at York University under the sponsorship of the Ministry of Agriculture's Department for Rural Development. I worked for a rural extension project in support of poor peasants and women of Chokwe in Gaza. In 1989, a grant from the University of Illinois enabled me to return once more to Chokwe as well as to do archival research in Lisbon, Portugal. Further research in the 1990s was cofunded by the University of Illinois and the John D. and Catherine T. Mac-Arthur Foundation. My work was made possible by the support I received from the Ministry of Agriculture.

My field experience was focused initially at the local level, where the apparent disregard of peasants' interests and needs was most obvious. From 1981 to 1983, I lived and worked in twelve cooperatives on Ilha Josina Machel, a locality in the District of Manhiça in Maputo Province. Ilha Josina Machel was one area of activity of Project CO-1, Mozambique's first cooperative development project. A strategic project of the Mozambique Nordic Agricultural Program (MONAP) at the Ministry of Agriculture, it was approved by the Frelimo government in January 1981. Funded initially for a three-year period, and then extended for another year, the purpose of Project CO-1 was to strengthen selected pilot cooperatives by creating conditions that ensured the participation and the influence of the members in the development of cooperatives.

As a researcher with Project CO-1, I resided with a team of six Mozambicans trained in agriculture and small animal species and a Portuguese technician on Ilha Josina Machel. At the cooperative level, my job was to assist peasant members with the organization and management of production (record keeping, remuneration distribution, developing techniques and organization of political participation, and planning agricultural production). Some of my other responsibilities were establishing working relations between the cooperatives and the state officials at the Ministry of Internal Trade, the Ministry of Education and Culture, and Mecanagro, the state-owned machinery park; as well as organizing visits of foreign delegations to Ilha Josina Machel. These efforts required weekly meetings at the cooperatives, monthly meetings with local committee leaders, and periodic meetings at the district level with party and government officials.

At the project's regional center in Namaacha in Maputo Province, I participated in the organization and instruction of formal training courses for cooperative members, national technicians of the project, local cadres of the party, and state workers in planning agricultural production and cooperative management. I also attended a series of seminars on the role of cooperativization in Mozambique's socialist rural development strategy. My position in Project CO-1 provided a unique opportunity to work at the ground level with peasant farmers who confronted a complexity of issues involved in a dramatic shift of production from family farming to collective production, and to work at the ministerial level with a staff who clearly saw themselves as enthusiastic supporters of the revolution but did not act consistently on behalf of those who were the objects of state agricultural policy.

The principal source of information was oral accounts. These included individual and collective interviews with peasant farmers (members and nonmembers of cooperatives), private farmers, and district officials, but I did not limit myself to them. Interviews with village residents were conducted almost always in the Shangaan language, while those with government and party officials were in Portuguese.[35] While older men of the community were the main informants for the oral historical data, most of the individual interviews were with women, the majority of peasant farmers. Some structured interviews, in a questionnaire format, were used in order that certain data and methods of fieldwork could be systematized. Unstructured individual interviews were also conducted with 270 cooperative members (a 20 percent sample of total cooperative members). They were selected based on contrasting criteria: class, gender, age, and family size. Initially, for each interview I tried to tailor questions to draw out both work and life histories. Return interviews were less dependent on a question-and-answer format and took more the form of open-ended discussions. These interviews typically took place at the home of each person involved, often with other family members or close friends present.

In addition to interviews, other ways of investigating complex social issues were devised. They consisted of: (1) frequent open discussions with as many different representatives of the community as possible—miners, political organizers, school teachers, judges, elders, ex-*régulos, curandeiros* (traditional healers), members of the women's and youth movements, shopkeepers, and local militia; (2) attendance at committee meetings; and, at times, (3) participation in manual labor with peasant farmers. On Ilha Josina Machel, a village survey was carried out in the seven neighborhoods. This survey included questions on family composition, marriages, land, cattle, agricultural production, commerce, and social services. It also sought other information on the wider district political economy within which this community is situated. Finally, a prolonged period of residence on Ilha Josina Machel contributed to my own appreciation and understanding of Mozambican rural society. I lived in a renovated ex-colonial warehouse with the Project CO-1 brigade, traveling mainly on foot or by bicycle from one end of the island to the other.

I carried out subsequent field research in rural communities in Chokwe, Gaza Province, in 1986 and 1987. During this period, I observed and conducted interviews with peasant and private farmers, most of them recipients of redistributed state farmland. I worked particularly closely with rural producers in Lionde, one of fifteen villages near the Chokwe irrigation scheme. Furthermore, I interviewed key government officials at the Ministry of Agriculture and both local and national Frelimo party members, and I attended numerous official meetings. I also interviewed local agricultural and aid personnel. During research trips to Mozambique in 1989, 1991, and 1993, I conducted multiple follow-up interviews with peasant and private farmers in these rural communities.

In addition, I consulted materials in governmental archives in Mozambique at every level—local, district, provincial, and national—and at agricultural research stations. Valuable colonial agricultural production data for the area were found in the former warehouse of the Instituto dos Cereais de Moçambique (ICM; Grain Institute of Mozambique) located in the Palmeira. Important collections of writings, notes, maps, and diaries were viewed at district administration centers. Colonial archives were also consulted in Lisbon, Portugal. Unfortunately, a rule of fifty years' confidentiality is still being applied in Portugal, which means that complete documentation from the colonial era will only become accessible in year 2025.

A final note needs to be made with respect to statistical data sources. The principal colonial sources used were the *Recenseamento agrícola de Moçambique* (agricultural censuses) for 1965 and 1970, which have built-in weaknesses. Not least of these is the rigid separation of "modern" (i.e., settler farms and plantations) and "traditional" (i.e., peasant farming) agricultural sectors, with no attempt to describe their interrelationship. In addition, colonial data collection was almost always inaccurate, and although they may be used to indicate trends, the absolute totals are unreliable. Similarly, macroeconomics data for the postindependence years are extremely scarce, poorly collected, and often incomplete. No consistent series of data exists for the period 1973–1993 with respect to the evolution of production and of its distribution over sectors (agriculture, industry, and services). As in other third-world countries, the most problematic area consists of the data on agricultural output. I constructed a pattern by employing different sources and carefully relating them to one another. The bias in statistical sources was overcome by cross-referencing scarce data sources and from knowing the practices and lacunae of data collection through formal and informal discussions. Apart from party documents on economic policy, official economic reports and policy documents were few in number.

Ilha Josina Machel is a rural community in southern Mozambique. Its history illustrates the various phases of rural development in Mozambique from the 1950s to the 1990s. The community experienced the successive stages of agricultural policy, from colonial settler domination (i.e., settler farms, plantations, and forced cash-cropping) to postindependence socialist agricultural collectivization (i.e., cooperative and state-farm agriculture) to the recent move toward capitalism (i.e., private agriculture and more market-oriented policies).

In some respects, Ilha Josina Machel was typical of the rural setting in the southern region, encompassing Maputo, Gaza, and Inhambane Provinces. Although settler agriculture was important in these provinces during the colonial period, there were no settler farms on Ilha Josina Machel. Rather, the village served as a labor reserve, with peasants supplying their labor to settler farms, plantations, civil construction projects, and the mines in South Africa. It was and continues to be a community with a differentiated peasantry. While the majority of residents are poor peasants, there always has been a significant stratum of middle peasants and a smaller number of wealthier ones. The inhabitants were subjected to all major forms of colonial capitalist exploitation—labor migration, forced labor, and forced cash-crop production. The mixture of these forces differed from region to region but they were evident in all provinces. In the postindependence period, state officials mobilized peasants to form producer cooperatives, and peasants combined collective farming with their other economic activities. Some peasants also were seasonal laborers at the nearby sugar estates.

In other respects, Ilha Josina Machel was very different from other areas in the south and the rest of the country. Its experience with colonial marketing cooperatives is exemplary. In the 1950s, the middle peasants—mostly men—were given an opportunity to participate in a wheat-growing cooperative or be likely targets for forced labor, known as *chibalo*. The colonial state established more than thirty marketing cooperatives nationwide, including three in the Manhiça District, of which Ilha Josina Machel was one. Marketing cooperatives were part of Portugal's effort to foster the growth of a rural middle class who would contain any popular movement for independence. Portugal also hoped that these cooperatives would reduce the colony's dependence on imported wheat. With state assistance (e.g., material inputs, storage facilities, transportation, and a guaranteed market), the middle peasants of Ilha Josina Machel seized the opportunity to increase their output. Unlike most rural communities in the south, where the majority of peasant households depended more on the income earned from migratory work than on agriculture, these middle peasants were able to make a decent living from the sale of their crops. The wages from mine labor were initially critical in establishing their rural households. However, these middle peasants also marketed large surpluses of maize, sweet potato, and cassava, foods consumed by African workers in both the rural and urban areas. The income from crop sales was as important for their households as it was for peasant households in northern Mozambique. At the end of the colonial period, regional economic boundaries still existed, but the state also promoted specialized peasant commodity production across all regions of the country.

In the postindependence period, Ilha Josina Machel received extensive support for cooperative development. Both the Ministry of Agriculture and Project CO-1 provided technical expertise, new technology, and agricultural inputs. Unlike in the north, there was no forced villagization; people remained in their homes and worked on their individual farms and at the cooperatives. In the late 1980s the war between Frelimo and Renamo forced them to seek shelter in the neighboring towns. The question of land redistribution was not a major issue in this area because the colonial state had not confiscated peasant property for settlement schemes, European farms, or plantations like in Gaza, Zambézia, and Tete Provinces. Ilha Josina Machel is an example of a rural community where both the colonial and postcolonial state intervened on a wide scale in the peasant economy.

My field research occurred under conditions of great material shortages and some personal danger. The drought conditions in southern Mozambique from 1981 to 1984 meant food and water were extremely limited, especially in the countryside where rations did not exist. One of Renamo's priority targets was rural development projects, and Project CO-1 was not exempt. During the four-year duration of the project, Renamo rebels killed three employees, including a Portuguese national, destroyed six project buildings with equipment, burned five large trucks, and kidnapped or killed a large number of peasant farmers. Many of them were members of cooperatives.

In early 1983, local militias were assigned to guard the Ilha Josina Machel brigade's headquarters at night because of a rising incidence of random attacks in nearby villages. In 1984, after the brigade's land rover was ambushed, leaving the driver dead and two technicians wounded, project personnel were forced to sleep in the nearby town, Xinavane. Several months later, Renamo staged the first of several attacks on the community, brutally axing several residents to death and setting fire to one of the four rural stores. Two other shops were destroyed in 1989. By then, most residents lived in towns close to the village—Xinavane, Palmeira, and Manhiça—returning only during the day to farm their fields. Over the years, many of my Mozambican colleagues who continued to work in the countryside lost their lives—victims of land mine explosions, road ambushes, and predawn raids. As the war accelerated in the south, I was unable to return to Ilha Josina Machel except for short day trips and always under well-armed protection. After the October 1992 Frelimo-Renamo agreement opened some prospects of peace, refugees and displaced persons began to return slowly to the area to resume their lives. Residents moved back to Ilha Josina Machel to find their homes destroyed, fields land mined, and cattle gone. By May 1993, most persons had resettled in the village, with the exception of those who moved to Maputo City. But they had difficulty farming, especially given the shortage of draft animals needed to prepare the heavy clay soil.

The research site in Chokwe was relatively more secure than Ilha Josina Machel because of the nearby Frelimo military base. Military convoys accompanied all long-distance travel outside the irrigation scheme. While Renamo rebels never controlled the town, they frequently attacked the margins of the irrigation scheme, killing civilians and disrupting production. In 1989, I barely managed to escape a Renamo incursion that left more than eighty people dead. On several occasions they entered Lionde, the village where I did my work, forcing the inhabitants to flee and live for months in the bush. These were just some of the tragedies that had an impact on me and affected my research.

The chapters that follow examine both colonial and postcolonial agricultural policies that resulted in peasant dissatisfaction and alienation from the state. The analysis is presented in three parts. Part 1 focuses on the specific policies and processes by which the state discriminated against the peasantry. While careful not to treat the Portuguese- and Frelimo-ruled states as if they were the same, it systematically traces the continuities in policy and practice between the colonial and postcolonial periods. Part 2 examines these policies as they impacted the rural community of Ilha Josina Machel. Through a detailed case study, the work documents the process of differentiation of the peasantry in a part of southern Mozambique. Part 3 investigates the changing relations between the state, private capital, and the peasantry as Mozambique made its transition from socialism to capitalism.

It has not been possible to arrange chapters in a purely chronological manner. Two or more chapters sometimes cover the same years, an overlap that is unavoidable since the objective of the study is to examine both the national and local-level perspectives from the colonial period to the postindependence period. Moreover, each chapter displays variations in the time periods covered, reflecting strategic shifts in state policies and practices. Therefore, some chapters, notably those on Portuguese colonialism, cover more than twenty years, and others, such as those on Mozambican socialism, cover less than five years.

Chapter 1 examines the major characteristics of the colonial economy, which shaped the context in which agricultural policy was debated, and analyzes the factors that affected the choices of the first independent government. Chapter 2 analyzes the Frelimo government's agricultural policy during the phase of socialist transition and its impact on the rural population. The next four chapters illuminate the historical development of the peasantry on Ilha Josina Machel. The case study examines the continuities in the treatment of the peasantry from the Portuguese to Frelimo. These chapters trace the rise and fall and rise of a stratum of middle peasantry from 1950 to 1983, thereby challenging the tendency in some of the literature on Mozambique to treat the peasantry as a homogeneous mass. Focusing on the last decades of colonial rule, chapter 3 analyzes the agricultural changes that took place in this rural community, exemplifying the extent to which the rural areas were mobilized under the colonial state and peasant farmers conditioned to respond to its initiatives. Chapter 4 illustrates several levels of policy and development problems in a changing situation; it shows that long before the war accelerated in the countryside, chronic commodity shortages and lower producer prices set by the Frelimo state were destroying incentives for crop marketing. Chapter 5 examines the impact of Project CO-1 on cooperatives and illuminates the influence of NGOs on policy and their role in development. Chapter 6 takes the analysis from issues of national policy to the practical decisions of peasant farmers. It shows how state policies affected peasant survival strategies and, in turn, how these family household strategies affected state policies.

There is no chapter that covers Ilha Josina Machel from 1983 to 1993 because the war accelerated in the area, resulting in the collapse of agricultural production and other economic activities. During this period, most residents fled the community and were displaced in nearby towns. Hence, changes in agricultural policy and relations between the state and peasantry of Ilha Josina Machel in the post-1983 period are examined within the national context of Mozambique's transition from socialism to capitalism in chapter 7. The conclusion draws out the important lessons to be learned from the study, which are relevant to the formulation and implementation of agricultural policy not only in Mozambique, but also in the rest of Africa. It illuminates the relationship between my study and the larger debates on the state and peasants, as well as on the state and rural development.

# Part 1

# The State and Policy Issues

# 1

# Portuguese Colonialism and the Early Postindependence Years, 1950–1976

**The Portuguese colonial system** imposed in Mozambique made the task of transforming agriculture in the postindependent nation unusually difficult. Colonial Mozambique was integrated into a regional southern African economy under the domination of South Africa.[1] Its economy was structured primarily to serve the needs of South African capitalism. Although Portugal was the official colonial power, Portugal's own economic weakness restricted its ability both to exploit and to develop its African colonies for its sole use. The first section of this chapter focuses on the major characteristics of Mozambique's colonial economy, which defined many of the challenges that the Frelimo government confronted after independence.

Unable to forge an integrated national economy in Mozambique, Portuguese colonialism established three distinct economic regions, each with its own structure of agricultural production. These regions differed in terms of the processes of peasant exploitation, patterns of social differentiation, and class structure. The integration of the peasantry into the money economy—on terms regulated by the colonial state—did not leave peasants as a homogeneous class of agricultural producers. Rather, there was a differentiated peasantry, which organized its livelihood in diverse ways. Some peasants were engaged in small-scale production or the sale of cash crops for subsistence and reproduction and at the same time dependent on wage income. The mix varied from region to region, as did overall strategies for sustaining family agriculture.

The second section of this chapter analyzes the breakdown of the colonial structures in the early postindependence years (1975–1976). Confronted with a multifaceted crisis, the government nationalized social services, housing, and land ownership. While the agrarian policy remained undefined until 1977, Frelimo created institutions that prioritized the state sector and set precedents for some disastrous trends in state relations with broad sections of society.

## The Colonial Economy

The main features of the colonial economy included subordination within the international division of labor as a producer of primary products; subordination within the southern African economic subsystem as a provider of services (i.e., transport, tourism) and labor such that the Mozambican economy adjusted to South African capitalism (and not vice versa); and colonial distortion of production such that output was geared to the consumption needs of the European community.

Within the southern African subsystem, Mozambique inherited a very specific position of subordination. It became a service economy dependent upon the provision of transport services (ports and railways) for the South African and Rhodesian economies, and it was also a major source of migrant labor to the South African and Rhodesian mining sectors and to the settler farms in these countries. In the late 1940s, the number of Mozambican workers in Rhodesia was estimated at 200,000, although in the later period, 1955 to 1974, there was a significant reduction of migrants.[2] The number of Mozambican workers recruited for the South African mines from 1950 to 1975 averaged 100,000 men per year.[3] Labor export was of great importance in terms both of labor utilization and of foreign exchange earnings.

The major foreign exchange earner was consistently the ports and railway sector. In 1972 this sector brought in about 30 percent of total income on the current account of the balance of payments, considerably more than income from each of the major cash crops—cashew (15 percent) and cotton (14 percent). Foreign exchange earnings from migrant labor are more difficult to assess. However, by 1970 obligatory deferred payments of miners' wages amounted to about 4 percent of foreign exchange earnings.[4]

Another characteristic of the colonial economy was an internal market shaped to the consumption pattern of the Portuguese community. In the last years of colonialism, approximately two-thirds of total manufacturing production was directed toward the domestic market in Mozambique and only one-third was exported. Protective tariffs ensured the growth of colonial force-fed industrial production for the home market, and three economic sectors emerged: an export sector, consisting exclusively of agro-industries processing agricultural products available in Mozambique; a mass-consumption goods sector; and an intermediate goods sector. These sectors represented an industrial infrastructure and significant linkages between agriculture and industry.

The colonial economy relied on agriculture, which accounted for over 40 percent of gross national product (GNP) and employed 70 percent of the active labor force in 1970. Of the country's total area of 80 million hectares (799,380 square kilometers), about 5 million hectares or 6.23 percent were devoted to agricultural purposes.[5] These hectares were evenly divided between two sectors: traditional family agriculture and commercial enterprise agriculture, the former consisting of peasant landholdings and the latter including plantations, large estates, and settler farms.

The peasantry produced about 70 percent of the total agricultural production, of which 55 percent was subsistence production, while the remaining 15 percent constituted their marketed production (see table 1.1). The plantation and settler farms sectors each accounted for about 15 percent of total output or one-third of the total marketed output. The plantation sector was geared toward the export market, and settler production specialized in the supply of food for the Portuguese urban population. In contrast, the peasantry produced for the domestic and export markets as well as for their own consumption.

Two qualifications to these agricultural production estimates must be made. First, the estimates represent national average data and do not take account of regional differences. Second, contrary to the colonial statistics, the peasantry was not a homogeneous class. Rather, it was subject to patterns of socioeconomic differentiation and class formation.

### Rural Social Differentiation and Regional Agricultural Economies

The peasantry was subjected to forced labor and to expropriation from their fertile land by the colonial regime for settler agriculture and plantations, but colonial policy underwent significant changes after the Second World War.[6] The reasons for shifts in state policy were both economic and political, ranging from the declining competitiveness of colonial exports to emerging nationalism. Beginning in the later 1940s with cotton production, Portugal was forced to make concessions in Mozambique. The colonial state actively fostered a process of commodification and differentiation among African producers. From the 1950s onward, Portugal provided incentives for middle and wealthier peasants to grow maize, rice, and wheat in an effort to reduce the colony's dependency on imported food staples.[7] Colonial authorities also experimented with the introduction of new forms of property for selected strata of the peasantry. For example, cooperatives were encouraged for specialized peasant producers in cotton-growing areas in Cabo Delgado and in areas of the south.[8]

In addition to the colonial state's policies, the very process of integrating the peasantry within the world market led to differentiation, and sometimes to class formation. The peasantry became proletarianized to a considerable ex-

Table 1.1 The regional structure of the colonial rural economy, 1970

| Region | Plantations | Settler Farms | Peasantry— Marketed Output | Peasantry— Own Consumption |
|---|---|---|---|---|
| North (Cabo Delgado, Niassa, Nampula) | sisal (67%)* | cotton (17%) tobacco (50%) | cashew (78%) cotton (37%) food crops | cassava (67%) groundnuts (56%) (also sorghum, millet, maize) |
| Regional Importance‡ | 2% | 12% | 26% | 60% |
| Center (Zambézia, Manica, Sofala, Tete) | sugar (73%) copra (69%) tea (l00%) sisal (33%) | potatoes (67%) tobacco (27%) (also maize, cotton, vegetables) | cotton (28%) cashew (9%) food crops | rice (28%) maize (64%) groundnuts (17%) cassava (25%) (and other minor crops) |
| Regional Importance‡ | 28% | 11% | 9% | 52% |
| South (Inhambane, Gaza, Maputo) | sugar (27%) | rice (56%) potatoes (32%) (also vegetables, wheat) | cashew (13%) food crops | maize (16%) groundnuts (27%) cassava (8%) |
| Regional Importance‡ | 2% | 39% | 10% | 49% |
| National Importance | 15% | 15% | 15% | 55% |

*Source:* Marc Wuyts, *Money and Planning for Socialist Transition: The Mozambican Experience* (Aldershot, U.K., and Brookfield, Vt.: Gower, 1989), p. 27. Reprinted by permission.
* Percentages in parentheses refer to percentage of national production of the particular crop.
‡ Percentages at the bottom of each block refer to relative importance within regional production by value of production.

tent, either to constitute an industrial reserve army for the South African mining industry, or as a rural semiproletariat for the plantation sector. The relation between wage labor and the agricultural base of the peasant worker was complex and subject to various patterns of differentiation.

Table 1.2 provides a crude indication of the degree of differentiation in peasant agricultural production. About 5 percent of the peasant holdings occupied

20 percent of the land cultivated by peasants. The top quintile of holdings occupied over 50 percent of the cultivated area, while the bottom accounted for only 4 percent; 44 percent of the holdings occupied only 16 percent of the area. The average size of a peasant holding was 1.5 hectares, with variations between provinces from 1 hectare to 2.2 hectares; the top 5 percent of holdings were all larger than 4 hectares up to the 10–20 hectares range. At the bottom end, nearly 20 percent of the holdings were less than 0.5 hectares, and 40 percent were less than 1 hectare.

The colonial agricultural statistics did not break down the regional distribution of peasants with more than four hectares. It is impossible to know whether their distribution was proportional to peasant distribution within each zone (in which case "nascent class conflict" was not regionally specific) or whether the peasants with large holdings were disproportionally concentrated in one of the three zones. From the data presented in table 1.2, the Gini coefficient, a measure of inequality, can also be calculated; its value turns out to be about .425, suggesting that there was real inequality and differentiation.[9] On a region-by-region basis, some, such as the south, would have been even more unequal. The inequality, such as peasant differentiation, was not staggeringly high, but it was significant.

Table 1.2 Land distribution of peasant holdings, 1970

| Classes in Size of Holdings (hectares) | Number of Holdings | | | Area | | |
|---|---|---|---|---|---|---|
| | Number | Percentage | Cumulative percent | Hectares | Percentage | Cumulative percent |
| 10–20 | 6,813 | 0.4 | 0.4 | 88,852.2 | 3.6 | 3.6 |
| 5–10 | 37,925 | 2.3 | 2.7 | 244,249.4 | 9.8 | 13.4 |
| 4–5 | 35,850 | 2.2 | 4.9 | 158,574.2 | 6.4 | 19.9 |
| 3–4 | 75,313 | 4.6 | 9.5 | 259,531.1 | 10.4 | 30.3 |
| 2–3 | 232,871 | 14.0 | 23.5 | 561,169.3 | 22.5 | 52.8 |
| 1–2 | 540,608 | 32.8 | 56.3 | 781,297.3 | 31.3 | 84.1 |
| 0.5–1 | 412,245 | 25.0 | 81.3 | 307,714.9 | 12.3 | 96.4 |
| Less than 0.5 | 306,077 | 18.6 | 100.0* | 92,116.5 | 3.7 | 100.0* |
| Total | 1,647,702 | 100.0* | | 2,493,504.9 | 100.0* | |

Source: Missão de Inquérito Agrícola de Moçambique, Estatísticas agrícolas de Moçambique 1970 (Lourenço Marques: Ministério do Ultramar, 1973), p. 1.
*Totals based on unrecorded numbers.

Three fairly distinct zones of agricultural production emerged, with the north (Cabo Delgado, Niassa, and Nampula Provinces) predominantly being a peasant economy, the center (Zambézia, Manica, Sofala, and Tete Provinces) representing a plantation economy, while the south (Inhambane, Gaza, and Maputo Provinces) was a settler farm economy. In terms of total agricultural output, the north, center, and south regions accounted for 40, 43, and 17 percent, respectively. In terms of marketed production, the center was clearly the most important region; it accounted for 46 percent of national marketed output, followed by the north and the south, with 35 percent and 19 percent, respectively. The difference between relative share in total production and in marketed production was a result of the different patterns in the social structure of production between regions, a topic that we shall examine next.

## THE SOUTH

In the south, the medium- and small-scale settler farms were the dominant elements in the structure of production. These farms, which were characterized by irrigation, mechanization, and some level of technical expertise, relied on settler family labor and a seasonal peasant workforce to produce such staple food crops as rice, wheat, and potatoes, and specialized in a variety of vegetables and fruits as well as in dairy products and in animal husbandry. The plantation sector consisted of only two sugar plantations, both in Maputo Province. Peasants produced mainly for their own consumption and marketed a small surplus. Their major cash crops were cashew, maize, and groundnuts.

Although the dominant feature of the regional agricultural structure of production was settler farms, it was not the major force operating on the transformation of the peasantry into a rural semiproletariat. Adult male peasants in southern Mozambique became semiproletarianized as suppliers of migratory labor to the South African mining industry. The migrant patterns that emerged in Mozambique and other southern African countries were determined both by the mining industry and by local economic conditions in African communities.[10] State-to-state agreements gave the South African mining industry a stable workforce and control over the recruits. South Africa received access to Mozambican ports and railways in exchange for promising to hire workers from Mozambique. In turn, Portugal collected an emigration tax for each migrant laborer and benefited from a deferred payment scheme for migrants' wages that ensured that the migrants did not spend most of their earnings abroad. Under this scheme, about one-third of the workers' salaries were paid directly to the Portuguese government—at fixed rand gold prices after 1928—which then repaid the workers in local currency upon return to Mozambique.

Income from migrant labor fueled the processes of differentiation among the peasantry in this region. A stratum of middle peasants emerged that relied on migrant wages to invest in agricultural means of production, which were combined with small-scale artisan activities or trade, to stabilize its position within the rural economy. Through a combination of a developed agricultural base and nonfarm activities, these peasants managed to establish themselves within commodity production (by producing food surpluses for sale to the towns) or within the local community (by plowing the farms of other households with their oxen in exchange for payment, by engaging in petty trade, or by undertaking various crafts such as house building, brick making, carpentry, or tailoring). A larger group in the south, however, consisted of poor or marginalized peasants who did not own sufficient means of production to assure the family's livelihood and for whom migrant wage labor was a constant necessity.[11] They used their wages to purchase seeds, to pay for plowing, and to buy food in the local markets, as they were often deficit producers of food. Mine wage remittances formed the main basis for the separation between middle and poor peasants. Contrary to the literature on the "rise and fall" of peasantries in southern Africa—consequent on the dominance, first of merchant, and subsequently of mining capital—the development of the mining industry did not lead to the uniform decline of the Mozambican peasantry.[12] Migration took place for various reasons for different strata of peasants.

The importance of mining capital in shaping the social formation of southern Mozambique hindered the development of other forms of capital located within the area. In particular, settler farming was restricted in its development in the south by the competition for labor migrating to the South African mining complex. Economically, the settler farms could not afford to pay wages competitive with those prevailing in the mines, and politically, the settler community was unsuccessful in monopolizing the labor supply. The contradiction between the different types of capital was resolved partially through relying on *chibalo* or forced labor to assure the supply of workers to the farms. Given the harsh conditions of forced labor, the system pushed increasing numbers of men to South Africa and other neighboring countries where they could earn higher wages than at home.

In spite of Portugal's exploitation of the Mozambican peasantry as miners and workers, the colonial state promoted specialized peasant production in the 1950s and the 1960s. Because the Salazar government wanted to create a class of African peasants who would be supporters of the regime through incorporation into the colonial state, the colonial authorities admitted a small number of *assimilados* in the Colonato do Limpopo, a settlement scheme established in

Gaza.[13] Similarly, in the Lower Limpopo, the colonial state provided a middle stratum of peasants, known locally as *machambeiros,* with technical assistance, regular inputs, and material incentives enabling them to expand their agricultural base.[14]

## THE CENTER

In the central region, the major agricultural area of the country, the dominant feature was the plantation economy. Due to the historical development of the colonial economy in this region, however, a mixture of a labor-supplying and a cash crop–producing peasantry developed in a predominantly plantation economy. In the period 1880–1926, foreign-owned concessionary companies were given political and administrative powers to develop a plantation economy in the center and the north.[15] Subsequently, in the period 1926–1960, the Salazar government limited foreign economic influence and abolished the political and administrative powers of the companies, restricting foreign capital to the plantation economy in the central region.

By 1938, the colonial regime had imposed a brutal system of forced cotton cultivation throughout rural Mozambique to supply the expanding textile industry in Portugal. In the central region, it meant that peasants were forced to grow cotton on their family farms and to supply labor to the plantations. Labor demands on the peasantry were exacerbated in the 1940s with the arrival of settler farmers who were also in need of a seasonal labor force. The colonial administration provided forced labor for these farmers as it had done for the plantations, with men performing most of this work and women continuing to grow the cotton on their own farms.

The patterns of social differentiation within the peasantry varied considerably. Plantations needed seasonal workers and food to feed their labor force. The peasantry supplied both the labor and the food, but the dominance of each element varied by region and by stratum. Those peasants who lived in proximity to plantations and had been expelled from their farms with the establishment of the plantation sector were more proletarianized and dependent upon wages for their subsistence than those who lived in more remote areas.[16] Those areas further distanced from plantations had more complex differential patterns in which some peasants became more specialized in supplying food and others in supplying labor power, but neither exclusively so. It was mostly within the food-supplying areas that a stratum of middle peasants emerged, based on the sale of maize, beans, and other food crops to the plantation sector.[17]

In those areas characterized by cash-crop production, the state's control of both producer prices and the marketing system severely limited the scope of peasant social differentiation. It was only in the 1950s, with an increase in producer prices for cotton combined with regular technical assistance and inputs provided by the state, that a middle peasantry began to consolidate its position.[18] By the end of the colonial era, in this region as in the south, an increasing number of middle-peasant farmers were able to improve their socioeconomic status.

## The North

In the northern region of the country, the cash crop–producing peasantry was the dominant feature in the structure of agricultural production. The major cash crops were cashew and cotton, and the principal food crops, of which the surpluses were sold, were cassava and groundnuts. Compared to the other regions, less research has been conducted in the north, especially in Niassa, but some generalizations can be based on data from cotton studies.[19] After 1930 the peasantry no longer served principally as laborers on plantations but was forced to grow cotton. The government established the Colonial Cotton Export Board (JEAC) during the first phase of cotton production, 1931–1961. As a technical and supervisory body, JEAC's role was to increase production and improve the quality of cotton. The JEAC along with colonial administrators established the minimum area that a peasant household had to cultivate in cotton as well as a timetable for planting. The government set prices that the Portuguese concessionary companies paid to the peasants for raw cotton at artificially depressed levels to maximize the profits of the state. This policy minimized social differentiation among peasants.

But after the Second World War, the cotton production system underwent dramatic changes, as the Portuguese state adopted an incentive-based system alongside forced cotton production, offering producers bonuses for high output, price increases, technical supplies, and improvements in infrastructure.[20] The reasons for the shift in state policy were both international and national in scope, ranging from criticism of Portuguese labor practices by international organizations to the poor quality of cotton.

In the second period, 1962–1974, the organization of cotton production and marketing changed. Portuguese settler farms, dependent on peasants as seasonal wage workers, became dominant. The ginning companies lost their monopoly on the purchase of cotton; the settler farms exported their cotton fiber directly; and the Mozambique Cotton Institute (IAM), which replaced the JEAC in 1961, established agricultural extension and credit programs for both Portuguese and Mozambican farmers. While the number of African producers fell in this period, a tiny stratum of peasant farmers established themselves as specialized producers of cotton, often hiring tractors and regularly using insecticides.[21] At the same time, they increased their marketing of groundnuts, cassava, and cashew nuts.

Labor migration was not as predominant in this region because the returns on migrant wages were not as high as in southern and central Mozambique, but the colonial policy of forced labor ensured that it still played a significant role. Large numbers of men preferred to work at higher wages in Tanganyika's sisal plantations and others went as far north as Kenya to construct the port of Mombasa. Moreover, in the 1960s, it became common for young men to seek wage labor. They sought employment in the construction of the Nacala-Malawi railway and in the expansion of the Nacala port, as well as in the expanding industry and service sectors in the cities of Nampula and Nacaroa. The increasing dependence on cash-crop production and wage labor, as well as the expansion of settler farms, led to greater peasant differentiation, as in the rest of Mozambique.

### The Impact of Colonialism on the Rural Economy

The colonial system operated in the countryside in two major ways. First, it institutionalized a system of migrant labor to South Africa, Southern Rhodesia, Malawi, and Tanganyika.[22] Internally, labor flowed to the mainly foreign-owned plantations in the center of the country. Second, the system forcibly transformed Mozambican peasants into a cash-cropping peasantry. Through migratory labor, *chibalo,* and forced cultivation of cash crops, the peasantry was made to fuel capital accumulation and was integrated into the world economy. Primitive capital accumulation at the expense of the peasantry was the norm.

In most parts of the country, forced crop production led peasants to change from the cultivation of grains such as sorghum, a labor-intensive subsistence crop, to cassava, a less labor-absorbing and less nutritious crop. Cassava also interfered less than sorghum or millet with the agricultural calendar of export crops like cotton and rice. The introduction of forced cash-crop production and labor migration fundamentally altered the division of labor between men and women on the family farms, absorbing male labor power and leading to a decline of subsistence production. Within the family household, women became responsible for subsistence production or cash-crop production and men supplied wage labor or tended the cash crop.

In the south, given the average length of a migrant contract abroad (twelve to eighteen months) and the high intensity with which adult men were involved in such work, it was impossible to integrate their wage work into the agricultural cycle of the peasant household. With the majority of men effectively separated from family farming, the burden of agricultural work and other family responsibilities shifted to women. These changes in the organization of family labor took place within a context of increased commodification in the rural community. Income from wage labor not only paid for consumer goods, but also financed inputs such as seeds and fertilizers and allowed for the purchase of oxen and plows, water pumps for irrigation, and tractors. In addition, certain tasks previously performed by men within the household became commodified. A large proportion of households cultivated with oxen and plows without actually owning them, by renting them from those peasants who did. Similarly, house building and the construction of water wells and tanks were financed out of migrant remittances. Finally, a proportion of earnings went to nonagricultural petty commodity producers (e.g., carpenters for furniture and tailors for clothes), giving rise to a division of labor in the local economy.[23]

Despite internal contradictions and distortions, the Portuguese private wholesalers, the rural petty bourgeoisie (private Portuguese and Asian traders, shopkeepers, and transporters), and the state helped the colonial economy to function in the countryside. These groups controlled marketing and transport. In the south, private Portuguese traders and transporters, many of them also landowners, controlled and conducted almost all of the marketing of produce from the settler farms to the urban centers. Thus, the Portuguese traders marketed the cash crops of the peasantry and the distribution of food imports, as well as the distribution of produce from the settler farms.

The Portuguese traders and *cantineiros*, rural shopkeepers, were linked to a network of private wholesalers, most of whom were Portuguese. These wholesalers linked shopkeepers and consumers, often providing capital to the shopkeepers for the necessary infrastructure (shops, warehouses, and transport facilities) to market produce as well as to introduce commodities into the rural areas. For peasants, the rural shopkeepers not only provided a major outlet for crops, but also were the main incentive for surplus production in the form of the enticements of well-stocked stores. This merchant capital was able to control the terms of trade vis-à-vis the peasantry through which the surplus produce was appropriated by virtue of its de facto monopoly over rural commerce and the exclusion of Africans from private trade. Frequently barter supplemented monetary exchange. By restricting part of the transactions to barter, the shopkeepers were able to depress the terms of trade; commodities bartered at much less than market value could be resold at a profit. Moreover, the provision of currency to peasant producers was bundled together with wholesale and retail commodity transactions. Shopkeepers wanted to limit currency supplies to peasants, thereby preventing them from trading their produce with others.

Through various statutory marketing boards, the Mozambican state played a leading role in the marketing and processing of export crops and an active role in the marketing of selected food crops. The IAM and the ICM were monopoly purchasers of cotton and cereals. For several decades, these institutes set fixed prices for cereals, soybeans, groundnuts, and cotton seed; prices reflected quality differences but could only fluctuate within ranges fixed by the administration. For crops grown on plantations (e.g., tea, sugar, copra, and sisal) and marketed by them, the international market determined prices. Given the extent of state intervention in internal and external trade as well as in other commercial activities—which broadened and deepened in the later stages of colonization—and the restriction of private trade to Europeans and Asians, there was little opportunity for African entrepreneurs. The exclusion of Mozambicans from commerce constituted a serious constraint on development after independence.

The economic gains that Portugal drew from its colony—foreign exchange from forced peasant cash crops and plantation export crops, transit incomes, and migrant labor fees and payments—depended upon its administrative control. The colonial state intervened in almost all aspects of people's lives, leaving behind a legacy of authoritarianism, violence, and repression. In contrast to the British and French colonies, where some Africans had access to limited participation in government, even if only late in the colonial experience, Portuguese colonialism in Africa was politically very repressive, based on a fascist regime in Portugal. At independence this grim historical legacy would pose several immediate challenges to the Mozambican government.

## The Crisis of the Peasant-Worker Economy

The disintegration of the colonial structures characterized the period of the transitional government (September 1974–June 1975) and approximately the first two years after independence. Massive emigration of the Portuguese settler population, representing the majority of the skilled and administrative labor, combined with capital flight occurred. The Portuguese settlers practiced economic sabotage in various forms—destruction of equipment, trucks, and economic infrastructure; killing of cattle stock; large-scale dismissal of workers from productive enterprises; and complete production standstills—on a large scale all over the country. The export of capital assumed enormous proportions and took various forms: foreign exchange was used to import goods without any imports subsequently materializing; and cashew, cotton, and other cash crops were exported without the foreign exchange returning to the national bank.[24] The illegal exportation to South Africa and Rhodesia of trucks, tractors, equipment, and cattle further depleted the available means of production in the country.

In the urban areas, the settlers' exodus caused the colonial economy to collapse. Medium and small enterprises closed down; the construction industry stagnated; the service sectors linked to tourism stood still; and domestic wage labor ceased. The impact of industrial production decline was cumulative since the fall in output of one sector (especially in such key sectors as transport, servicing, and repair of equipment) provoked pronounced falls in the output of other sectors.

In the countryside, as the Portuguese farmers and rural traders left, the systems they had instituted for agricultural marketing collapsed, along with those for the supply of agricultural inputs and equipment, spare parts, and service. With their departure, such incentives as the peasants had for market production disappeared, and outputs fell accordingly. From 1973 to 1975, total production of agricultural crops dropped 13 percent and total marketed agricultural output fell 43 percent. Marketed agricultural production of the settler farm and plantation sectors declined approximately 54 percent and 16 percent, respectively.[25]

For the peasantry, the departure of the settlers also meant loss of an outlet for agricultural surpluses, as peasants were unable to market their produce because of the breakdown in the marketing and transportation systems. From 1973 to 1975, peasant-marketed production fell by approximately 60 percent. The failure of the commercial sector or the state to buy peasant crops and to supply them with consumer and capital goods led to a longer term problem, with peasants producing less for the market in future years. For the Mozambican economy as a whole, the net effect of the rural crisis was a reduction in export earnings, derived predominantly from cotton and cashew, and an increasing need to import basic foods such as grains and maize.

The impact of the crisis was not uniform throughout the countryside because of the significant differences in the structure of production in the three different regions. The prolonged breakdown in the marketing network particularly affected the cash-cropping peasantry of the north and central regions. Their cash income from cotton, rice, and surpluses of maize and other food crops fell dramatically as they reduced commercial production in response to unreliable marketing conditions and the insufficient supply of basic consumer goods. Furthermore, the collapse of the economic base of urban centers such as Nampula and Nacala meant unemployment for both wage workers and the self-employed. Many migrants returned to the countryside, and many would-be migrants could find no employment. In the central area, foreign-owned plantations did not fold immediately but operated with decreasing managerial staff and technical workers, as well as fewer migrants.[26]

In the southern region, the massive abandonment of the settler farms, which produced predominantly for the internal market, resulted in acute food shortages in the urban centers, especially in the capital, Maputo. The productive capacity of the Incomati Valley, as in other parts of southern Mozambique, was reduced, transforming the once food-exporting area into a net importer.

Throughout the country, the lack of trained African entrepreneurs to fill the vacuum left by the exodus of Portuguese rural shopkeepers and traders partially accounts for the near collapse of internal trade. Other reasons were related to state policies. For example, the Frelimo government did not encourage Mozambicans (including Asian traders) who were capable of maintaining the marketing and transportation systems to replace the departing settlers. Instead, the leadership sought a complete transformation of commerce whereby the state assumed total control over wholesale and retail trade. This policy was reversed only in 1980, after a decision that state retail trade was too costly. Henceforth, private traders began to play an important role in rural marketing, though within a framework of planned pricing and wholesale distribution, organized and directed by state planning.

From early 1976 onward, the number of miners recruited to South Africa dropped suddenly to 43,000 men, about one-third of the previous year's figure. The immediate reason for this reduction was a recession in the South African economy that sharply increased urban unemployment, a problem that South Africa resolved by increasing its proportion of domestic labor in total labor and therefore exporting part of its unemployment. With the sharp decline of Mozambican labor migrating to South Africa, the economic situation of the peasantry in southern Mozambique worsened.

The impact of the reduction of migrant labor on the peasantry was unequal. The most severely affected were the young peasants for whom wage work was the only way they could establish a household and finance their initial investment in family agriculture. The poor peasantry, whose day-to-day necessities depended heavily on income from wage labor, found itself suddenly cut off from its principal source of subsistence. The sudden end to mine labor also rendered precarious the middle peasants' position. Although they had a more secure agricultural base than the poor peasants, middle peasants often relied on artisan activities to supplement their incomes and earned extra income through renting ox-plows to miners' families or selling their food surplus. Moreover, the decrease of remittances from the South African mines further reduced the internal circulation of money and goods in the rural economy. The disintegration of the South African connection came to reinforce the already existing breakdown of peasant agriculture.

The combined effects of a reduction of income from mine labor and from marketed agricultural production was a severe income and unemployment crisis for the peasantry. Unemployment in the countryside resulted in an accelerated flow of men, especially young men, to the urban centers in search of wage work; rural-urban migration was to be a chronic feature in southern Mozambique. In the urban centers, industry was unable to absorb more jobless persons after 1976, for the collapse of the colonial economy had produced unemployment in the tourist and service sectors. Conditions were not improved by Frelimo's agricultural policies, which failed to address the fact that the young men of the southern provinces flowed into Maputo City and other urban centers because they needed wage income to finance their initial investment in family agriculture.

In the first two years after independence, however, what appeared to be a problem concerning only miners was in fact the result of the two combined movements that characterized the crisis of the economy in the southern region: the disintegration of colonial capitalist agriculture and the breaking up of Mozambique's integration with the South African economy. The drop in the mine-labor recruitment did not imply that a migrant laborer could fall back on his agricultural base, since the latter, apart from being eroded during the first stage of the crisis, depended for its very reproduction on wage labor to supplement its basic consumption needs and to finance essential inputs.

The government's immediate response to the multifaceted crisis was the creation of politically organized mass-based groups, known locally as *grupos dinamizadores,* or dynamizing groups (GDs), and the nationalization of social services (e.g., health, education, and the provision of legal services), housing, and land ownership. With no organized state apparatus to direct the economy and few cadres thinly spread at the government level, Frelimo entrusted the GDs, committees of approximately a dozen Frelimo sympathizers, with complex political, economic, and social responsibilities. In the countryside, the GDs were supposed to prevent private land seizures of abandoned settler farms and estates. This state directive, however, already contained a definite strategic interest with respect to rural transformation: the abandoned property was not to be distributed to the peasantry, but was to constitute the basis for an emerging state agricultural sector and cooperatives. From the beginning, Frelimo's agenda did not include land reform in the rural areas. While no absolute land shortage existed in any part of Mozambique, there was a relative shortage of good land—that is, land that was fertile and where rains were plentiful and regular, or where irrigation facilities existed. The question of land redistribution was not a major issue in the Manhiça District of Maputo, but it was critical in those regions where land had been a problem in the colonial period such as Gaza, Zambézia, and Tete, where the Portuguese authorities had set up settlement schemes, European farms, and plantations.

Another task of the GDs was to mobilize peasants for production in cooperatives. Initially, the GDs managed to organize broad mass participation in collective fields and other reconstruction activities, but enthusiasm quickly evaporated, as cooperatives were beset by difficulties including lack of clear objectives, minimal organization, low production results, and ineffective relations with the state agricultural extension service. Overall, the progress of the GDs was uneven for a variety of internal and external reasons.

While the agrarian policy remained undefined from 1974 to 1977, several features and trends were evident. First, while in theory state farms and cooperatives were both key aspects of the government's rural development strategy, the state sector was given priority from the start. In 1976, the Ministry of Agriculture reorganized itself and created a National Directorate for the Organization of Collective Production (DINOPROC), which consisted of two branches: one dealing with state farms and the other for cooperatives. The former employed a team of fourteen agricultural specialists or economists, and the latter consisted of three members mainly skilled in political organization and the preparation of propaganda material.[27] Behind the ministry's allocation of a small proportion of its nontechnical staff to cooperative support was the assumption that merely increasing peasants' knowledge and control of the production process in a political way could lead to productivity increases. Thus, state assistance for the dissemination of scientific knowledge and material investment to make greater productivity possible, as well as production planning to enable peasants to take control of decision-making in the cooperatives, was not forthcoming. These activities required organization and coordination, implying the need for a more elaborate institutional setup at the ministerial level than three politically trained cadres.

Second, the resolution of the 1976 Central Committee meeting restricting cooperative membership exclusively to poor peasants—and those middle peasants prepared to hand over their oxen, plows, and other means of production to the collective unit—meant that the latter were not seen by Frelimo as having a significant role to play in the new Mozambican rural society.[28] As illustrated in table 1.2 (above), of the nearly 1.7 million farmers, there were approximately 390,000 middle farmers, or 25 percent of the total, who were responsible for most of the commercial production toward the end of the colonial period. Contrary to the Frelimo criteria, several case studies on cooperatives in southern Mozambique—including this work—show that middle peasants dominated these institutions, and that in some instances they came to have a disproportionate influence upon the functioning of the villages as well.[29] Instead of formulating guidelines to include the different groups of peasants in a rural development strategy, Frelimo's political line only sharpened contradictions between the state and those middle peasants who came to control the very institutions from which they were supposed to be excluded.

Third, according to Frelimo's development strategy, communal villages were central, fulfilling two objectives: the concentration of the rural population to provide basic social services (schools, stores, and health posts) and political facilities (party cells and state apparatus) while simultaneously laying the foundation for new forms of collective production. As in Tanzania—where the Frelimo leadership was based at the time when *ujamaa* (communal villages) and forced villagization came into effect—villagization also was seen as the most efficient method for bringing the peasantry under direct state control.[30] In practice, the formation of communal villages and cooperatives proceeded at a slow but steady pace in the rural areas, with people moving into them only gradually. By the end of 1977 cooperatives numbered fifteen hundred, of which the majority was based outside communal villages. The estimated eight hundred villages were distributed unevenly over the country, with three-quarters in Cabo Delgado, while the remaining two hundred villages were in Niassa, Nampula, Gaza, and Maputo.[31]

The most obvious problems of communal villages in this early period were organizational and technical—the same difficulties that challenged neighboring Tanzania's village settlement program in the 1970s.[32] Often these villages were poorly planned in terms of having insufficient water supplies to meet farming and family needs, great distances between residences and family farms as well as collective fields, limited possibility for future production expansion, and no access to roads. Many of these villages also lacked an economic base to establish or maintain the anticipated social services, and villages were established independently of collective production, despite the original intentions of becoming centers of residence. This discrepancy between village residence and cooperatives reflected wariness on the part of the majority of peasants to participate in a new production form whose economic results were uncertain.

Most villages were formed voluntarily in this period, with the major exceptions being those forced resettlements in Maputo and Gaza Provinces after the flooding of the Limpopo and Incomati Rivers in 1977 and 1978. Families displaced by the floods were not permitted to return to their farms afterward but were forcibly relocated in communal villages to provide labor on state farms and cooperatives. Some peasant farms were incorporated into the largest state agro-industrial complex in the country, CAIL, further exacerbating tensions between the state and sections of the poor and middle peasantry in the Limpopo Valley.[33] Frelimo assumed that these displaced persons would become agricultural laborers for the state farms, but peasants resisted, bitter that the new government continued with the colonial policy of depriving them of their land.

Last, with the collapse of marketing and distribution systems, Frelimo sought to develop a new marketing policy aimed at state control of wholesale trade, while retail trading was to be undertaken through a mixture of state, private, and cooperative outlets. In 1976, the government established consumer cooperatives and *lojas do povo*, people's shops run by the state and modeled on those developed in the liberated areas. Both enterprises operated on a system of rationing schemes, but the former included an accounting system based on ration cards that guaranteed family quotas while the latter organized sales on a first-come, first-served basis. Overall, consumer cooperatives established a system of distribution superior to people's shops. By 1980, Frelimo recognized that these state shops were inefficient and handed them over mainly to private traders.

It was not until 1977, at the Third Party Congress, that the Frelimo rural development strategy was clearly articulated. Nevertheless, from 1974 to mid-1977, there were strategic components built into some political, economic, and social policies. The framework was established for the next stage of state-led socialist agricultural transformation in the countryside.

# 2

# Frelimo

## From the Liberated Zones
## to Rural Socialism, 1964–1983

**The economic situation** began to deteriorate several years before Mozambique gained independence in 1975. Even before the fall of the Portuguese dictatorship in April 1974, the 250,000 settlers (who represented the majority of the skilled and managerial labor) had started to desert the colony—40,000 had left between 1971 and 1973.[1] Between the coup in Portugal and independence, at least another 100,000 left. The balance in 1975 was about 100,000, the bulk of whom left within one year. The departure of these settlers was combined with economic sabotage and flight: private businesses had begun to smuggle their capital out of the colony in 1970, a practice that accelerated between 1974 and 1975, the years of the transitional government, when an estimated U.S. $360 million was illegally exported.[2]

With the near collapse of the colonial economy, which implied a complex mix of income-earning and welfare-generating strategies for peasants, new alternatives in the agricultural sector had to be explored. The key question was not whether some form of transformation was necessary—this was a given— but whether the appropriate options would be selected. This question would almost certainly require a debate that was open enough to shape arguments for alternative policies toward a regionally diverse and socially differentiated rural society. When Frelimo came to power, the movement was predisposed to rural socialism based on its revolutionary experience and ideology, and the economic crisis reinforced the leadership's decision to implement a socialist strategy of development in both industry and agriculture.

There is consensus among scholars that Frelimo's agrarian policy during the phase of attempted socialist transition from 1977 to 1983 was a dismal failure, both economically and politically. State farms performed poorly, cooperative production was negligible, and peasant production declined. Furthermore, the development of a centralized hegemonic party excluded the peasantry from the political process. The reasons for the failure of its socialist project, however, have been a topic of academic debate. Until recently, the dominant explanation concentrated on external forces and intervention, mainly South African destabilization. While not minimizing the role played by Frelimo's policies in shaping the country's crisis, scholars in this school were inclined to blame the collapse of socialism in Mozambique on the war waged by the South African-backed Renamo.[3] In the mid-1980s academic interest shifted to focus on Frelimo's policy of villagization and the extent to which it may have contributed to Renamo's successes in rural Mozambique.[4] Critics of Mozambique's collectivization strategy argued that communal villages either created or exploited social tensions already present between different traditional political and kinship groups. According to this argument, the state further alienated sections of the rural population by excluding traditional authorities from political power and by rejecting their diverse cultural traditions and religious practices. Moreover, Frelimo tried to imprint upon peasant society a single strategy of national development. According to these scholars, henceforth referred to as the traditionalists, villagization was more a means of constructing the state apparatus in the rural areas than a strategy for development.

The traditionalists are only partially correct: Policy and political errors are key to understanding the demise of rural socialism in Mozambique. But Frelimo's fundamental policy errors were not its villagization policy or its alienation of traditional leaders. Over time Frelimo retreated from many of the central aspects of its rural program.[5] The traditionalist account is ingenuous in attributing Frelimo's villagization policy to the spread of the war because so little collectivization of peasant residence and production was ever realized. Frelimo continued to invest heavily in the state-farm sector until the Fourth Party Congress in 1983, but it retreated from its attempt to implement villagization at a national level, adopted a gradual and vacillating approach to cooperativization, and accepted a role for private trade and production in rural areas. The reasons for this retreat had to do with the different ways rural people and government officials on the ground responded to Frelimo's program.

Studies show that the major problems of the cooperative movement were its marginality and its low productivity.[6] But to understand the successes and failures of cooperatives, it is also necessary to examine more closely their internal dynamics, that is, how peasants shaped the composition, authority structure, and activities of cooperatives. For example, peasants' struggles over resources, labor allocation, and income distribution decided the history of Ilha Josina Machel's two cooperatives in the late 1970s. After that, the survival of the project-sponsored cooperatives came to depend on their ability to provide for the needs of poor and middle peasants. Household production held the key to the structure and pace of peasants' participation in wage labor and the cooperative movement during the 1980s.

The objectives of Frelimo's villagization program varied over time and there were radical differences between areas. In their attempt to discredit Frelimo's rural development strategy, the traditionalists ignore the pre-1983 achievements that enhanced the lives of the village dwellers. Notwithstanding the technical and logistical problems associated with communal villages, a genuine effort was made by the Ministry of Health, Ministry of Public Works and Housing, and Ministry of Education toward improving village conditions in the late 1970s and early 1980s. By 1982 more than 60 percent of the 1,360 communal villages had benefited from water supply systems and were provided with schools, while more than 30 percent had health posts administered by a basic health technician.[7] The situation had changed dramatically by 1983. Renamo was operating in all of the central and southern provinces and communal villages were transformed into protected villages, as part of a wider counterinsurgency strategy in Nampula, Sofala, and Manica. In these provinces, peasants saw Frelimo not as a development agent but as an embattled agent of control.

Party and state institutions were established in areas both with and without communal villages. Christian Geffray's traditionalist critique goes beyond a denunciation of Frelimo for creating communal villages to an attack for imposing new political institutions to replace the *regulado* system in the countryside. For Geffray, "the state and the party could only be present in the rural context through a village-secretary, a village party-cell, village youth and women's organizations, etc. whether the villages existed physically or not."[8] His argument, then, applies to rural communities like Ilha Josina Machel that did not build communal villages but established government and party structures.

In Mozambique, as in other African colonies, Europeans created political dualism: the sharp jural separation between colonial and "customary" authority enforced in rural and urban areas. All Africans were legally subject to a customary ruler *(régulo)* unless they were *assimilados*. At independence, Frelimo's agrarian policy explicitly attacked the system of local governance based on *régulos* through which both labor recruitment and peasant access to land were regulated. The government eliminated the dual system that gave traditional authorities control over the rural population and replaced it with a unitary system of local government based first in GDs and then in the elected political structures of local assemblies and party cells.[9] In Ilha Josina Machel, the elimination of the *regulado* system meant that poor peasants were no longer forced to provide free labor on traditional authorities' farms; middle peasants no longer had to give a portion of their harvest to the *régulo* and his *cabos*, junior chiefs; and migrant workers no longer had to give a portion of their wages to traditional chiefs upon their return. Frelimo's policy regarding *régulos* had a rural constituency among those who had suffered (and were excluded) from political authority in the past.

New scholarship has presented a nuanced view of the *regulado* system, chieftaincy, and its related institutions. In her 1994 study on Manica Province, Jocelyn Alexander described the *régulo*'s duties and responsibilities as part of the colonial administration.[10] Yet her interviews with peasants also suggested that the *régulo* had some popular legitimacy, having a traditional title and working and living in African languages and cultures. This does not negate, however, the fundamental point: the *régulo*'s tasks were colonial, not precolonial or traditional in nature. Traditional leaders were part of an inherently undemocratic and inequitable system. Indeed, Mahmood Mamdani singles out the colonial legacy of political dualism—a bifurcated power that mediated racial domination through tribally organized local authorities, reproducing racial identity in citizens and ethnic identity in subjects—as the major obstacle to democratization in postindependent African countries.[11]

The problem was not the elimination of the *regulado* system but that Frelimo replaced chiefs and traditional authorities by one-party state officials. Thus, the structural characteristics of the colonial system were carried over into independence although the nomenclature changed and the autocratic role of chiefs was taken over by single-party officials. Party and state officials were not easily distinguishable, as party members filled many of the posts left vacant by the departed Portuguese bureaucrats and managers. The result was that positions such as locality administrator and locality party secretary were frequently invested into one person.[12] Furthermore, given the hierarchical political system, local officials found that they had no systematic way to influence political decisions at the provincial and national levels.

What I highlight is the contradictory and complex process that led to Frelimo's evolution from a popular victorious liberation movement into a bureaucratic, antipeasant one-party state. I also analyze Frelimo's socialist policies, showing that there was little socialist content to them. The leadership chose a rapid strategy of agricultural development dependent on modernization through mechanization that was not different from other third-world countries' attempts to promote economic development. While a strand of non-Marxist agricultural-modernization theory also identifies agricultural development with mechanization, Frelimo's decision to pursue this strategy rested on a particular notion of socialist development that prioritized state farms and devalued peasant farming.[13] Furthermore, foreign donors—both socialist and capitalist—supported the strategic course chosen by Mozambican leaders, as they preferred to finance large-scale, capital-intensive agriculture for ideological and economic reasons. And internally, influential government bureaucrats supported state farms for the economic benefits generated by a collectivization policy.

This chapter begins with the war of national liberation and the experiences of the liberated zones, where the relationship between the postindependent state and the peasantry is rooted. Frelimo could pursue its own economic policies after 1975 because it came to power uncontested and with strong support among the peasantry in areas in which its guerrilla forces operated. The leaders no longer heard peasant voices, a standard theme in revolutionary societies in Central America and Africa.[14] Instead, the leadership came to depend on the modernizing state bureaucracy.

Following a brief résumé of the period from 1964 to 1974 (the beginning of the armed struggle to the end of Portuguese colonialism), this chapter examines Mozambique's agricultural policy, indicating the main trends and shifts in two periods: from 1975 to 1980 (the early postindependence years including the Third Party Congress of Frelimo); and from 1981 to 1983 (the years of policy reforms up to and including the Frelimo's Fourth Party Congress). In the first five years of independence, or "the triumphalist phase," Frelimo believed it was moving from one victory to another. Cooperatives were part of the government's rhetoric but never the main thrust in reality. After the Third Party Congress in 1977, the government gave priority to the state-farm sector and let cooperative, peasant, and private farming evolve on the basis of their own internal resources. The second period, 1981–1983, was characterized by Frelimo initiatives and policy changes to correct the mistakes of previous years and by South African intervention. At the Ministry of Agriculture, for example, two cooperative projects were established (Projects CO-1 and CO-2) to assist selected pilot cooperatives. Subsequently, at the fourth congress, in 1983, Frelimo officially recognized the high political and economic costs of concentrating investments in the state sector while ignoring the cooperative and family sectors, and it decided to reallocate some resources from the state sector to private and family farming and to cooperatives. The policy shift in the second period toward small-scale agriculture reflected the party's desire to adapt to failures on the ground and to a more difficult external situation.

## The Experiences and Interpretations of the "Liberated Zones," 1964–1974

On June 25, 1962, Frelimo was founded, and three months later, at the first congress, Eduardo Mondlane was elected president. Frelimo was a "front" in two senses: first, it was the product of three ethnically based parties merging together, and second, it was an alliance of different classes (workers, peasants, and the petty bourgeoisie).[15] The movement's platform for creating unity was simple: opposition to colonialism and the demand for national independence. Given Portugal's refusal to negotiate a decolonization settlement with its colonies, Frelimo was forced to take up arms, as the nationalist movements did in Angola and Guinea-Bissau. The scholarship on the Mozambican revolution has dealt with the formation of Frelimo and its achievements during the war of liberation.[16] But what is not so clear is why and how Frelimo was transformed from a popular liberation front into an antipeasant one-party state. It is possible to detect some of the problems that emerged after independence in this previous period.

In 1964 the armed struggle began in Cabo Delgado. During the next ten years, the guerrilla movement came to control large areas in Cabo Delgado, Niassa, and Tete Provinces, territories Frelimo declared as "liberated zones," indicating areas where the colonial administration had been eliminated and partially replaced by institutions of popular participation, as well as new programs in health, education, and agriculture. Nampula played only a marginal role in the liberation struggle because Frelimo's attempts to establish a military front there met with only limited success. This resulted in part from the power of some traditional political leaders, who discerned Frelimo's anti-traditionalist orientation, and in part from the historical distrust that characterized ethnic relations between the Makua, people of Nampula, and the Makonde, people of Cabo Delgado, who constituted the majority of Frelimo's guerrilla army.[17] As in other areas, the Portuguese manipulated ethnic and religious differences as a tactic to divide rural support for Frelimo. Although Frelimo managed to advance into central Mozambique in 1972, these provinces remained only semiliberated—that is, territories where the Portuguese had left but where Frelimo was not quite functioning. The armed struggle for independence never reached the southern provinces, which produced all three of Frelimo's presidents—Eduardo Mondlane, Samora Machel, and Joaquim Chissano.

In the context of administering its territories, Frelimo leaders were forced to deal with contradictions internal to the movement. They had to decide whether to continue with the same colonial economic, social, and political structures and relations or build alternative forms. According to the literature, it was in working through this issue and other such decisive questions that the movement expanded its sole initial objective of gaining national independence to the transformation of Mozambican society. Its radicalization (which culminated in the death of Eduardo Mondlane in 1969) is usually described as the outcome of an intense internal struggle between the narrow nationalists on the one hand and the popular revolutionaries on the other, generally referred to as the "two lines" in Frelimo, who disagreed on fundamental issues of gender, race, and class as well as on the question of the character of the new state.[18] The most prominent spokesperson on each side was Lazaro Nkavandame and Samora Machel, respectively.[19]

Nkavandame was one of the founders of the Mozambican African Voluntary Cotton Society, a peasant cotton-growing cooperative formed in Cabo Delgado in 1957 that Makonde peasants established with little input from the colonial administration, distinguishing it from those marketing cooperatives in the south. In the early 1960s, when Portuguese authorities hindered the growth of this cooperative movement, the co-op leaders, most of whom were middle and wealthier peasants, joined Frelimo. However, the Makonde leaders showed little interest in social revolution. Many of them, including their leader, Nkavandame, were not radicals but social conservatives who wanted more access to land, labor, and markets as well as fewer state restrictions. Although they held different objectives from the revolutionary militants, these Makonde leaders and their supporters represented a political economic group that had a material basis inside Mozambique.

In 1962 Nkavandame was appointed Frelimo's provincial secretary of Cabo Delgado and director of the Department of Commerce. According to Frelimo's official historiography, by 1966 peasants were complaining that Nkavandame was using his party position for personal profit and was underpaying the workers on Frelimo's cooperative farms. As matters came to a head, the argument broadened. Nkavandame and his group came to see the struggle almost exclusively in racial terms ("that only the white man was an exploiter"), while Machel and his followers increasingly perceived the conflict in class terms. Eventually the crisis of leadership degenerated into violence: Mateus Muthemba and Paulo Kankhomba, Machel supporters, were assassinated, and, a month after Nkavandame was ousted from Frelimo, Eduardo Mondlane was killed. With the expulsion of Nkavandame and other northerners, the Frelimo leadership was dominated by educated southerners—an issue that Renamo and other opposition groups would stress in the 1990s.

Under Samora Machel, who succeeded Mondlane, and influenced by the blowout with Nkavandame and by the Stalinist Russian and socialist Tanzanian experiences, the leadership grew suspicious of the middle and wealthier peasants. Familiar with Stalinist ideas in Russia, the leaders came to see all better-off peasants as "protokulak" farmers. Many of these Frelimo militants had studied abroad in communist countries and/or had strong ties with communist parties in Western Europe, and they were influenced by the prevailing orthodoxy. Political developments in Africa also had an impact on shaping Frelimo's ideology. During the 1960s, notions of "African socialism" dominated postindependence political discourse on the continent, and Frelimo was particularly influenced by the African socialist project in Tanzania, where the movement had been based since 1962. Following the Arusha Declaration of 1967, the key strategy of the ruling Tanzanian African National Union (Tanu) was to create *ujamaa* villages, communal setups where voluntary collective production was to be encouraged. But the program ran into trouble, and by 1970 forced villagization was begun, despite peasants' continuing resistance to collectivization.[20] The massive social dislocation caused by forced villagization, combined with poor weather, led to a food-production crisis, which required grain imports.

One of the key lessons that the Frelimo militants drew from the Tanzanian experience was that its leaders had not taken the class struggle seriously. According to their analysis, *ujamaa* failed primarily because it did not allow for class struggles, which in the Tanzanian context meant pitting the poor peasants against the rich peasants. Predicated on the supposed nonexistence of social differentiation in African society, Tanzania's "African socialism" failed to account for kulak resistance. Frelimo concluded that class struggle was a prerequisite for the development of socialism and thus sought to eliminate future "Nkavandames" and other well-off farmers, using Nkavandame and his legacy to repress the wider social base that he was supposed to represent. In the aim of destroying his legacy, they exaggerated the threat of a kulak class and categorized wealthier peasants and capitalist farmers as enemies of the revolution.

New members who joined Frelimo in 1974, including those Mozambicans who held junior positions in the Portuguese civil service and those who sympathized with the nationalist struggle but were not Frelimo activists, reinforced this anti–middle-peasant line. They joined the liberation movement because they understood that the colonizers were not going to win the war and wanted to be on the victorious side, not because they held the same socialist political and ideological objectives. In addition, Frelimo started to recruit people for technical reasons, and many of these individuals came to occupy key positions within the party and the state after independence. Frelimo came to depend on the skills and advice of these bureaucratic "modernizers" (as well as foreign experts) and placed more emphasis on technocratic solutions than on "peasant know-how" to develop the country.

Moreover, the peasant support for Frelimo during the war led to the incorrect view that this support also represented a full endorsement of its socialist programs. It resulted not only in an overstatement of the degree to which new social relations had grown in the liberated zones but also in an understatement of the continuing importance of family-based agricultural production. Four forms of production relationships existed inside Frelimo areas: (1) individual production, (2) precollective fields, (3) collective fields, and (4) collective production. Of these, individual production by peasant families remained dominant even to the end of the war.[21] Second in practice were the precollective fields, where the peasants continued to cultivate on individual plots as was normal before the war, although as a result of new organization, part of the harvest was set aside to feed the soldiers. Simultaneously, and more common, peasants contributed by cultivating some fields reserved for the soldiers, just as they shared their marketable surpluses with Frelimo. Next were collective fields, which were worked in addition to private plots; peasants worked collectively a designated number of days each month on a communal field. Each person's labor time was recorded and the harvest was distributed according to the number of days worked. And finally, there was collective production organized within Frelimo's own structures (e.g., schools and health posts). The least practiced form of production was one in which peasants worked the land jointly with the guerrillas and shared the produce and profits equally. While the movement succeeded in introducing new and varying forms of production, these units did not reach the same level in all the fronts of the struggle. Full cooperative production emerged only in the liberated zones of Cabo Delgado, and even there not extensively.

The experience gained in the liberated areas frequently has been referred to as a model for the development of postindependence Mozambique.[22] Frelimo's tendency to romanticize its own accomplishments by holding up as a model for agrarian policy the most radical and exceptional transformations attained in very few sites clearly promoted a distorted idea of collective agriculture. In the end, this contorted image came to dominate popular accounts of the collectivization experience for two reasons: (1) it served to reinforce the sense of common purpose, of identity, and of solidarity between peasants and Frelimo; and (2) it helped to maximize state bureaucratic power.

## The "Triumphalist" Years, 1975–1980

For the first two years of independence, Frelimo relied on decentralized decision-making and mass mobilization practices. By 1977 the dominant Marxist faction in Frelimo decided to centralize power. Subsequently, Frelimo reconstituted itself from a national liberation movement to a self-defined vanguard party in preparation for socialist transformation.[23] As Mozambique's single party, Frelimo became almost an extension of the state, eliminating the distinction between party and state. Despite Frelimo's rhetoric about being a workers' and peasants' party, the modernizing state bureaucracy was making most of the key decisions, and those who came to hold state power represented the class interests of government bureaucrats, concerned mainly with their own survival and political power, and accumulated wealth eventually. These included the heads of operational divisions at the Ministry of Agriculture, directors of state farms, and central planners at the Ministry of Planning.

At the third congress of Frelimo, in 1977, the newly self-proclaimed Marxist-Leninist party adopted a series of social and economic directives that set out the main lines of Mozambique's socialist program for development.[24] Agriculture was to be developed to provide resources for industrialization, a common conception in socialist and nonsocialist development strategies. The means for transforming and increasing production in agriculture were to be the organization of peasant farmers in cooperatives and state farms. Family or small-holder agriculture was to be collectivized, and peasant farmers were to be employed on mechanized state farms or on semimechanized producer cooperatives. The labor force for the state farms and cooperatives was to come from communal villages, where the rural population would be concentrated.

Frelimo's socialist development strategy antagonized the peasantry. Poorer peasants resented the government's intent to transform them into agricultural workers for state farms and producer cooperatives. Middle and wealthier peasants resented the government's plan to control their capital accumulation. And, given the importance attached to state farms at the third congress, small-scale peasant farms were accorded the lowest priority in the national development strategy. At the same time, the countryside as a whole was downgraded in relation to the urban sector and seen as a source of accumulation to fund and feed heavy industry, which Frelimo had decided was the key to development and the creation of a working class.[25] Frelimo's social base thus shifted from the countryside to the town and cities, and it came to depend on a burgeoning state bureaucracy.

Subsequently, three features came to characterize the period from 1977 to 1980: (1) the channeling of agricultural investment toward large-scale state farms and agro-industrial complexes; (2) the consolidation of bureaucratic privilege and power; and (3) the operation of a centrally planned economy. At no time did Frelimo commit major resources to the cooperative or family sectors, although sometimes it spoke as if it might do so. Of agricultural investment between 1977 and 1983, about 90 percent went to the state sector, 2 percent to cooperatives, and virtually nothing to small-scale family farming.[26]

Those individuals who controlled the state apparatus and a bureaucracy whose political power depended on the primacy of state enterprises came to determine the agricultural policies pursued after the third congress, and their policies reflected a strong bias toward identifying the socialist sector with mechanization of large units. The decision to invest heavily in the mechanization of the state sector was linked to an oversimplified concept of agricultural modernization. Development was seen as the process of building a new and separate modern sector in both agriculture and industry, marked by the use of the most modern techniques and organizational structures available. This view of development was influential among the most powerful government and parastatal decision-makers and was supported by international donors.

At the Ministry of Agriculture, the heads of operational divisions favored the large mechanized farms, arguing that higher productivity had to be based on modern technologies and methods of organization rather than simple tools and shifting cultivation patterns. The managers in the parastatal enterprises created to manage the large farms reinforced the government's bias toward the state sector. Despite the disastrous economic results of state-farm production, the directors argued each year that a reversal in performance was imminent once problems of inadequate rainfall, nonarrival of crucial supplies, reliance on untrained personnel, and newness of organizational system were resolved.

Compounding these difficulties were international donors that supported the large, mechanized state-farm strategy. For a number of Eastern European countries, the strategy fit their own governments' policies, and it also made Mozambique a market for their machinery and management systems. The same was true for some of the Western donors and for private firms with agricultural interests, such as suppliers of agricultural chemicals and fertilizers.[27] In 1978, the Mozambique Nordic Agricultural Program, MONAP I—a joint effort by the five Nordic countries and the United Nations Food and Agricultural Organization, FAO—was started to support the Mozambican government's takeover of abandoned settler farms and plantations.[28]

Another factor that facilitated the consolidation of technocratic privilege was government planners' control of the annual state plan and resources allocated under it. As the state sector grew, economic planning was developed and organized under a National Planning Commission (NPC) to which all the major ministries, such as agriculture, internal commerce, and transport, were subordinated. The state budget, which centralized all state financial resources, provided for the allocation of resources among the ministries in accordance with the central plans drawn up by the NPC.[29] State planners justified the need for centralized decision-making by reference to the low productivity and organizational problems in every sector and by the scarcity of trained labor power. Yet there were costs: the highly centralized system at the national level left little scope for flexibility in planning and in economic policy at the regional, provincial, and district levels.

The main losers under Frelimo's development strategy were the majority of peasant farmers. Government decision-makers identified the state sector as modern agriculture while portraying the family sector as "backward subsistence farming." Adherents of this classically dualist position explained that in the colonial era, the peasantry's integration into market exchange was due to extraeconomic factors such as forced cultivation or contract labor, forms of exploitation that did not fundamentally alter the precapitalist character of peasant production. With independence, their argument goes, the peasantry had returned to their precapitalist subsistence economy, retreating from the production of surplus and withdrawing from the market, rejecting the production of cash crops as well as labor migration. Like certain neoclassical economists, these Marxists analysts saw the eventual disappearance of peasant agriculture as a goal to be valued.[30]

The opponents of this dualist position were a minority of government officials and academic researchers at the Center of African Studies (CEA) at Universidade Eduardo Mondlane.[31] They maintained that the objective conditions in colonial rural Mozambique were characterized by a deep involvement of the peasantry in market relationships and their dependence on it, either as suppliers of labor power or as cash-crop producers. According to this perspective, forced cultivation of cash crops and migrant wage labor significantly altered the Mozambican agricultural system. Peasant production was organized to produce consistently subsistence plus surplus value, which accrued to capital in Mozambique, in Portugal, and in South Africa. The cheapness of colonial labor power depended on the peasant family's being able to feed itself and to produce a surplus.

Hence for the peasantry, their subordination to wage labor in the colonial period did not mean total separation from the land. Rather, the income derived from wage work and cash-crop production became a necessary element to meet subsistence and for the reproduction of family agriculture. To these analysts, the dual economy advocates seemed to underestimate the extent to which the agrarian family units needed material inputs and investment from outside simply in order to keep going, and minimized the peasantry's historically conditioned responsiveness to commercial or monetary incentives.

The relation between force and market, however, varies from place to place and time to time, depending on a variety of factors. On Ilha Josina Machel, for example, both were present and intertwined to different degrees: a partial and growing market integration existed alongside a relative peasant autonomy.[32] That autonomy was effectively breached, not by the market but by force. The agency of that force was the cadre of chiefs and traditional authorities aligned with the colonial state.

With independence, Frelimo did not resolve the crisis for the peasantry, which confronted the disintegration of colonial capitalist agriculture and, in the south (where most peasant families depended on money from migrant labor), the sharp cut of Mozambicans working in the South African mines. Instead, the government's agricultural policy set up extreme tensions in the rural areas between representatives of the state and its state farms, on the one hand, and the peasantry, on the other. These tensions took many forms, including forced labor under the rubric of "voluntarism" and appropriation of peasant land for state use. The functionaries of the single-party state became the chiefs of the new order, embodying fused power and applying force to crack open the relative autonomy of peasant households. The incorporation of some peasant farms into state enterprises and later the forced collectivization of other peasants were practices that set the context for further difficulties leading to peasant resistance and eventual alienation.

## The Reform Years, 1981–1983

The years 1981-1983 marked a period of much more overt struggle in Mozambique than the preceding five years. The economic trends continued to be contradictory: On the one hand there was the reinforcing of the earlier command-based tendencies, best illustrated with the country's first ten-year plan, known as the Prospective Indicative Plan (PPI). On the other hand, this increasingly centralized and authoritarian trend went along with new initiatives and changes in government policies, particularly in agriculture. After the Fourth Party Congress in 1983, the government began to dismantle state farms and to redistribute land to peasant and private farmers.

The forces that brought about a reconsideration of policy were twofold: the economic performance of the state farms continued to be dismal, and agricultural producers themselves made their own unhappiness known to the leadership. At the nationwide discussion sessions organized in workplaces and neighborhoods to discuss the themes or "theses" of the Fourth Party Congress at the end of 1982, Mozambicans had opportunities to articulate their concerns to party members. Given the deteriorating economic situation and the widening of the war waged by the Renamo forces, the Frelimo government found it politically expedient to respond to farmers' grievances and those of other rural dwellers.

The decade began, however, with Frelimo still pursuing ambitious programs of rapid political and economic change. The leadership proclaimed the 1980s as the "Decade of Development," sure that Mozambique would be transformed into a developed industrial country by 1990. This objective was incorporated in the PPI, which outlined the development guidelines for 1981–1990. For numerous reasons — including the lack of foreign investment and the collapse of the market combined with the growing economic destruction wrought by Renamo, which made an increase in exports impossible—the PPI was never implemented. But the insistence on mega-projects was maintained, an indicator of the ideological, institutional, and class forces that created the emphasis on huge state farms and were strengthened by them.

Despite the financial investment and human resources that went into the state agricultural sector, the huge farms failed to meet the very pressing economic needs of the country. In 1981 the Ministry of Agriculture admitted that not one state farm was profitable. Indeed, the government's agricultural policies were not having the required economic effects: state farms performed poorly, cooperative production was negligible, and peasant agricultural production declined. Agricultural production as a whole had not recovered to preindependence levels as intended, and agricultural exports remained generally low. Family agriculture remained the productive base of the majority of communal villages.

From 1981 onward, Mozambique confronted a more difficult external situation and was subjected to the increasing terrorism of the South African–backed Renamo. In addition to targeting ordinary citizens, the rebel group attacked key infrastructure, aggravating already severe economic problems and social and political tensions.[33] From 1981 to 1983, Renamo destroyed 140 villages, 840 schools, 200 health posts, and 900 rural shops, and caused thousands of deaths and hundreds of millions of dollars of damage to the Mozambican economy.[34] By disrupting the production and distribution networks, Renamo effectively halted the already inadequate supply of industrial commodities and consumer goods into the rural areas, which further hindered the capacity and willingness of farmers to produce for the official market. Education and health facilities, institutions seen as the two achieved gains of the Mozambican revolution, were singled out. It also systematically targeted roads, railway, warehouses, and other infrastructure, as well as persons (i.e., government officials, party members, and expatriates) associated with rural development. During this period, Mozambique's economy was undermined by a combination of Frelimo policy errors, but the real devastation was caused by the low-intensity warfare of Renamo.

Frelimo leaders conceded that in some regions, even if the local population was not actively cooperating with Renamo, they no longer supported the government and allowed Renamo to operate unchallenged. Unhappy with Frelimo's agricultural policies but fearful of Renamo, the bulk of the rural population chose neutrality as a survival strategy in the war between the government and the rebel group.[35] The exceptions were found in some districts in Nampula, Manica, and Sofala Provinces, where the government used coercive measures to enforce its villagization program.[36] More people in these areas became receptive to Renamo and actively supported the rebels against Frelimo.

Following a self-critical assessment of its policies and practices, Frelimo proposed fundamental changes at the Fourth Party Congress in 1983. These included decentralization of planning, organization, and implementation in agriculture and industry and a corresponding shift in emphasis away from large-scale, capital-intensive projects, toward small-scale local projects based on appropriate technologies, both in agriculture and manufacturing.[37] To achieve these goals, the congress concluded that mega-agriculture projects were at the time beyond the technical and organizational capacity of the country's labor force. New investment in the state-farm sector was to be halted and big farms were to be reduced and consolidated, with land redistributed to peasant and private farmers. The congress further instructed state institutions to provide much greater support to the cooperative, family, and private sectors. Toward this end, the congress emphasized the need to improve the rural marketing system and the supply of consumer and producer goods to agriculturists. Small local industries were to provide manufactured goods for local consumption, thus linking industrial and agricultural development strategies. To market agricultural products, both the number of fixed posts and mobile brigades were expanded.

How to improve cooperative and family farming was not an obvious matter. The congress documents remained vague, leaving room for various interpretations about what constituted a policy of aiding small-scale production. Authorities often combined these two sectors into one, assuming that the family sector could rapidly be transformed into the direction of cooperative farming, overlooking the fact that the existing cooperative sector was an adjunct to family farming and that it could hardly survive unless the family sector was healthy. The issue of assistance to family farming was complicated further by the failure of the congress to analyze the class or social context in which a shift in resources would take place.[38] In party documents, the peasantry appeared as a homogeneous mass instead of a group heterogeneous and socially differentiated in character. By leaving the class and gender features of the peasantry vague, Frelimo set the stage for further struggles over land and other resources. The allocation of material resources was not neutral and, therefore, a policy that aimed to shift resources to the peasantry needed to be assessed in specific terms.

The Fourth Party Congress policy changes were offset by repressive measures that included Operation Production, public executions, and floggings. In 1983 Frelimo enforced Operation Production, a program of forced removal of urban unemployed that was meant to curb the ongoing rural-urban migration. In the south, the relocated included a diverse group of persons ranging from young men who could no longer go to the South African mines, persons engaged in the informal sector, and single women with children who were vulnerable to prostitution charges. Once resettled in the countryside, many were forced to harvest crops on the labor-deficient state farms or given small landholdings, usually without adequate seeds, tools, or other inputs to farm. Operation Production was one of Frelimo's major political blunders: it destroyed what was left of the government's urban and rural base and facilitated the recruitment of ordinary Mozambicans into the Renamo forces.

By the end of 1983, the economic and political situation in Mozambique looked very bleak. Drought, war, and the foreign exchange crisis had drastically reduced Frelimo's control over the economy. Politically and administratively too, the government was losing control. In this context, Frelimo began negotiations with the IMF and the World Bank.

## Conclusion

All governments make policy errors, but their impact is greater in poor countries—given the scarcity of both economic and political capital. Frelimo was no exception. As the leaders of a developing country under siege since independence, their mistakes took on great significance and proved costly. With hindsight, it can be argued that Frelimo's attempt at rapid modernization was terribly misguided; many African countries had followed a similar path and failed. Influenced by an ideology that placed emphasis on large-scale, capital-intensive state enterprises, Frelimo invested its resources in one pole of development with disappointing results. Overly confident of the widespread support from the rural population, earned during the armed struggle, the leaders assumed that the majority of Mozambicans would endure hardship and sacrifices to build a modern socialist society. Simultaneously, the policy chosen benefited a minority in control of the state and party apparatuses who thereby increased their political power and private consumption. Thus Frelimo's policy errors were due to a combination of "wrong ideology," bureaucratic bias, and class interests that reinforced the bias.

The new state basically ignored the needs of the peasantries and tried to appropriate as much surplus production as possible for industrialization and state agricultural projects, a standard theme that forms the basis for development policy and practice in most of Africa.[39] Priorities were given to large-scale infrastructure when what would have been more helpful was a program to renovate ports and rail transport and construct secondary roads throughout the country, as well as an import policy that gave precedence to consumer and capital goods required by peasants, spare parts, and the reestablishment of rural-urban trade networks.

Even when it became obvious that its rural development strategy was not working, Frelimo did not immediately change its policies because those in control of the state apparatus favored large farm projects for their own political and economic gain. A combination of peasant dissatisfaction with agricultural policies and political pressures created by the war accounted for the government's reorientation away from state agriculture to family and private farming, but by the time the fourth congress sought to correct policy errors, it was too late. The war drastically limited the government's options.

Evidence of the difficulties that characterized Mozambique's rural development strategy since independence is provided in the subsequent chapters, which examine Ilha Josina Machel. These chapters analyze a case study of the impact of Frelimo's changing policies at the local level. The next chapter focuses on the last two decades of colonialism, analyzing the agricultural changes that took place in Ilha Josina Machel.

# Part 2

# The Case Study
## Ilha Josina Machel, Maputo Province

# 3

# Agricultural Change on
# Ilha Josina Machel, 1950–1974

**T**he last decades of colonialism in the Portuguese African colonies were characterized by the administrative and labor control policies initiated under the fascist government of António Salazar. The distinctive feature of the state was the expansion, rationalization, and institutionalization of forced labor into a system that became the cornerstone of colonialism. In the case of Mozambique, this feature should not obscure crucial shifts of state policy from the 1950s onward brought about by emerging African nationalism and by the declining competitiveness of Mozambican exports.

In the 1950s the colonial administration began to actively foster the selective development of specialized peasant commodity production in some areas. The objectives were both political and economic. On the one hand, the state wanted to develop a small stratum of commercial agricultural producers that would align itself with Portuguese rule; this aim gained impetus in the 1960s with increasing popular demand for independence and the advancement of the armed struggle. Consequently, the colonial state was compelled to become simultaneously more repressive toward individuals or classes that constituted a threat to it, and more reformist toward those who were most amenable to the perpetuation of colonial rule. On the other hand, economic contradictions forced Portugal, as other colonial powers in the southern African region, to reconsider its agrarian policies in the 1950s and 1960s. Portuguese development planners were concerned with rural unemployment and the influx of men into the cities, the negative impact of imported food staples on the balance of payments, and the reduced competitiveness of colonial cotton on the world market.[1]

In the countryside, state reforms were directed toward a tiny but politically significant stratum of middle peasants who produced mainly cash crops. While the success of this strategy was limited, there were groups that benefited from state concessions. In Gaza and Manica, for example, a few Mozambicans were brought into some smallholder settler schemes aimed at encouraging specialized production of maize, rice, and wheat.[2] Colonial authorities also experimented with the introduction of new forms of property for selected strata of the peasantry in certain areas, encouraging cooperatives for specialized peasant producers in cotton-growing areas in Cabo Delgado and in areas of the south.[3]

Among the latter, Ilha Josina Machel, a locality of Maputo Province (formerly Lourenço Marques) figures prominently. The period from 1950 to 1974 was one of agrarian change and relative prosperity for many of the residents of this inland island: peasant family farms were marketing large surpluses of maize, cassava, groundnuts, and beans consumed by African workers on the nearby plantations and large estates and by the African urban population. The colonial agricultural marketing cooperative, Cooperative Moses, was consolidating a middle stratum of peasants dependent on cash-crop production, and in the 1970s, more men from Maputo Province, including island residents, were recruited to work in South African mines than from Gaza or Inhambane. At Ilha Josina Machel, a traditional undifferentiated peasantry producing mainly for subsistence did not exist. Over the years, a growing number of middle peasants purchased oxen, plows, hoes, and other hand tools from the proceeds of their marketed crops.

The colonial state was critical to the development of family agriculture and cooperative farming in this rural community: it provided services, supplies of inputs, and technical assistance with the aim of increasing productivity. Under colonialism, the peasantry (like the European capitalist farmers and plantation owners) could not advance primarily on its own internal resources. The state's agricultural modernization strategy served to "lock in" peasant commercial farmers—through higher and controlled levels of input and credit use, and through the organization of marketing and processing, thus achieving greater commodification, specialization, and standardization.[4] Colonial practices accelerated regional differentiation (as between high-potential areas with higher and more reliable rainfall vs. lower-potential or marginal areas) as well as class, gender, and generational differences within and across rural households.

Though the colonial state wished to promote the development of a middle stratum of commercial agricultural producers, as a buffer against the advancing liberation struggle, it was intent on ensuring that this development should not be at the expense of settler farmers. Contradictions often emerged in rural communities as the colonial state tried to balance its racist agenda of protecting European settler and plantation agriculture and, simultaneously, promoting African agriculture.

## The Physical Setting

Ilha Josina Machel, an area of approximately 300 square kilometers, is one of six localities that form the District of Manhiça, situated in Maputo Province, shown in map 2.[5] The locality is about 130 kilometers from the city of Maputo, the capital. According to the first general population census of postindependence Mozambique in 1980, there were 6,971 men, women, and children living on the island.[6]

An island of alluvial soils, Ilha Josina Machel is situated at the junction of the Incomati River and one of its tributaries, the Matseculi River. The fertile soils are very productive, as they have a high organic content and are well supplied with water. Dispersed throughout the island there are also large pockets of clay soil, which is much more difficult to work because when it rains, the water is slow to penetrate the clay, and once penetrated, the soil remains moist for a long time. This heavy soil requires the use of a plow and thus cannot be cultivated easily by those peasants who own only hoes.

The combination of soil and temperature permit agricultural activity throughout the year, including two harvests of maize. Agriculture remains possible even in periods of drought, because the six major lakes on Ilha Josina Machel and the surrounding Incomati River offset the worse effects of drought years. The rainy season begins in October and ends in January, and the dry period is from March to May. Ilha Josina Machel, like the rest of Maputo Province, has a tropical climate: July generally experiences the lowest temperature, about 24.1°C (75.4°F), and the warmest months are January and February, with summer temperatures ranging from 25°C to 30°C (77°F to 86°F).[7]

## The Colonial Political Economy: The Political Context

In the 1930s, as part of the policies of Salazar, a uniform pattern of administrative divisions was imposed in the colonies of Portugal. The Province of Sul de Save (South of the Save), was created in 1934, containing the Districts of Lourenço Marques (including the present-day Maputo and Gaza Provinces) and Inhambane. The districts were subdivided into *conselhos* or councils, areas where the Portuguese presence was already important, and *circumsçricões* or subdistricts, areas with little Portuguese influence. The councils and subdistricts were formed from administrative posts or localities that were themselves divided into *regedorias* or chieftainships.

Ilha Josina Machel, known as Ilha Mariana during the colonial period, was one of nine chieftainships responsible to the administrative locality of Xinavane (established in 1940), located approximately 18 kilometers from the island. This administrative locality along with that of Calanga fell under the jurisdiction of

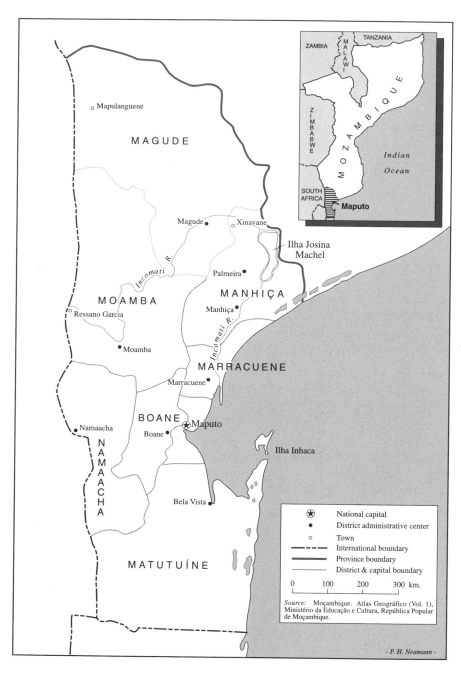

Map 2. Maputo Province: District Boundaries

the Council of Manhiça, an area that covered 2,343 square kilometers, which, in turn, was part of the District of Lourenço Marques.

The system of public administration in the Portuguese colonies was characterized by political dualism—a common feature in colonial Africa. The European system of administration and code of law applied to Europeans and *assimilados* while a state-enforced customary order was imposed on the African majority. In the countryside, local-level administration often recruited legitimate local chiefs. Where others were named in their place, the accoutrements of power were reestablished on traditional ruling lines to promote a semblance of legitimacy.

Typically, an administrator was appointed by the governor-general of Mozambique (the supreme colonial authority) to run the council, and his subordinates, the *chefes do posto*, subadministrators, managed the localities. As administrators of African areas and agents of the Native Affairs Department, the district and subadministrators were responsible for native affairs: census taking, tax collection, implementation of the labor laws, supervision of peasant agriculture, and punishment of infractions of the law. A hierarchy of African chiefs assisted these Portuguese bureaucrats: *régulos*, the senior African chiefs, and *cabos*, the junior chiefs. These and other traditional holders of political office were incorporated into a colonial administrative structure, which made their customary position of privilege dependent on the state rather than the support of their followers.[8] As part of the colonial apparatus, they received a salary for the day-to-day management of the chieftainships and for assisting the subadministrator with his specific duties.

On Ilha Josina Machel, the *régulo* and his three *cabos* were subordinated to the subadministrator of Xinavane. With the establishment of formal Portuguese rule in 1897, the Portuguese appointed the first *régulo* of Ilha Josina Machel from the Timana family, one of the traditional noble families in the area. Eduardo Moses Timana, the only surviving ex-*régulo* of Ilha Josina Machel, described the process of succession and its transformation under colonialism: "The Timana family would meet with the elders of the area to select a *régulo*. They would then present the person to the population. The choice was not open for popular discussion. With the establishment of colonialism, the Portuguese authorities had to agree to the choice."[9] While the indigenous population never directly chose their senior chief, the colonial system further diminished the latter's accountability to them. The last *régulo* of Ilha Josina Machel was Adriano Chimbutana Timana, who governed the island from 1957 to 1975. Together with his chiefs, they administered the four designated neighborhoods of the island (Cutane, Mapsana, Zonguene, and Régulo Proper), with Régulo Adriano ultimately responsible for the entire chieftainship.

The colonial government's interference in the succession process also pre-vented women from holding positions of power. Local oral accounts and offi-cial documents show that in cases where women were selected as the legitimate heirs in the succession process according to the cultural traditions of rural people in the area, the Portuguese intervened to secure the line for men. For example, in a memo dated February 23, 1961, sent from the district secretary of civil administration of the Lourenço Marques District to all administrative di-visions, a succession process was described whereby the population of an un-named locality in the district chose a woman over two male candidates (a well-known drunk and a nurse) to succeed the deceased *régulo* who had left no legitimate heirs.[10] Given the outcome, the colonial authorities annulled the election and gave orders that a new process should be initiated to select a man. Subsequently, a dispatch was sent from the same central office to rural admin-istrators stating, "It is determined by the order of his Excellency the Governor of the District as given in the dispatch of the 3rd day of the current month [March] that whatever the circumstances in the future, be it verified, that the preparatory acts of succession and investiture of the native authorities will be carried out in a manner that a woman will never be able to come to be desig-nated to the position of *régulo*."[11] The restriction and codification of the *régulo* post to men was a rigidity to serve the colonial interests of order and stability, and, simultaneously, it became part of a new and unchanging body of "tradi-tion" to deprive women of political power.

The local-level administrators, intermediaries between the native popula-tion and the Portuguese authorities, were responsible for collecting taxes set by the state, in addition to other tasks. Ex-régulo Eduardo Moses Timana de-scribed his responsibilities:

> The first was the organization of the population in order to resolve the social problems. The second was the annual tax collection. The *indotas*, subordi-nates to the chiefs (and there were many), were responsible for collecting the tax and giving it to the chiefs who passed it along to the *régulo*. The *régulo* then presented the money to the subadministrator of the locality. The third was the organization of *chibalo* labor. The *régulo* usually received a list handed down by the administrator of Manhiça with the number of men and women needed for *chibalo*. The demand varied from months to years. Al-though the list sometimes included labor for public works, more often in the case of Ilha Mariana, *chibalo* labor meant hard labor on private settler farms.[12]

For carrying out these tasks, not only did the *régulo* and his subordinates re-ceive a monthly salary, but also they and their immediate families were exempt from taxation and forced labor. Together with *sipais* (sepoys who formed the

African police force), administration interpreters, and guards, the *régulos* and chiefs formed a privileged stratum among the African population. As an employee in the colonial state apparatus, the *régulo* used his political position to advance economically through monopolizing good commercial lands or through the recruitment of labor for his own use. On Ilha Josina Machel, Régulo Timana owned the best tracts of land, close to the river and easily irrigated, and peasants were obliged to pay him a labor and product tribute (chickens or some other small animal as well as a portion of their harvest). If one failed to pay tribute, additional labor was required, often with a threat to be sent to do *chibalo*. Migrant labor was not exempt; in the 1970s, miners paid one hundred escudos to the *régulo* upon their return.[13] Similarly, peasants were required to pay a tribute to the junior chiefs of the area after each harvest.

The privileges of the *régulos* and other African administrators depended on the rigorous application of the colonial policies. *Régulos* who opposed the policies were often dismissed and replaced by someone more compliant. During the administration of Régulo Eduardo, for example, the Portuguese authorities accused him of stealing a portion of the hut tax and they replaced him with his cousin, Adriano Chimbutana Timana. According to the popular local account of the event: "The district administrator, António da Novoa Cortes, arrived on Ilha Mariana and called a general meeting. The population had to give testimony that they had paid their taxes but they had not received receipts. The meeting ended and Eduardo was taken to jail."[14] The residents of Ilha Josina Machel maintain that a power struggle existed between the cousins and that it was Adriano who invented the story that Eduardo had stolen part of the hut tax. Because of his great popularity on the island, Eduardo did not spend more than five months in jail, and the local population sold more of their maize to pay his debt to the Portuguese government. As in other parts of colonial Mozambique, peasants made a distinction among state-appointed chiefs in terms of how closely they were allied with the colonial system.

The relationship between colonial administrators and traditional authorities was not entirely coercive. The Portuguese understood that chiefs had to maintain some legitimacy within their communities to execute their tasks and achieve order, and not be simply collaborators with the colonial government. Thus, alongside the brutalities of Portuguese administration, colonial officials also made gifts of wine, sugar, cloth, and ivory, in support of rainmaking and other traditional ceremonies.[15] Still, the organization of the local administration system, which underlay forced labor and forced crop appropriation, compromised their positions.

In most cases, it was the *régulo* who initially gave the farming land to the peasants or their families. According to island residents, there was no shortage of land in the community, but there was competition for the better-irrigated and more fertile holdings. The relationship of the peasant and his family with the *régulo* and the peasant's means of production were the two determining factors in the distribution and size of landholdings. Former *régulo* Eduardo Timana elaborated: "First a person would choose the land and then approach the *régulo*. The *régulo* would make the final decision and designate the quantity of land too. Usually a present was given in return for the land, for example, a goat, pig, or chicken. Although the land was limited as the island was populated, the quantity varied according to whether the peasant was a friend of the *régulo* and his means of production."[16]

With the new appointment of Régulo Adriano Timana in 1957, the system of land distribution became decentralized: his three chiefs were given the authority to allocate small landholdings to peasants who owned, minimally, a pair of draft animals and a plow. However, when it involved a large quantity of land, the chief first went to speak to the *régulo*. The case of Vasco Juma Sumbana, one of the few African *agricultores* or "evolved" farmers (i.e., rural producers who had capital resources, cultivated large areas, made regular use of wage labor, and marketed most of their production), is illustrative:

> From 1958 to 1962 Vasco Juma Sumbana worked in South Africa. At the end of his last contract, he returned to his home in the Gaza District of southern Mozambique where he purchased two oxen and a plow. In 1963 he moved his residency from Gaza to Ilha Mariana, facilitated by a letter from the administrator of the Xinavane post, Amandio Augusto Russo. Prior to his arrival, well-irrigated and fertile land was arranged by one of the traditional African chiefs of Ilha who had spoken to the *régulo* on Sumbana's behalf. Sumbana's first farm of 15 hectares was situated in Cutane, a central area of the island. After proving to be a successful farmer, Sumbana arranged a second farm of 150 hectares, located in Zonguene where he employed a large number of peasants: twenty regular workers and a number of seasonal laborers whom he employed for two or three months during the harvest seasons for wheat and maize.[17]

The factors crucial in Sumbana's initial acquisition of land were the ownership of a team of oxen with plow and an amicable relationship with the local authorities. In the case where a peasant did not own an ox-plow and had not established a relationship with the local administration, a relative already settled on the island acted as a liaison. Once the *régulo* gave the land to a peasant, the most common method of land distribution was through inheritance.

## Agricultural Changes: Labor Demands on the
## Peasantry and Transformation of Social Relations

During colonialism, Ilha Josina Machel was an indigenous labor reserve; Portuguese settlers were not permitted to establish residence on the island, as it was a special area of recruitment for the colonial state. The population of Ilha Josina Machel constituted a labor reserve primarily for the South African mining economy, the surrounding Portuguese settler farms and estates, the Incomati sugar plantation, as well as state public works. No statistics are available on the flow of labor from Ilha Josina Machel to the South African mines because the regional organizational divisions of the Witwatersrand Native Labour Association (WENELA), the South African recruitment organization, did not coincide with the colonial administrative districts of Mozambique. The issue of migrant labor to South Africa is subsequently discussed within the context of southern Mozambique in general.

For the greater part of seventy years, between 80,000 and 100,000 men from the three southern provinces were annually recruited as migrant laborers to the South African mines.[18] The average length of the miners' contracts was from twelve to eighteen months, and they spent approximately 50 percent of their active working life on the mines. Between contracts, migrant laborers remained at home about seven months on average. This large-scale and long-term mine recruitment had a marked effect on peasant agriculture and work patterns on the family farms. Prior to the institutionalization of the migrant labor system in the 1890s, men had very clearly defined tasks in the agricultural cycle: Their principal functions were to clear the land, fish, hunt, and look after cattle. Often men kept their own small fields, and the harvest was saved as an emergency reserve. They also planted tobacco for their own use and for local sale.[19] In periods of natural disasters, male labor constituted an important reserve for intensifying production. In addition, men's activities included the construction of houses, storage places, water pits, and carpentry in the rural economy. The division of labor in the agricultural sphere clearly benefited men: seasonal tasks were reserved for men, and the everyday agricultural labor (hoeing, sowing, and weeding) was done by women.

At the beginning of the twentieth century, peasant women of southern Mozambique confronted a difficult situation. Labor migration and internal forced labor kept more than half of the adult males away from home at most times. With a large part of the labor force separated from participation in the agricultural production cycle, family agriculture became exclusively women's work. Although young boys herded the cattle, women learned to plow the fields with ox-plows that appeared in southern Mozambique at the end of the

1940s, and women increasingly performed tasks that had been earlier handled by men—in addition to their regular domestic workload that included cooking, fetching water and firewood, and child care. Over time, some of the migrants' families came to use the wages of migrant laborers to hire workers —many of them elderly ex-miners—to perform former male tasks, reducing women's burdens. Light construction work and carpentry were increasingly left to them.

Since the contract of Mozambican migrants did not consider the agricultural needs and necessities of family farming, it was not always possible for the miners to assist family farming between contracts. Although the data are scant, the migrant workers who returned to Ilha Josina Machel between contracts and invested their wages in instruments of production tended to participate in family farming. Those mine workers who did not acquire agricultural equipment with their earnings frequently did not engage in farming activities.[20] Other migrant laborers described how they spent this time between contracts avoiding forced labor. Often they reached their homes only to spend the seven-month period in the fields and swamps hiding from the *régulo* and the African police force, making it difficult for them to assist family farming.[21] Although migrant laborers were legally exempt from forced labor, exceptions were frequent.

A more complicated issue is the relationship between migrant labor and peasant agricultural productivity in southern Mozambique. The argument generally made is that peasant agricultural development was constrained by the region's transformation into a labor reserve for South Africa's mining-based economy. Research by the CEA, for example, concluded that migrant labor seriously undermined the reproductive base of the Mozambican peasant economy and agricultural production diminished over the years to a level where it could no longer sufficiently support the family.[22] Peasant households became principally dependent on wages from mine labor and not on the proceeds of agricultural production. In 1967, for example, money income from the mines in the three southern provinces was nine times that resulting from crop sales, about U.S. $28 million and U.S. $3 million, respectively.[23]

In his study of the Lower Limpopo Valley, Otto Roesch substantiated the CEA's central thesis.[24] According to his analysis, migrant labor had the contradictory effect of being both a source of capital for African agriculture and a drain on available labor supplies. African capitalist farms, like their Portuguese counterparts, were unable to pay wages that could compete with those paid on the mines in South Africa, and thus, they found their productive capacities constrained by a chronic shortage of labor. These structural constraints imposed on African agricultural development by the migrant labor system in combination with the Portuguese administration's preference for settler farmers impeded the state's attempt to foster the growth of capitalist and peasant commercial agriculture in the Lower Limpopo Valley.

The experience on Ilha Josina Machel partially supports these views. For poor peasants, who were the majority, migrant labor did undermine their reproductive base—the first point made in the CEA study—and they remained marginal agricultural producers. But the situation was different for a growing number of middle peasants, for whom the Portuguese agrarian reformist policy combined with labor migration to South Africa created a vibrant economy. Ilha Josina Machel patterns of peasant involvement in mine labor varied considerably. Some men migrated to South Africa and then returned to Mozambique to farm, while others farmed and supplemented their income with artisan activities for a number of years, returning to the mines after a poor harvest, a drought or flood, a loss of livestock through disease, and so on. In the 1950s, many miners invested their income in ox-plows and joined the colonial cooperative. From the proceeds of their agricultural surplus on the family farms, they purchased more ox-plows, hoes, and other agricultural hand tools, and a few paid for the construction of masonry houses.

The case of Fernando Chavango is illustrative:

> From 1946 to 1949, I worked as a cook in South Africa. My first mine contract was in 1950, but it was not until my third contract that I bought three head of cattle (two oxen and a cow) and a plow. My last contract ended in 1958. With the money from South Africa, I bought oxen, a bicycle, and paid *lobolo*, bride price, for my first wife. In 1958 I returned to Ilha Josina Machel and farmed sixteen hectares of mostly maize, beans, and wheat. With the money from the sale of these crops I paid *lobolo* for the second and third wives, a radio, a hand mill for maize, three more teams of oxen, another plow, and I paid a person to build a masonry house for my family.[25]

Although Fernando Chavango bought most of his agricultural equipment and cattle from income earned from crop sales, the argument made by the CEA is pertinent—mine wages were essential for peasants to establish themselves in family agriculture.

The second part of the general case made by the CEA, that agricultural production diminished over the years to a level where it could not support the family, did not fit the situation at Ilha Josina Machel. In Ilha Josina Machel, as elsewhere in the countryside, a growing stratum of middle peasants emerged that the colonial state, for political and economic reasons, had to support. From the 1950s onward, middle peasants and evolved farmers received state support in the form of supply of seeds, purchase of crops, marketing, and transportation, but this support had its limitations: the colonial state wished to promote the development of commercial peasant agriculture but not at the expense of Portuguese settler farmers.

Forced labor and the forced cultivation of cash crops further depleted the workforce available for peasant farming in southern Mozambique. The colonial state controlled the linkages between the peasantry and these units of production through labor legislation. The 1928 "Código do trabalho dos indígenas nas colónias portuguêsas de Africa" (Native Work Code in Portugal's African Colonies) was the basic legal document of the system, which remained operative until 1962.[26] It was supplemented by a set of 1930 regulations, the "Regulamento do trabalho dos indígenas" (RTI), which covered every aspect of "native employment."[27] The RTI made it obligatory for all but a small minority of men to take up wage work for six months of the year either for a private employer or for the state. The only exceptions from contract labor covered those Africans given *assimilado* status, those in permanent wage employment, and those engaged in migrant labor abroad. These *provisos,* however, were frequently ignored, and miners on their way back from working contracts in South Africa were often forced directly into *chibalo.* Still others were prevented from returning to the mines as they had acquired skills needed in the colonial economy.[28]

Most peasants from Ilha Josina Machel who performed forced labor were sent to the nearby Portuguese settler farms and the agricultural estates, which extended from the Marracuene Valley to the Manhiça and Incomati Valleys. One of the largest estates, separated from the island only by the Incomati River, was the banana plantation owned by Inacio da Sousa. According to ex-régulo Eduardo Timana: "The administrator of Manhiça would request *chibalo* for Inacio da Sousa but the latter would usually pay his workers."[29] Other local residents were less fortunate; they were forced to work without pay for six months at the Sociedade Marracuene Agrícola Commercial Limitada, which produced bananas for export to South Africa as well as some cereals and purebred cattle. The estate owners had a contract agreement with the administrator and the transport bus lines to recruit labor from Inhambane and Gaza Provinces. As the colonial economy grew, the contradictory demands of labor compelled peasants to cut their costs of reproduction.

The local peasantry also supplied labor to the Incomati Sugar Estates, the largest sugar plantation in southern Mozambique, located sixteen kilometers from Ilha Josina Machel. In 1952, the Espirito Santo Group, a Portuguese monopolist group, bought the plantation from an English firm. With approximately seven thousand hectares under sugarcane cultivation at the time, it required an abundant supply of cheap labor from the peasantry on both a regular and a seasonal basis. In 1958, the subadministrator of Xinavane estimated that the number of Africans working at the Incomati was about six thousand, of whom five thousand were contracted for six months while the remaining one thousand were full-time workers.[30]

The agricultural cycle at the Incomati Sugar Estates conflicted with the labor needs of peasant farming. At certain times of the year, crucial tasks had to be done on farms at the same time that labor needs were highest at the sugar plantation. The peak labor periods on the family farm were during the land-preparation months of August and February; the sowing of maize in September and March; the weeding in September, October, March, and April; and the harvest in February and August. Sugar had to be harvested from May to November. The months of March and April, when the Incomati specifically hired seasonal women laborers to weed and make mounds around the cane, was a critical period for weeding the second crop of maize.[31] Thus, peasants were forced to work on the sugar plantation at the expense of subsistence production.

The Incomati used both *chibalo* labor recruited by the state and regular contract labor supplied by its own recruiting agency. Most of the recruited and forced labor came from Inhambane and Gaza, with some from the Moamba area of Maputo Province. The local population in the vicinity supplied the voluntary labor, including the peasants of Ilha Josina Machel. The accounts given by the island residents suggest they were not coerced to work at the Incomati plantation, although it is probable that some volunteered to avoid the threat of contract labor.[32] Volunteer labor, in this sense, was part of the "moral obligation" for all natives to work, as stipulated in the RTI. A more important factor, in the case of Ilha Josina Machel, was the recruitment of women, which began in the 1940s. According to the local inhabitants, during colonialism there was a chronic lack of men at the plantation due to competition for labor from WENELA and the Mozambique railway, and so the company began to recruit women.[33] Initially, these women were widows or those who were divorced or abandoned by their husbands. Without a regular wage income to help out, especially during the time lapse between planting and harvesting, these peasant women of Ilha Josina Machel sought employment at the sugar plantation.

Originally, when women were hired, a division of labor existed whereby the men did the cutting and women did only the weeding and making of mounds around the sugarcane. Management claimed that the cutting was too difficult for women, but there was an economic motive for this division of labor: women were paid less for weeding than they would have been for cutting the sugarcane. As more women were recruited, they broke down this division of labor and eventually started cutting sugarcane, reflecting their need of a wage income despite the physical hardship of the work. The proletarianization of women thus enabled the colonial system to extract more labor from the peasant economy. The only other way to increase production was to turn to the middle peasants.

The establishment of the colonial cooperative at Ilha Josina Machel in the 1950s was related to an increase in the number of island women seeking work at the sugar plantation. The common pattern was for ex-miners who were middle farmers to work on their landholding with one wife and children, and to send another wife to work at the Incomati Estates, a labor strategy that assured the household a regular wage income. In addition, the sugar plantation chose to replace sick or old workers with members of the same household in order to reduce recruitment costs.[34] Peasant households thus internalized the recruiting system because they feared losing a steady income. Due to the close proximity of Ilha Josina Machel to the plantation, the residents generally worked the morning or day shift in the sugar-cane fields and returned to their homes at night. They provided their own food, which meant that management did not have to pay the full reproduction costs of these workers. The plantation provided food and shelter for those workers contracted from outside the immediate area.

With the official ending of forced labor in 1961, the Incomati Estates started to mechanize some of its field operations. Yet progress was slow, and at the end of the 1960s the sugar plantation still relied mainly on seasonal labor to cut sugarcane and to expand production. At independence, half the process was mechanized and half remained labor-intensive. For women peasants on Ilha Josina Machel, the plantation's attempt to mechanize its field operations had a minimal effect on their employment; they continued as seasonal workers to weed and to cut the sugarcane. The impact of the Incomati's adoption of more mechanized technologies was different, however, for men, for whom this period was characterized by the full-time employment of ex-mine laborers as technicians, usually working with irrigation equipment.[35] The differentiated work experience of women and men at the Incomati Estates underscores how colonial practices enhanced gender differences, giving more men than women new skills in working with machinery, full-time wage employment, and, in some cases, the knowledge of the national language, Portuguese.

## The Colonial Marketing Cooperative:
## Peasant Differentiation and Commodity Production

In the 1950s, the colonial state promoted peasant commodity production in Mozambique on a large scale. The Ilha Josina Machel peasantry became a cash-cropping peasantry first through the cultivation of rice and cotton on an experimental basis, and later through the production of wheat and surpluses of maize, groundnuts, and beans. These food crops were geared to the growing demands of African workers in the towns, plantations, and large agricultural estates.

With the increase in agricultural commercial production, there developed more pronounced social stratification among the peasantry. The establishment of a marketing agricultural cooperative, predominantly for wheat but also for maize and beans, on Ilha Josina Machel reinforced this peasant differentiation, as the percentage of peasant farmers who qualified as members was low in comparison to the active labor force of the community. In 1959, for example, there were 318 members registered, of whom 90 percent were men and 10 percent were women.[36] The total active population (individuals eighteen years and over) was approximately 3,684, which means that only 8.6 percent of the residents qualified as cooperative members.[37]

In the post–Second World War period, the colonial government introduced rice cultivation on Ilha Josina Machel. The crop was grown on an experimental basis that lasted only two agricultural seasons because production results were low, after which agents of the Junta de Exportação dos Cereais (JEC; renamed the Instituto dos Cereais de Moçambique, ICM, in 1961) returned to the island in 1950 and introduced cotton and wheat cultivation. The local inhabitants explained that cotton production, too, was discontinued after a few years because of low yields. Wheat, however, was considered a viable economic crop in the regions of the Lower Incomati Valley and in the Lower Limpopo Valley. Subsequently, from 1953 to 1974, wheat cultivation was practiced on a large scale in three chieftainships of the Council of Manhiça: Ilha Mariana (Ilha Josina Machel), Movana (Taninga), and Delhote (Palmeira). Each of these chieftainships was obliged by the colonial government to establish a cooperative to grow wheat: Cooperative Moses, Freire de Andrade, and Mouzinho de Albuquerque, respectively.

The establishment of these cooperatives, as well as of those created in other parts of Mozambique, was an initiative by the colonial state to exploit systematically the economic potential of the countryside and to control peasant production.[38] The objective was to create a middle stratum of peasants, organized by and dependent on the state, who would collaborate with the authorities to govern the local population more effectively. In the 1950s, the proposal to foster a rural middle stratum of African farmers gained a new impetus due to the ineffectiveness of the 1944 Estatute do Agricultor Indígena (Statute of the Native Farmer), and it manifested itself in a new series of options—the establishment of colonatos; large land-settlement schemes, financed by the state for European and African farmers; as well as the creation of marketing cooperatives. António Rita-Ferreira, an administrator of a subdistrict in Lourenço Marques, described the advantages of native cooperatives for the colonial state: "The creation of a middle class of rural proprietors is, since there are many, judged indispensable to the process of complete integration. It is one general way that these responsible leaders recognize that they gain creating a real interest in the economic life [of Mozambique] and to reduce the migrant flow; it is the one satisfactory solution to combat without respite to the rural misery and to improve production and efficiency of native agriculture without repressive political and administrative measures."[39] In 1957, Governor Gabriel Teixeira recommended that cooperativization be a priority applied "South of the Save where the native for reasons of race, as well as perhaps from being a part of the province where the presence of our occupation was most thorough since the war of 1895—has attained a higher level of civilization than his brothers north of the Save."[40]

The three cooperatives of Manhiça grew mainly wheat to supply the domestic market. In Mozambique, as in neighboring Tanganyika, the colonial government encouraged peasants and settlers to grow wheat and other cereals for European household consumption and to reduce imports.[41] In 1952 the Matola Industrial Company (CIM), a mill factory in the suburb of the capital, Lourenço Marques, was built to process the wheat. By 1953, selected zones of the district South of the Save as well as in the District of Manica/Sofala were producing wheat. Subsequently, in 1961 the ICM established a rural branch at the Palmeira, a locality situated approximately thirty-eight kilometers from Ilha Josina Machel, with warehouse facilities, agriculture equipment, a machinery park, a transport fleet, and a technical and administrative team. Despite the efforts of the government, the Agronomic Inquest Commission concluded in 1968 that the total production of wheat in Mozambique was so low that it did not even cover 10 percent of domestic needs. In order to compensate for this deficit, Mozambique resorted to further imports of wheat: in 1969 it increased its imports of wheat flour by about 95 percent in relation to 1968 imports.[42]

For those middle-peasant farmers—referred to as *machambeiros* on Ilha Josina Machel—who joined the wheat-marketing cooperative, the primary incentive was their release from forced labor.[43] The identification pass given to each member showed how much seed was distributed, the area cultivated, total production in kilos and escudos, payments due, and the total income received per year. There were also economic incentives, which followed once peasants acquired a pass. The ICM provided them with technical assistance, an advance supply of seeds on credit, machine and equipment rental, credit to purchase oxen, agricultural equipment, storage facilities, and an effective transport and commercialization network to market the crop. Although the price of wheat paid to the peasant farmers was low, 2.5 escudos per kilo in comparison to 10 escudos per kilo paid to Europeans, they were guaranteed a steady income for their production.[44] With the earnings they received from wheat production, the peasant families bought producer and consumer goods available at the local stores.

To be a member of the cooperative, a peasant had to meet specific criteria: he or she had to be a resident of the area where the cooperative was established; had to live predominantly from the income of the farm; and had to have cultivated no less than three hectares of crops each year for the past three years. In addition, the peasant farmer had to own at least an ox-plow and three hectares of land of which one hectare was set aside for the cultivation of wheat. No farm workers outside household labor were to be employed, thus there would be no competition between these middle peasants and settler farmers for African laborers.

The first ox-plow of these peasant farmers was normally purchased out of the wages earned in the South African mines. The peasants who grew wheat went to the mines fewer times than the norm of seventeen contracts and then returned to Ilha Josina Machel, established themselves on good land, and joined the marketing cooperative. It is likely that before the worker-peasants returned to Mozambique, they had already acquired a favorable position with the *régulo* and/or administrator and were guaranteed good land. Those who volunteered to grow wheat were given better land, and those who distributed the seeds received even better land.

The membership criteria had two major effects: they ensured that only the wealthier peasants in the chieftainship joined, and they increased peasant differentiation between the middle peasants, who were recipients of state assistance, and the majority of poor peasants. The few island residents who were considered to be "evolved" farmers by the Portuguese government did not have to produce wheat, although most did. Once these middle farmers owned the necessary means of production, they had to go through an obligatory apprenticeship of one agricultural season before they were considered cooperative members. Fernando Chavango, a former member, described his apprenticeship: "I began my apprenticeship in 1956 with Josef Tlemo. I was not paid but I learned the skills of planting and harvesting wheat. The following year, I did not become a member as there were problems in the cooperatives and all the leaders were dismissed. In 1958, I joined the cooperative and became the leader of group 3. At the time, there were about 58 members in this group and about 150 premembers waiting to finish their apprenticeship and join the cooperative."[45] Although the data for total membership for the 1959 wheat season are incomplete, table 3.1 provides a crude indication of the different strata of peasants who cultivated wheat. Approximately 84 percent of the 169 members cultivated three hectares or less of wheat, while at the top end of the scale, slightly more than 4 percent cultivated 6 hectares or more.

Cooperative Moses had its own internal organization, with a central directorate consisting of a president, treasurer, and secretary chosen by a general assembly that included all the members. The directorate, elected for a three-year

Table 3.1 Number of members and hectares cultivated, Ilha Josina Machel, 1959 wheat campaign

| Membership | | Size of Landholding (hectares) | Total Number |
| Number | Percentage | under Wheat Cultivation | of Hectares Cultivated |
| --- | --- | --- | --- |
| 169* | 100.0 | Total | 415 |
| 45 | 26.6 | 1 | 45 |
| 49 | 29.0 | 2 | 98 |
| 48 | 28.4 | 3 | 144 |
| 16 | 9.5 | 4 | 64 |
| 4 | 2.4 | 5 | 20 |
| 6 | 3.5 | 6 | 36 |
| 1 | 0.6 | 8 | 8 |

*Source:* JEC, "Mapa da produção de trigo. Campanha 1959" (Lourenço Marques: JEC, 1960).
* The total number of members in 1959 was 318. The figure 169 reflects only those in groups 2, 3, 4, and 5; data on groups 1, 6, and 7 are not available.

term, could be dismissed by the Portuguese authorities, as was the case in 1957, for reasons discussed below. Two of the main functions of this structure were to mobilize the members to cultivate more wheat and to increase the membership. The president also acted as an agent for the ICM. Although he did not receive a salary for distributing the seeds, it is probable that he made a small income from the members through bribes, since he determined the allocation of seeds, giving more to those he favored. Below this central structure, the members of the cooperative were geographically divided into seven groups, each with a leader. The members of the directorate would meet with the leaders of the seven groups and discuss the required quantities of seeds prior to the distribution. The central structure then distributed the seeds to the leaders, who in turn divided the seeds among the members.

The members of the cooperative—who numbered from 143 to 395 between the years 1953 to 1974—regularly met to discuss the organization of the cooperative and membership fees:

All members were required to pay annual membership dues. At the beginning, the membership was only 2.5 escudos per year and this was to cover the cost of the paper and pen for the treasurer. Then it was increased to 110 escudos per year. Then it was raised again to 120 escudos for 6 months or 240 escudos per year. When payment was due each leader of the group called a meeting and members paid their fees. The leaders collected the fees from the members and gave the amounts to the treasurer who kept a simple account of the books. The money was then deposited into a safety box at the post office in Manhiça.[46]

The three signatures of the president, the treasurer, and the secretary were required for a bank withdrawal. One of the ostensible reasons for the creation of a common fund was to loan money to a member when it was necessary: funeral expenses, the replacement of old or dead oxen, purchase of a new plow, and so on. Yet according to former member Josef Tlemo, "The members were never able to use the money for their own purposes. Rather, the money was used by the administrator, Cortes, and the ICM agent, Rodrigues, to buy a threshing machine, a machine to cut the wheat, and another to cut the weeds. The Portuguese bought these machines without asking the members and then took the money out of the account."[47] The Portuguese authorities were prepared only to let middle peasants have access to second-rate mechanization.

The members also held secret meetings apart from the Portuguese authorities to discuss the organization of the cooperative and how to produce more and better wheat. Josef Tlemo elaborated, "The management directorate and all three cooperatives in the area met regularly and studied the problems. For example, they discussed a problem and then brought it back to their areas to discuss it with all the members and then reported back at the next central meeting of all three cooperatives. For example, they all studied the matter of buying a tractor and discussed how to increase production. They came to the conclusion that the only way to increase production was to buy a tractor and a water pump."[48] The main objectives of the members were to increase wheat production and their contributions to the collective fund (which explains the rise in dues over the years) in order to purchase a tractor, a water pump, and other machinery. From their perspective, the only way to increase production was through mechanization and improved technology; the idea of purchasing oxen or plows collectively was not even raised at these meetings. Thus, prior to independence, these members strongly identified agricultural development with mechanization—a position in sharp contrast to Frelimo's cooperative policy of "self-reliance" with an emphasis on the maximal utilization of available labor power and ox-powered equipment.

The local Portuguese authorities opposed the idea of the cooperative members purchasing a tractor and sought to restrict the cooperative's access to first-rate mechanization (i.e., tractors) because they wanted to control both the development of African agriculture and the process of capital accumulation for this middle stratum of peasants. The colonial administration's priority was

always settler farms: settlers had privileged access to labor supplies and received the limited technical and financial resources of the state. Though this
commitment to settler agriculture did not prevent Portuguese officials from
trying to promote an indigenous class of capitalist farmers, it was within the
parameters of a controlled racist colonial agenda, and contradictions and tensions were bound to exist between the colonial agenda and practice on the
ground. Thus when cooperatives showed signs of fulfilling the political aims
for which they had been created—economic advancement of a middle stratum
of Mozambicans—the colonial administration at the local level interfered with
the process to protect the interests of settler farmers. A former cooperative participant recalled the reaction of local officials to the members' request:

> When the Portuguese heard that we wanted a tractor, they called all the
> members from each of the cooperatives and asked why we wanted a tractor.
> They said that a tractor had many expenses like gas and how would we, the
> members, be able to arrange gas? Then they said that blacks could only use
> the plow with oxen. Then the Portuguese told the rest of the members that
> those who wanted the tractor planned "to eat their money." After the meeting
> ended, the Portuguese ordered those who wanted a tractor to remain in one
> group and said that these individuals would go to jail. People became nervous
> and said they did not want a tractor. All the leaders of the three cooperatives
> were changed. Nobody went to jail; the Portuguese just tried to intimidate
> everyone.[49]

The agricultural season for wheat was from March to November. The preparation of the land and the sowing of seeds were generally completed by the end
of April or May, depending on the variety of seed, which meant that the agricultural calendar for wheat overlapped with the peak labor period at the Incomati Sugar Estates. The wheat season also coincided with the peak labor
months of maize production, which was cultivated twice per year. The first
crop of maize was sown, weeded, and harvested in September, October, and
February, respectively, and the second crop was sown, weeded, and harvested
in March, April, and August, respectively. The voluntary cultivation of wheat
(voluntary in the sense that it was the only way for peasant farmers to avoid
*chibalo* short of migration) exacerbated the labor demands already placed on
the local peasantry, especially women, by the state and private capital. The
major implication was less labor for family farming.

Co-op members produced wheat on their own farm, controlling their
production process and organizing their labor force. Unable to hire outside
agricultural workers, the peasant farmers were dependent on family labor
complemented by seasonal child labor during the months preceding the harvest. There is no information on the recruitment system for children, but it is

probable that it included child labor outside the immediate and extended family. A former member described the use of child labor: "Young children, as many as ten, guarded the wheat in the individual fields. Their job was to scare away birds and to assist the harvest. The peasant farmers provided the food for the children and after the harvest, there was a small feast."[50] During the agricultural season, there were regular visits by the administrator of Manhiça and by the subadministrator of the Xinavane locality as well as agents of the ICM to control and supervise wheat production. Those members who neglected their fields were often beaten by the *capataz* (the African overseer) using a *palmatoria* (a wooden pronged instrument).[51]

The wheat harvest, beginning in September, was the only phase executed collectively by the members. The local authorities obliged the members to assist with the harvest of individual fields in order to minimize yield losses from birds and other predators. Once the wheat was collected, it was cleaned, threshed, and stored in the ICM warehouse on Ilha Josina Machel until November, when agents returned with trucks to transport it to the ICM warehouse at the Palmeira. From the Palmeira warehouse, the wheat was transported by railway to the factory in Matola where it was processed.

For the members, the final stage was in mid-November when ICM agents at Ilha Josina Machel held the wheat markets. Before a member could sell any wheat, several deductions were required: repayment of seed plus 10 percent annual rate as well as the corresponding amount of wheat to cover the threshing cost (8 to 10 escudos per ninety kilos). The peasant farmer then sold the remainder to the ICM at 2.5 escudos a kilo, a price that the members considered low in relation to the expenditures and labor input.[52] The members also knew that the price they received was one-quarter of the price paid to Europeans.

From 1954 to 1969, wheat production varied from 231 to 931 kilograms per hectare, with an average of 445 kilograms per hectare. Membership also fluctuated from 190 in 1954 to 395 in 1961, 272 in 1963, and then 168 in 1969.[53] Irregular climatic conditions, uneven soil fertility, different seed varieties, increased demand for migrant labor from South Africa after 1961, and the advancement of the liberation war, as well as service and technical cutbacks by the ICM, account for the varied production results and the changes in membership over the years.

To improve the productivity of Cooperative Moses, the government planned to establish an *aldeamento piloto* or a model village on Ilha Josina Machel in 1970. In the north and center, *aldeamentos* were built to control the movement of Mozambican peasants and to isolate Frelimo from the population. In the case of Ilha Josina Machel, the Portuguese authorities hoped it would facilitate more efficient ICM services to peasant farmers. Of secondary importance was the provision of more social services (a first-aid post, a school, a social center, a bathing place, and some water fountains). The community already had a health post and a maternity clinic built in 1955, as well as two schools with approximately 150 students. In the end, the financial support did not materialize, largely as a result of the intensification of the war, and the *aldeamento* was not constructed.

The colonial state, through the ICM, was an active agent in the management of wheat production at Ilha Josina Machel. The ICM organized the marketing of wheat (supply of seeds and buying of the crop) and provided the transport. In some cases, credit was advanced—that is, seeds were distributed without payment—with the general understanding that repayment of seeds would include interest, likely at usurious rates. The rental of machinery and other supplies as well as veterinary and agronomic technical assistance were other important services provided by the ICM. The state-owned ICM thus ensured the smooth functioning of the cooperative through its direct control of all aspects of wheat production on Ilha Josina Machel, from the distribution of seeds to the purchase of the crop at a fixed price. The ICM agents also distributed maize, beans, and groundnut seeds to the peasants through the cooperative. Those peasant farmers who were members of the cooperative were guaranteed seeds of the staple food crops, and after the harvest, the ICM marketed their surpluses of beans and groundnuts.

As the war advanced in Mozambique, the ICM became cautious about further investment in the indigenous cooperatives, and agricultural production declined. With independence, the colonial cooperatives in the Council of Manhiça collapsed, but wheat production did not end immediately. A number of peasant farmers sowed wheat on their family farms, and the first collective fields on Ilha Josina Machel cultivated wheat, but the harvest was not marketed and the wheat rotted in the warehouse as a result of the collapse of the colonial economy. According to some members, in 1974, the departing local Portuguese administrators embezzled the cooperative's collective fund, a situation repeated in other parts of the country.

The colonial cooperative proved to be an experience in which the members learned crucial bargaining and organizational skills relevant to cooperative development in postindependence Mozambique. From a sample of 169 members of the marketing cooperative in 1959, 31 peasant farmers (18.3 percent) were members of the agricultural producer cooperatives in 1983; 20 former members (11.8 percent) farmed their own landholding, normally complemented with small artisan activities; 4 persons (2.4 percent) were employed as regular wage workers at the district sugar plantations; 15 individuals (8.9 percent) had moved away; 60 people (35.5 percent) were dead; and there was no information on the remaining 39 members (23.1 percent).[54] Nearly all the members of the management commissions of the twelve agricultural producer cooperatives on Ilha Josina Machel were former members of Cooperative Moses, and those cooperatives that produced the most during the 1980s were the ones with the largest proportion of members from the colonial cooperative.

There are five aspects of the colonial marketing cooperative experience that should be considered in relation to collective activities on Ilha Josina Machel since 1975. First, the members were self-trained peasants who were relatively prosperous in comparison to the majority of the local population; poor peasants did not meet the membership criteria. Cooperative Moses effectively accentuated interhousehold differentiation in favor of those commanding the resources to reap the benefits from wheat production, as well as maize and other commercial food crops marketed by the ICM. Second, this kind of "modernization" initiative augmented gender differentiation: of the total membership, fewer than 10 percent were women in any given year, due both to administrative bias and to female resistance. On the one hand, colonial administrators preferred to work with male farmers, who with the confidence and organizational skills they had gained from experience in wage labor and greater exposure to the official education system were better equipped to take advantage of the agricultural services. On the other hand, peasant women resisted wheat cultivation because it was labor-intensive. Given that they were expected to shoulder the responsibilities of food production and family welfare, women chose to grow maize and other food crops rather than wheat, which directly interfered with the production of food crops. Women were not against commodity production, but they were unwilling to grow a crop that threatened the family well-being and whose earnings they might not have claims on, as generally men controlled the income from the sale of cash crops.

Third, the members worked individually on their own fields, which tended to be dispersed from one another. Each member controlled the production process with the exception of the harvest, when it was obligatory for the group to act as a unit and collect the wheat from the fields, and each member had the right to rent the machines bought from the collective fund, to credit, to warehouse facilities, and to marketing and technical assistance. This period gives evidence of considerable change in the relations of production in agriculture, with the use of more purchased inputs and markets as well as changes in technology. Fourth, the smooth functioning of the cooperative depended upon considerable state assistance on a regular basis.

Fifth, the members held a strong bias favoring mechanization and improved technology to develop agriculture. The heavy soil could not be cultivated easily, even by ox-drawn plows. Moreover, for many members, agricultural development implied the use of combine harvesters, tractors, and other motor equipment, as well as hybrid seed. The problem with the colonial marketing cooperative, from their perspective, was state intervention, via the local Portuguese authorities that prevented the members from accumulating capital and modernizing their agricultural base.

Given the contradictory colonial efforts—combined with the weakness of Portuguese economic power and the sale of Mozambican labor to neighboring states—the marketing cooperatives confronted substantial challenges in their attempts to meet the colonial state's political objective. In the final phase of Portuguese rule, a growing middle stratum of peasants coexisted with settler agriculture—which was granted privileged access to resources by the colonial administration. The relative prosperity of settler agriculture depended on its access to the most fertile land and availability of labor power, as well as subsidized prices for its crops. Yet native labor was scarce because the colonial state was dependent on the export of labor power to earn foreign exchange, to balance the colony's budget, and to subsidize its balance of payments. Unable to compete with the wages offered in the South African mines, settler farmers relied largely on forced labor. In this context, the colonial state's concession to Portuguese settlers was to constrain the development of a Mozambican middle peasantry (who might compete for laborers at a wage competitive to that offered by Portuguese farmers), even if it meant restricting agricultural development in the colony. Consequently, the cooperatives could not fulfill their second objective—to control and direct the process of rural class formation so that it would not threaten the existing setup. Thus, a growing contradiction between an indigenous middle peasantry and the colonial administration was left unresolved.

Similarly, a minority of Mozambicans who qualified as evolved farmers confronted obstacles in their attempt to expand their agricultural base and to accumulate capital. Information is limited on this stratum of Mozambican farmers, who since independence are referred to as private capitalist farmers. Before the creation of ICM, few Mozambicans were exempt from the six months' obligatory labor period outside the family holding. In the 1950s and 1960s, however, to be classified as an evolved farmer qualified one for exemption from such labor, but the process of becoming an evolved farmer was difficult because it depended on an individual's means of production, on family links, and on relations with the *régulo* of the chieftainship and the Portuguese administrator.

In the 1960s, only two peasants on Ilha Josina Machel were recognized by the Portuguese authorities as evolved farmers.[55] As such, they purchased wheat, maize, beans, and groundnut seed from the ICM and received their services. There were about twenty other farmers in the community considered *pequeno agricultores,* small farmers, who met some of the criteria, and hence they also received regular assistance from the ICM.[56] Unlike the middle-peasant cooperative members who were denied access to tractors, evolved and even small farmers had opportunities to buy or rent tractors and other first-rate mechanized equipment from the ICM or other state-owned enterprises, as well as from some colonial settler merchants and capitalist farmers. In Ilha Josina Machel, as elsewhere in rural Mozambique, class stratification was greatly aided by a colonial settler stratum of merchants and farmers who served as a market outlet for commercial surpluses and as a source of credit, technical inputs, consumer incentive (in the form of well-stocked stores), entrepreneurial example, and laissez-faire ideology.[57]

Vasco Juma Sumbana, the only surviving evolved farmer on Ilha Josina Machel, described his agricultural activities during colonialism, comparing them with his situation after independence:

> My first farm was in neighborhood Cutane. Until today I am the owner of 15 hectares there. My second farm was located in Zonguene. I was a great farmer having 150 hectares. Now my total farm is only 60 hectares. I bought my seeds from ICM. In the past, I sowed thirty sacks of wheat [about 30–40 hectares] and twelve sacks of maize. I was the first one to experiment with 148 [a variety of wheat from Angola]. At that time Melhomen was in charge of the ICM warehouse at the Palmeira. In 1970–1971, I planted 12 hectares of this type but it didn't grow well; Senvalocho [from Argentina via Rhodesia] is much better. I also planted beans and vegetables. Now I keep my maize seeds and beans. Vegetable seeds are more difficult; I bought some in Maputo but there are none now. Before I bought a tractor, the ICM in the Palmeira helped me by sending a machine. In the past, when the tractor came from the ICM, I had priority. The tractor drivers did not stop work until the job was done. Now, the tractor works a couple of hours for a day or two and then leaves whether or not the job has been completed. I understand, as the demand is so great. I eventually bought a tractor that still runs today. It works sometimes and then breaks down; it is difficult to acquire spare parts. I was very good friends with the Portuguese rural shopkeepers and would borrow their tractors, even oxen and plow when my tractor broke down. In the past, I rented my tractor regularly to the peasant farmers of neighborhood 6. Only in the last two years when parts have been difficult to arrange, the tractor has been working less and less. I also employed a large number of workers: twenty regular people and during the harvest season (two or three months) of maize and wheat I employed seasonal laborers. I paid them with both products and money. Twenty kilos of maize, for example, meant one week of work during the harvest time. Now I employ eight regular workers at the cost of 2,000 meticais each per month. In the past, I sold my goods to the ICM. I transported my wheat directly to Matola while the peasant farmers sold their crop to the ICM during the wheat fairs. Now I sell my surplus production of cassava, maize, and beans in the neighborhood.[58]

As long as the growth of African capitalist farmers was not at the expense of Portuguese settler farmers, the colonial administrators accommodated their interests and promoted their development.

The account given by Sumbana as well as the analysis of the agricultural marketing cooperative on Ilha Josina Machel illustrate that the local peasantry and farmers were very integrated into the market economy as petty commodity producers. Between 1950 and 1974, there was an increase in peasant differentiation, with the colonial state playing an active role in accentuating this social stratification. Poor peasants, mostly women, suffered from the process of social stratification under colonial rule. Over time, they could only hire themselves out because they had become part of a labor reservoir for both white and black commercial farmers.

**Commercial Network**

Crucial in the countryside was the network of *cantineiros,* who linked city and country, peasant and plantation, and who were essential in the reproduction of family agriculture. Set against well-organized commercial monopolies and the interests of industrial capital, the profit margins allowed them were very low. Often these rural shopkeepers, including those of Ilha Josina Machel, combined their commercial function with the management of a farm and cattle breeding.

It was not until 1940 that Cutane, the business district of Ilha Josina Machel, was formally recognized as a commercial center. By 1967, there were nine commercial establishments, of which three rented their stores. These latter three employed family labor, as did two other merchants who owned their individual shops. The other four stores on the island were the property of members of the Portuguese rural petty bourgeoisie who maintained a number of establishments in the Council of Manhiça. These absent proprietors employed local Mozambican *assimilados* to manage their stores.

The commercial rural petty bourgeoisie provided the necessary infrastructure (which included shops, warehouses, and transport facilities) to market the agricultural produce of the peasantry as well as introduced commodities in general and the price system into the rural areas. According to Albino Bila, an *assimilado* who managed a local shop,

> The store at Ilha was the second store of Poças and Poças. Hence the owners purchased goods for both stores and then sent the goods from the store in Xinavane. The goods came originally from Lourenço Marques. The owners brought the goods to Ilha when they wanted and when they had goods to bring. However, it was on a regular basis and the store was always filled.

Transport was privately owned. At this store, the owners owned a lorry, a jeep, a delivery van, and two cars. Access to Ilha was difficult especially during the rains and floods. Each trader had a boat; they parked their car on the main road and brought their goods across by boat.[59]

The merchants bought and resold peasant crops, providing them in return with consumer and producer goods. One of the local residents described the marketing system of the store owned by Alfredo Luis: "He bought maize from the peasants at 2 escudos a kilo, storing the crop in his warehouse until he could transport it to his mill in Xinavane. The maize was processed into flour and then transported back to his store on Ilha Josina Machel where it was resold at 2.50 escudos a kilo to the peasants."[60] Luis also sold maize flour to the Incomati Sugar Estates, thus linking family production at Ilha Josina Machel to the reproduction of wage workers at the plantation.

In addition to maize, peasants traded beans, *riccino* (an ingredient in castor oil), and *mafurra* (an ingredient in soap) at the rural stores. By controlling the terms of trade, which were based on barter and cash, with the local merchants refusing to pay only cash for the peasants' crops, the merchants appropriated the economic surplus produced by the peasants. In the 1970s, for example, twenty kilos of maize, equivalent to forty escudos, was traded for a *capulana*, a piece of material worn by peasant women, or eight bars of soap.[61] The rural merchants on Ilha Josina Machel tied the peasants to their shops by providing the only outlet for the peasants' crops. One of the residents elaborated: "In the past, Mozambicans here did not have a say as to where and to whom they were going to sell their produce. Rather, the law on Ilha Josina Machel was that residents had to sell to the *cantineiros* who were Poças and Poças, Alfredo Luis, Bernadinho, and Albuquerque. These merchants set the selling prices for the seeds and the crops."[62] The merchants agreed collectively on the prices of goods and crops to avoid competition among themselves. In some cases, the shopkeepers extended credit to peasants, another way to tie the local population to individual shops.

Even though the marketing system was largely in the hands of a few Portuguese traders and merchants, there were particular moments when peasant farmers were able to exert some economic forms of defense. In 1964, for example, they refused to sell their beans for the low price of 2.10 escudos per kilo. Fernando Chavango recounted the incident:

> We met secretly and all agreed that we would not sell our beans. The consequences were high: the shopkeepers refused to sell their bread, oil and other products. Finally, we were called to a meeting in Xinavane. We expressed our discontentment with the low prices for beans. Alfredo Luis spoke and said that the peasant farmers did not dry the beans and they had to hire others to

perform the task. Plus he said there were bugs in our beans. The peasant farmers still refused to sell at such a low price. We were then taken to the administrator's office in Manhiça. After hearing our grievances, the administrator said we could sell our crops to whom we wanted in Xinavane, Gaza, or even Maputo. The shopkeepers of Ilha Josina Machel were very upset. A rural trader came from Macia [Gaza Province] and bought some of our beans. The shopkeepers then decided to buy our beans at four escudos a kilo.[63]

Peasant farmers were not entirely helpless in economic bargaining, but when the monopoly position of the traders and merchants was combined with their skills in bookkeeping and their inevitably strong connections with state power and political influence, the structural disadvantage of the producers stood out.

In the development phase of late colonialism, peasant households on Ilha Josina Machel came to depend increasingly on the state and merchants as sources of consumer and producer goods as well as outlets for marketed surplus. Well-stocked rural stores provided peasant farmers with commodities that they could not purchase elsewhere. An efficient transport and commercialization network ensured that their crops were marketed. Yet market incentives alone cannot explain the development of a commercial peasant agriculture. In fact, the low prices for crops paid to peasant farmers by the state and by private traders served as weak incentives. The colonial administration also placed restrictions on peasant economic activity and mobility. A more compelling argument—and the one made here—is that the colonial system of peasant surplus production worked because it was a very managed process. With the abrupt departure of the rural traders and shopkeepers in 1975, this rural community—which had been mobilized under colonialism and whose residents were conditioned to respond to its incentives and constraints—was thrown into disarray.

# 4

# Markets and Power
## Development Challenges, 1975–1981

**The peasant economy** of Ilha Josina Machel, like the national rural economy, was severely affected by the postindependence breakdown of the colonial system of marketing agricultural production, of transport, and of supply and service systems. Its trading network was greatly reduced, although it never closed down completely, as in many other rural areas. In 1976 and thereafter, the disintegration of the South African connection worsened the economic situation of most rural households, generating severe income losses and unemployment. This chapter illustrates several levels of policy problems in a changing situation. Three issues—the reorganization of local power and governance, the breakdown of the marketing system, and the development of collective farming—are examined within the context of Ilha Josina Machel for the period 1975–1981, the years before the Ministry of Agriculture launched its pilot cooperative development project, Project CO-1.

These issues had a profound impact on the political and economic organization of this rural community. The administration of the district and local levels, which was assured until then by the *régulo* structure, now was openly contested by Frelimo. The new government's decision to reorganize local power and governance affected different classes, genders, and generations in different ways. To the crisis of administration was added the disruption of the rural trade network and transport system. The exodus of the settler farmers, shopkeepers, and employees of the ICM meant for Ilha farmers unmarketed produce and shortages of consumer and producer goods. And the establishment of collective farms interfered with production in the family sector in a way that state farms did not. In the Manhiça District (of which Ilha Josina Machel is a part), where there was one state farm, Maragra, and one privately owned plantation, the Incomati Sugar Estates, only a small proportion of the local population became regular wage workers at these enterprises. Instead, in such rural communities as Ilha Josina Machel where state farms were few, co-operatives were supposed to play the key role in Frelimo's strategy of trans-forming peasant agriculture.[1] Peasants were expected to work initially in both cooperatives and family farms but over time to devote all their labor to collective farming.

One of the immediate challenges that Frelimo confronted with the departure of the Portuguese was the collapse of the colonial administration apparatus. Instead of reestablishing the colonial dual system of political administration characterized by the appointment of chiefs in the countryside and European law in the towns, the government introduced a democratic system based on choice and representation. For the first time, Mozambicans were given an opportunity to participate directly in the political process and to elect their own representatives, within the context of a one-party system. Frelimo denied rural people the right to choose traditional leaders as their representatives, however, because it viewed the latter as having compromised their positions under the colonial administration system.

Colonial administrative penetration had created a dependence on state structures; the flight of skilled labor and capital brought with it a collapse of these mechanisms, meaning that any government confronted staggering challenges. In this context, Frelimo's centralized economic policies, which included price controls unrelated to market conditions, aggravated deteriorating conditions and yielded widespread dissatisfaction. With low prices for crops and few commodities to buy, even as early as 1977, long before the acceleration of the war and its destructive effects became widespread, the peasantry had little commercial incentive to engage in surplus agricultural production. As a result, peasant farmers of Ilha Josina Machel, like agricultural producers in the rest of the countryside, reduced their farming areas under cultivation.

Frelimo's approach to rural development was flawed from the outset. In 1977, the government embarked on an overly ambitious rural transformation program, with neither the knowledge nor the material resources necessary to calculate, much less meet, the costs of transition. Concentrating the bulk of investment and resources in the state sector, Frelimo paid insufficient attention to developing relations between the state and the rest of the economy and gave no support to the family sector. Because of this, producer cooperatives lacked support, even where set up by local initiative.

Beyond the state's failure to invest in cooperatives, reasons for the movement's problems are found in the internal dynamics of the cooperatives and the way peasants shaped the outcomes of inherent struggles. On Ilha Josina Machel, the first collective fields were formed by a small group of middle and wealthier peasant farmers, the overwhelming majority of them men, who already had a firm base in agriculture as well as in other economic activities. Frelimo's expectation that poor peasant farmers would dominate the cooperatives was unrealistic given the state's failure to provide them with technical and material support; poor peasant farmers simply did not own or have access to the basic resources to initiate and control self-reliant cooperatives. On the ground, only those who had the means of production and organizational ability invested in collective farming. Initially, these better-off peasants formed cooperatives because they hoped these institutions could be used to accumulate capital. They assumed that state assistance would be forthcoming, like under the colonial regime, but that Frelimo would do away with the obstacles that prevented them from advancing in the past—for example, limited access to semimechanized equipment, low fixed prices for their crops, and restricted marketing practices. When Frelimo authorities intervened in 1977 and insisted that co-op membership be expanded to include poorer peasants, the majority of prosperous peasants deserted collective production. Resenting state interference, they concentrated on their own farms and, over the years, competed with cooperatives for poor peasant labor.

The formation of cooperatives did not by itself produce fundamental changes in the relations of production on the land. Even when cooperative membership was opened to the general populace, the few remaining male middle-peasant farmers dominated the leadership positions, leaving poor women, the majority of the members, as agricultural laborers without decision-making powers. This sexual division of labor and power reflected the predominant relations in family farming, with men maintaining their control over women and production. From the advent of the cooperative movement on the island, the new units of collective production were the terrain for discrimination on gender and class lines.

## Political Administration, Local Power, and Governance

Recent academic debate on the origin and spread of the war in rural Mozambique has focused on two issues: the exclusion of traditional authorities from political positions and peasant opposition to Frelimo's strategy of rural development.[2] It is argued that the government's attempt to install a single, country-wide system of public administration was driven by a desire to exclude chiefs and other legitimate traditional authorities from political positions, and to replace them with state functionaries, in order to control the rural population. Summing up Frelimo's policies in the countryside, this scholarship asserts that the postindependent state, with its collectivization policy, antitraditionalism, and technocratic and urban bias, was more authoritarian than the colonial state. But it fails to address the fundamental problem confronting the new Mozambican government: how local power and governance were to be organized.

After independence, the Frelimo government maintained a uniform pattern of administrative divisions, changing the colonial units of district, council, and administrative post to province, district, and locality, respectively. The southern province of Maputo was divided into seven districts, including the District of Manhiça.[3] In 1976, Ilha Mariana was renamed Ilha Josina Machel, and the locality was placed under the administrative authority of the Manhiça District. Circles and cells, political divisions, replaced the *regedorias* or chieftainships and the subchieftainships in the countryside. The overall effect of these changes on Ilha Josina Machel was to provide a system of political administration within which local power and governance could be organized.

In the Manhiça District, the local administration was greatly reduced with the departure of most Portuguese government officials, but it did not collapse entirely. Given the severe shortage of qualified and experienced personnel, Frelimo relied on Mozambican civil servants who had held subordinate positions in the colonial state apparatus and grassroots GDs to prevent a complete administrative breakdown. At Ilha Josina Machel, Régulo Adriano Timana died suddenly of a heart attack in 1975 and, given Frelimo's abolition of the chieftainships, he was not replaced.[4] Shortly afterward, the district party cadres chose thirteen residents of the community to form GDs in the seven neighborhoods.

According to the members, they initiated weekly mass assemblies with large attendance where discussions focused on problems of production, the nature of their collective activities, and the personal behavior of the GDs' representatives. They also took over the decision-making functions, ranging from land use to solving intra- and interfamily disputes. Although they retained popular support, the members were overworked, inexperienced, and ill equipped to deal with managing the economy as well as assisting various social and political demands. Mobilizing the peasantry proved to be a skilled, labor-intensive, and costly strategy, even using motivated volunteers. By 1978, eight of the original members of the GDs had returned to farming or other economic activities full-time, and five chose to stand for party elections.

In February 1978, as a means of expanding its political base beyond the fifteen thousand men and women who had participated in the armed struggle, Frelimo began a national campaign to create party cells throughout the country. Those persons who declared themselves candidates had to meet strict party membership criteria and were subjected to intense public scrutiny. Party cadres advised citizens not to elect former *régulos* or other traditional authorities who had collaborated with the colonial regime.

Frelimo's decision to bar all traditional chiefs and *régulos* from the system of governance generated substantial political discussion on Ilha Josina Machel.

Most residents supported ex-*régulo* Eduardo Timana's candidacy, perceiving him as a leader who was not as closely aligned with the colonial system as some of the candidates running for political office. During the election process, several persons recounted stories of how he had protected them from forced labor or extended their period to pay taxes. In contrast, a number of individuals who benefited from the positions they held during Régulo Adriano Timana's tenure and whom the residents viewed as being much more firmly integrated in the colonial system than Eduardo Timana stood for election. It was well known, for example, that one candidate had received a fertile tract of land to expand his production of wheat, maize, and other cash crops because he sold the *régulo*'s locally brewed alcohol, yet residents still voted for this prospective candidate because he was a prosperous farmer and they hoped he would promote their agricultural interests.

According to some scholars (i.e., the traditionalists), the government's decision to exclude local "traditional" authorities from political power alienated significant sectors of the rural population. In their analysis, Frelimo ignored or rejected the diverse cultural traditions of rural people. The government's prohibition of such rituals as headmen sacrificing to the ancestors was part of a consistent disrespect for the values of the peasantry implicit in Frelimo's conception of nation-building and socialization of the countryside. Renamo capitalized on this situation by appealing to the marginalized chiefs and religious leaders and their followers on the basis of ethnic and regional sentiments. Christian Geffray, a leading proponent of this thesis, argued that peasants supported Renamo because they wanted respect and recognition for their traditional chiefs. Traditional chiefs entered the war not to recover the privileges that *régulos* enjoyed in the colonial period, the argument goes, but to reclaim their dignity and the exercise of their authority that were repressed by Frelimo. By exploiting these grievances and by claiming that it had the support of the ancestral spirits in its war against Frelimo, Renamo succeeded in establishing a social base in parts of the countryside.

This scholarship challenged the long-standing argument put forth by earlier studies that Renamo was primarily a movement externally backed by South Africa and other countries, and that most Mozambicans were forcibly recruited into Renamo's army.[5] These studies offered considerable documentary evidence of the military and predatory character of Renamo and of its failure to establish itself as a genuine political movement inside Mozambique. A pioneering analysis by Robert Gersony described the scale and types of violence Renamo employed (namely burning of village homes and ransacking of shops and people's belongings, particularly food and clothes) and argued that Renamo kidnapped most of its recruits. William Minter provided further evidence that the main method of recruitment into Renamo was coercion, and that its military operations were sustained by regular supplies from South Africa as well as by a centralized system of command and communications.[6]

Detailed regional studies reveal that Renamo had a different set of relations to various Mozambican populations, and that the nature of its support was diverse both within a province and from province to province. In Nampula, Geffray stressed that the divisions among chiefs in support of Frelimo and Renamo fit the precolonial cleavages (i.e., traditional rivalries between communities). In contrast, Roesch found that the response of Nampula peasantry to exhortations from their chiefs varied according to their socioeconomic interests.[7] In general, the more educated and affluent sectors of the peasantry preferred to side with Frelimo against the chiefs, because Renamo's predatory and undisciplined actions represented a greater threat to the livelihood of this social stratum than Frelimo's policies.

In some regions in Manica and Sofala, where Frelimo used coercive measures to enforce its villagization program, traditional authorities crossed voluntarily to Renamo and organized their followers to do likewise.[8] But often their enthusiasm for Renamo was short-lived. In rural Manica people who came under Renamo control in Macossa District were quickly placed under severe movement restrictions and threatened with death if they tried to flee.[9] Renamo also resorted to kidnapping chiefs and spirit mediums in order to broaden its control over the rural population. Moreover, Renamo's relations with chiefs had a strong Portuguese resonance, combining support for certain aspects of "tradition" with violence and extraction. Chiefs were charged with providing food and labor (e.g., for porterage) and incorporating outsiders, generally captives. Though they resented carrying out these unpopular duties, chiefs were reluctant to go against Renamo's coercive demands.

Kenneth Wilson noted that Renamo was more selective in its use of violence in Zambézia than elsewhere, and that it emphasized coercive administrative control with a sophisticated political line, rather than simply intimidatory violence. Nonetheless, his work showed how central a "cult of violence" was to Renamo, and how it was used instrumentally to conquer huge areas in northern Mozambique in the 1980s.[10] While some chiefs became political clients of Renamo, others engaged in passive resistance, drawing upon support from their subjects to resist overexactions by Renamo. According to Wilson, most chiefs appointed by Renamo were those who had collaborated with the Portuguese as *régulos,* contrary to Geffray's findings in Nampula. Furthermore, the local population who joined Renamo did so as an act of revenge against the power of an arrogant "modern" elite who managed to retain authority from Portuguese rule to independence under Frelimo. Loyalty to traditional authorities and resentment of communal villages were nonissues in Zambézia.

Southern Mozambique, a region regarded as under Frelimo control, experienced the most large-scale violence committed by Renamo soldiers. There rural people, even those disillusioned with government policies, saw Renamo as a Ndau project, with the predominantly Ndau speakers of central Mozambique composing its military leadership, and resisted the movement's overtures. In Gaza, Roesch found that the issues Renamo successfully exploited in the center and north—villagization, traditional authorities, and peasant culture—did not carry the same weight.[11] By 1983, when the war began to spread seriously in Gaza, the government had already ceased actively promoting villagization in the province and was allowing people to return to their land. Unlike Nampula, Manica, and Sofala, traditional authority structures in Gaza had lost much legitimacy during colonial times. Chiefly power was undermined by labor migration to South Africa that gave families access to regular wages and made them less dependent on agricultural income, and, hence, less subservient to local authorities who controlled access to land. While some people resented the state's disregard for local traditional culture, high levels of enthusiasm for Frelimo exceeded it, especially in the early years. Without popular support, Renamo operated as a predatory army, terrorizing and plundering the rural population.

On Ilha Josina Machel, the residents did not turn against Frelimo and support Renamo for several reasons. First, most people did not resent cooperatives, although they were frustrated that Frelimo failed to invest in these new production units. The disillusioned members simply abandoned collective farming. Second, unlike in central Mozambique, there were no powerful-alienated traditional authorities antagonized over the loss of their power and imposition of cooperatives who were prepared to offer hospitality to Renamo. Furthermore, while some individuals may have favored an individual *régulo*, most residents disliked the *regulado* system. Third, the people did not feel that there was a general assault on their culture and religion. In the two years that I lived in this rural community, I did not find that peasants were ashamed or afraid to show their allegiance to traditional beliefs. When I arrived in the village, for example, one of the most powerful *curandeiros* informed me that she would extend her powers to protect me during my entire stay. Her reputation was so well known that despite the escalation of the war in 1983, people traveled from afar to serve as her intern; even the Frelimo village secretary openly sought the skills of the *curandeiro* to cure his illness. Fourth, Renamo's own brutal methods—mutilation (of ears, lips, noses, and breasts), castration, and crucifixion—that were an integral part of its control of civilian populations made it easy for Ilha residents to chose Frelimo over Renamo. Many had lost family members and friends to Renamo's savage attacks on nearby rural communities, which are described in graphic detail in Lina Magaia's short stories of the war in the Manhiça District.[12] They also were aware that Renamo targeted rural development projects for destruction, including the Project CO-1–supported cooperatives in Tete Province.[13]

The debate between those who explain Renamo's growth on the base of its Rhodesian–South African origins and those who consider Frelimo's rural policies as a major cause for the spreading of Renamo's influence over the countryside has reached a stalemate. By focusing solely on the predatory nature of Renamo and its involuntary recruitment methods, we cannot understand its changing social base. By focusing on the issue of traditional authorities and their supposedly popular power base—divorced from their historical complicity with the colonial regime—the revisionist literature creates serious distortions. Overlooked in this controversy is the question of local power and governance after independence: the fundamental question being not whether rural people could honor traditional authorities, but how local power and governance were to be organized. From the leadership's point of view, the colonial system of governance based on European law in the urban areas and on the appointments of *régulos* and chiefs in the rural areas was divisive, antidemocratic, and responsible for maintaining economic backwardness in the countryside.

Frelimo decided to dismantle the colonial dual system of political administration and to replace it with a structure of elected assemblies, the first step toward representative democracy. At the locality level, deputies were elected directly. Representative or indirect elections followed on higher levels—district, provincial, and national people's assemblies. By 1980, over thirteen hundred assemblies existed in administrative localities and in communal villages all over the country.[14] Simultaneously, party organs were created on provincial, district, and locality levels, with party cells implanted in places of work and residence. These new party and state structures were applied both in rural and urban areas. Notwithstanding the deficiencies of the single-party system, Frelimo offered the prospect of a more democratic political order than the Portuguese regime.

Frelimo's restructuring of local power and governance had different effects on different classes, genders, and generations, as well as regions and rural-urban divisions. In the Ilha community, the abolition of the *régulo* system meant that poor peasants no longer had to provide free labor on the farms of the chiefs and other so-called traditional rulers; that middle farmers ceased to present a portion of their harvest to the local authorities; that migrant workers no longer were forced to pay cash to former colonial functionaries upon their return; and that young men were not obliged to pay tribute to receive land, but instead submitted a request to the local administrator who then presented it to the People's Assembly for discussion. In general, the more affluent sectors of the peasantry, which had historically opposed the constraints that the colonial state and its local chiefly collaborators had imposed upon its capacity to accumulate, preferred Frelimo's representational forms of local government over the colonial system of chiefly rule. The only residents in the community who took a less critical position of indirect rule were old peasant farmers who experienced a drastic deterioration in their living standard after independence. Their privileges as elders—in particular, customary rights that gave them control over youth and women and hence patronage—were undermined.

Given that the structure of authority was highly patriarchal, women had the most to gain from a shift in political power from traditional rulers to representative democracy. In 1982, for example, of the thirty deputies elected to the People's Assembly on Ilha Josina Machel, thirteen (43 percent) were women, a figure that compared favorably with the national average of 24.5 percent women deputies elected to local assemblies. The lower national local average hid a wide variation over the country, from next to no representation of women in the northern provinces—where Islam was widely practiced—to an almost equal number of women and men in the southern provinces.

The Mozambican government implemented legislation mandating gender equality and created new institutions to build and broaden women's political experience. Yet rural women did not participate or advance in politics as rapidly as Frelimo envisaged, largely because they were not prepared to assume responsibility in the public domain without a reduction of their household duties in the private sphere. The sexual division of labor that legitimated the subordination of women remained in place, making it difficult for most women to become actively involved in the political process or to assume leadership positions in collective production. The latter was an issue that Frelimo did not seriously address. As a result, the same few women—typically those with a sound economic base—served on nearly every local body. Of the thirteen women deputies on Ilha Josina Machel, for example, five held positions on the twenty-member local committee that served as a forum for discussion of community issues.[15] These thirteen women also were members of the party and of the women's mass organization, the Mozambican Women's Organization (OMM).

Frelimo established a more democratic system of governance than the Portuguese did, but it did not manage to avoid the pitfalls of the one-party state. In particular, the party failed to constitute itself as a force separate from the state and capable of entering into opposition to it. Rather, Frelimo opted for a system of public administration in which the party secretary at a particular level was also the top official in the government hierarchy. The provincial first secretary, for example, was always the governor of the province; the district or locality administrator was simultaneously the first secretary of the party; and the highest state functionaries (i.e., the provincial governor or the district or the locality administrator) led the executive council elected within the assembly to direct the affairs of the government.

This hierarchical structure also meant that the power of the locally elected people's assemblies, to which the government was theoretically accountable, was very weak. The people's assemblies, which were created at the locality to give the masses a voice, did not serve the majority of rural dwellers. There was mass participation and a great deal of discussion and debate, as discussed above, but the assemblies made little impact without policy-making or legislative functions. Higher authority usually ignored decisions made at the base considered to be politically incorrect. In effect, Frelimo continued the tradition of an all-powerful administrative structure inherited from the Portuguese.

From 1981 onward, popular participation declined and the peasants' attitudes toward Frelimo began to change from support to disillusionment as their socioeconomic position worsened. The already weakened economic base of the peasantry in southern Mozambique was further debilitated by the onset of drought conditions that persisted through 1983, further reducing levels of consumption and the peasantry's standard of living. Although peasant production on Ilha Josina Machel was adequate to meet basic food needs, it was not abundant. As was the case elsewhere in southern Mozambique, many peasant farmers on the island suffered from skin and eye diseases associated with malnutrition. The decline in peasant farmers' productive capacity posed a severe constraint on the productivity and output of their labor.

### The Breakdown of the Marketing System

The supply of essential goods and agricultural implements declined initially because of the collapse of the colonial commercial infrastructure and subsequently due to the inability of the industrial sector to produce them and the unwillingness of the government to import them, soon creating a situation where demand greatly outstripped supply. From the late 1970s, Frelimo's development strategy of concentrating investment in public-sector enterprises accounted for the limited consumer goods in the countryside. The war exacerbated the goods shortage, but it did not initiate it.

By 1978, the traders and shopkeepers on Ilha Josina Machel had abandoned their commercial establishments and fled the country.[16] The Portuguese owners of the nine stores in the community had been linked to a network of private wholesalers. When the bulk of the colonial wholesalers emigrated to Portugal in 1975, supplies and credit flows to the rural commercial establishments were cut, creating a situation of disorganization and chaos and resulting in the near collapse of the marketing circuits.

Although the exoduses of capital and resources were important factors to account for the initial breakdown of the system, more significant was the managerial experience lost. The *assimilados* who managed the local stores had only limited knowledge of the market exchange system. The example of Albino Bila is illustrative:

> Bila, an *assimilado*, worked seven years at the Xinavane store owned by Poças and Poças [a family enterprise]. In 1962, he was transferred to Ilha Josina Machel where he was a sewing machine operator for twelve years. From 1974 to 1978, Bila worked behind the counter as a clerk and then took over management when the owners left. Despite his twenty-three years of employment with Poças and Poças, his knowledge of the marketing network was limited. He knew that the majority of the goods came originally from Lourenço Marques [Maputo] but he did not know the wholesalers. The owners transported the goods from Maputo in their privately owned trucks to their store in Xinavane. There, the Poças brothers divided the merchandise between the three stores, transporting the goods to each one. At no point had Mozambicans been involved in the process.[17]

The departure of colonial shopkeepers and the collapse of the marketing and transportation systems had a doubly negative effect on the Ilha Josina Machel peasants. Their outlet for marketing maize, cassava, groundnuts, and beans disappeared, as did the distribution system of other essential consumer goods, with the result that many peasant producers began dropping out of the market economy. The marketing cooperative, Cooperative Moses, also collapsed. The shutdown of the cereals and cotton institutes at independence instantly cut the production levels of those prosperous peasants whom these institutions had helped; without the coordination and extension services of the ICM, wealthier peasant farmers were unable to arrange the supply of inputs and services. During the 1975–1976 agricultural season, for example, some of them sowed their wheat seed from the previous season on the first collective fields, but without transportation the harvest rotted in the warehouse. The peasants did not cultivate wheat again until the 1981–1982 agricultural season, and then under state pressure. Without state programs to assist both poor and middle peasants, Frelimo pushed the weakest of the middle peasants down to the level of poor peasants. For both groups, the state's failure to back co-ops and family farms meant they had no route to economic development and they became poorer.

To reestablish production and commerce, the Frelimo government expanded state retail trade. In 1976, a parastatal organization, the National People's Shop Enterprise, was set up to coordinate, establish, and supply the people's shops with consumer goods. Shortly afterward, an abandoned store on Ilha Josina Machel was converted into a people's shop and the Manhiça District administrator sent a government official to manage it. According to the local residents, the goods at the people's shop did not arrive regularly in comparison to the three private stores still functioning at the time. The main problem with the people's shops was the government personnel, most of whom had limited knowledge and experience: Most officials lacked the basic mathematical skills required for effective marketing and accounting and the organization and management skills to coordinate and conduct the marketing and distribution process. They had little or no experience with price structures, inventory and storage systems, sales, personnel control, transport planning, and other general aspects of the marketing system. Administrative weaknesses, shortages of goods, and the limited number of functioning state-owned vehicles to transport the goods aggravated the situation.

There were other reasons to account for Frelimo's failure to reestablish rural commerce. From 1975 to 1980, government policies toward private traders and transporters were mixed, consisting of different efforts to control their activities and to co-opt them into the governments' distribution plans, while the government proceeded to build up parastatal structures. Frelimo's general antipathy to the private traders often meant that the government did not differentiate clearly between the different types of intermediaries or the resources at the disposal of each, such as the number of vehicles and storage facilities. A 1978 study on the marketing and distribution system concluded that the government still was largely unaware of the functioning of the private sector, their resources, and operations.[18]

In March 1980, the government decided state retail trade was beyond its capabilities, and the people's shops were handed over to private traders, transformed into consumer cooperatives, or simply closed down. In the southern rural economy, this policy change concerned mainly rich peasants and private farmers who already had a sound economic base and migrant workers abroad who had access to foreign exchange and could invest in the shop. Private traders and shopkeepers were encouraged to operate in the countryside at the retail level, but the state retained its control of wholesale trade in agricultural and industrial products and set producer and consumer prices for most goods. Instead of reestablishing the colonial agricultural pricing structure that was differentiated by area of the country, the government implemented uniform prices for reasons of equity and administrative simplicity. Thus, the state envisaged private retailers as local economic intermediaries rather than as a group that could develop as an independent economic force. At Ilha Josina Machel, a Maputo resident merchant bought the people's shop and transformed it into a private store, making a total of four privately owned shops in the locality.

The privatization of rural retail trade benefited the residents of Ilha Josina Machel because the local shopkeepers had gained some knowledge of the marketing-distribution process from experience as store clerks or warehouse employees. They also had monopolies of resources such as trained and experienced personnel, transport vehicles, and storage facilities, making them able to purchase, transport, and sell their goods with more efficiency than the people's shop. Although the quantity of goods at the private shops was not usually sufficient for the total population, the disparity reflected more the problem of supply at the national level than the incompetence of the shopkeepers in determining items and quantities. An example illustrates these points:

> The two Mozambican entrepreneurs, who took ownership of the rural store formerly owned by the Poças family in 1978, entrusted Bila with a half-ton truck to pick up and transport the goods from the privately owned warehouse in Xinavane. Although the state controlled and regulated the wholesale trade, the warehouse was still owned by the Alfredo Luis family, former owners of a commercial establishment on Ilha Josina Machel, meaning there were previous exchanges, if not a developed friendship, between Bila and the warehouse management. It is probable that the warehouse employees felt some security of payment for the goods forwarded to Bila. Twice per week, Bila transported the goods from the Xinavane warehouse to the Ilha Josina Machel shop, storing the goods in the warehouse until they were put on sale. He kept accurate bookkeeping records and an up-to-date inventory of the stock.[19]

The other three stores on Ilha Josina Machel were in a similar situation. Transportation was privately owned, meaning the owners planned pickup and delivery of the goods from the district warehouse; the counter clerks or managers were experienced employees or trained family members with some mathematical skills necessary for effective bookkeeping and accounting; and the owners had previous connections with the local warehouse personnel for the distribution of goods. This combination of factors guaranteed some marketing and distribution efficiency of consumer goods.

Government intervention in the marketing of peasants' surplus agricultural production on Ilha Josina Machel, as elsewhere in Maputo Province, was minor during the first few years after independence. Neither the state marketing brigades (set up in 1975 as an emergency measure to purchase peasants' crops) nor the parastatal organization National Economic and Agricultural Marketing Directorate, DINECA (created in 1976 within the Ministry of Agriculture to supply inputs for agriculture and to maintain the marketing systems), operated in the locality. The government gave priority to the continued operation of the marketing systems in the northern and central regions of the country, assuming that the remaining Portuguese private traders and transporters would market peasant farmers' surplus production in southern Mozambique.

In 1980 Agricom, a state agricultural marketing company setup, replaced DINECA. Agricom undertook wholesaling of agricultural produce (repurchasing crops bought from farmers by private traders) and purchased and sold at the retail level in rural areas where a private network did not exist. Given that its territory included all provinces in Mozambique with the exception of Maputo Province, the impact of Agricom was negligible in unblocking the marketing of Ilha peasants' crops. Subsequently, in 1981, the government established Hortifruta, an agricultural parastatal organization, to market fruits and vegetables produced by the private, family, cooperative, and state sectors in Inhambane, Gaza, and Maputo Provinces. Typically, administrative, organization, and management problems prevented Hortifruta from performing its marketing function. In 1981, for example, the only recorded produce marketed by Hortifruta in the Manhiça District was some bananas sold by a private farmer.[20]

By the late 1970s, the family sector on Ilha Josina Machel only had three main outlets to market their surplus agricultural production: private traders and transporters, a local store assigned by the Ministry of Internal Commerce as a marketing post, and the parallel market where trade occurred at prices other than those officially set. According to many Ilha residents, more miners returned to the area with vehicles to transport and market agricultural crops as well as to provide public transportation.[21] As private traders, these returning miners often offered commercial competition to the government market channels.

The only state marketing outlet for Ilha peasants' agricultural surpluses was a private store owned by Carlos Fernando Xerindza Majonane. In 1981, the administration of Manhiça selected his store to be a marketing post for the Ministry of Internal Commerce, so Majonane was able to purchase consumer goods at the ministry's warehouse in Manhiça and exchange them at his store for beans and maize produced by the family sector. It was the ministry's responsibility to supply the storage sacks for these crops and trucks to transport the agricultural products to Maputo. But within a year, Mozambican farmers throughout the countryside were unwilling to sell goods to the state buying agencies without receiving goods in return. The ministry responded to this by increasingly selling consumer goods only in return for crop sales; during the 1981–1982 agricultural season, Majonane traded sufficient quantities of sugar, soap, matches, and other basic rationed goods with peasant farmers in exchange for two thousand kilograms of maize and six thousand kilograms of beans.[22]

The 1981 results reflected the first year of recorded-marketed agricultural production by the family sector on Ilha Josina Machel. Majonane was convinced that these quantities of maize and beans represented a decline in production from the colonial era, and local farmers described how their maize had previously filled the Portuguese shopkeepers' warehouses.[23] Yet within the Manhiça District, these results were outstanding. Of the nine marketing posts in the district, only Majonane's store exchanged consumer goods for peasants' crops, suggesting that this was an incentive toward greater production.[24]

According to Majonane, there were three major problems with the barter system established by the Ministry of Internal Commerce: the late arrival of consumer goods; a scarcity of popular products to trade with the peasants, such as soap, batteries, and sugar; and the delay in state transportation to pick up the crops, which often meant that the produce rotted in his warehouse. Majonane elaborated on the second point, which he saw as the major stumbling block to marketing peasants' crops: "The major problem in trading beans and maize for consumer products is that the Ministry of Internal Commerce does not send sufficient supplies of the products which the peasants want. Specifically, peasants will trade crops for sugar and soap. Other goods like *capulanas* [cloths worn by women] and blankets do not sell as well because they compete with goods brought back by miners who offer better terms of trade [than the government].[25] The government's terms of trade were based on the national prices of consumer goods and agricultural products. In 1983, for example, a *capulana* priced at 350 meticais meant that a peasant had to exchange approximately fifty-eight kilograms of maize at the wholesale price of 6 meticais/kilo. Although the terms of trade in the parallel market were not known, the remaining bolts of cloth in Majonane's store at the end of the harvest indicated that peasant farmers were unwilling to exchange maize, the region's preferred food crop, for an item that could be obtained on better terms outside the official outlet.

After the decline of Mozambican recruits to the South African mines in 1976, many Ilha residents established a system of barter with miners and their families at the communal village 3 de Fevereiro, located nineteen kilometers from the locality. Since many of the communal village residents confronted severe land shortages, preventing them from growing their own food supplies, Ilha farmers found a ready market for their crops, which they traded for consumer goods brought back by miners. By the early 1980s, agricultural producers and wage earners depended on the growing parallel market for basic commodities.

It was common, for example, that workers from the nearby sugar estates exchanged their monthly quota of sugar for maize produced by Ilha farmers; in other cases peasant farmers exchanged crops and oxen in return for motorcycles purchased by miners in South Africa.

Three interlocking phenomena shaped the exchange between the state and the peasantry: the reduction in relative and absolute terms of official marketing of crops, as a result of the rapid expansion of parallel markets; the sharp increase of prices in the parallel markets; and the associated rapid depreciation of the currency and the increased reluctance of the peasantry to accept the metical in exchange for sale of crops. According to the official explanation of the problem, articulated by the Ministry of Internal Commerce, the peasantry had withdrawn from the market because money no longer bought goods. Rural wages and cash crops channeled money into the economy in excess of available producer and consumer goods directed to the peasantry. Therefore, the peasantry withdrew from the market and preferred to buy up supplies with available money rather than through production.[26]

The main problem with the government's policy was that it did not take account of the parallel markets and the accompanying process of commercial speculative capital accumulation. From the government's point of view, speculation was seen mainly as the activity of small producers and consumers to bypass the official channels: producers searched for a higher price and consumers searched for access to commodities. Speculative private traders, however, rapidly assumed an independent role. They managed to accumulate rapidly through price increases on the parallel markets and the control of alternative trade circuits.

Although some prosperous peasant farmers and traders accumulated wealth, the real problem was not the conversion of money into capital. More significant was the scarcity of consumer goods relative to the purchasing power of peasant farmers at state prices, which created a situation where differential access to scarce consumer goods accentuated social stratification in the countryside. Those who accumulated capital often were linked to external migrant labor, providing hard currency and access to irrigation pumps, tractors, motorcycles, and other goods. Through their access to certain commodities they were in a position to obtain cheap labor power from poorer peasants.

From 1980 onward, the class structure of agriculture and trade on Ilha Josina Machel came to resemble the colonial situation. There was a reintegration of trading and large-scale farming (that is, farms of fifty hectares or more that used regular wage labor) reminiscent of the previous integration of Portuguese settler farming and trade. With the exception of the one new shopkeeper from Maputo City, the three rural store owners in the community combined private farming and trade, enabling them to profit from the growth of the parallel markets. These Mozambican farmer-traders invested their profits in tractors and private transport, as well as in other nonagricultural economic activities. One of them, for example, established a popular restaurant in the community that served full-course meals, a rarity in the district, until Renamo rebels destroyed it in 1988. Finally, there was a process of concentration of trade taking place: the two most successful farmer-traders came to own a couple of shops in the locality and in the district.

The Frelimo government recognized the necessity to combat the growth of the parallel markets and speculation that eroded the control of the state over marketed surpluses of food. But its successes in controlling the internal situation were limited, since state policies gave private traders opportunity to assume control over food surpluses. Eventually, the control of private trade over food surplus eroded the coherence of the state sector. In the Manhiça District, the official market for food supply could not respond to the demand coming from Maputo City, the Manhiça town and its surrounding food-deficit rural areas, the army base situated in the nearby Palmeira, and the two sugar plantations that needed food for its workers. Thus, state enterprises and institutions resorted to buying on the parallel market to obtain the necessary supplies.

## The Development of Collective Fields on Ilha Josina Machel, 1975–1977

During the first two years after independence, peasant farmers established collective fields on a spontaneous basis throughout Mozambique as part of Frelimo's strategy to transform agriculture. The GDs of Ilha Josina Machel, like elsewhere in the countryside, led an active and extensive program of political mobilization to promote collective farming. The reaction of peasant farmers to these initiatives varied according to their social and economic status. In general, the more wealthy and educated stratum of peasant farmers seized upon the challenge eagerly, hoping that their participation in collective farming would lead to capital accumulation. They could participate in collective production during this early period, when earnings were very irregular and low, because they had a strong base in family production, usually in combination with alternative sources of income. In comparison, the poor peasants placed first priority on the family farm to assure subsistence. The two examples of collective fields established in neighborhood 1 (formerly known as Régulo Proper) and neighborhood 6 (previously Zonguene) are illustrative of the difficulties that beset this early period of collectivization.

At the beginning of 1976, the GDs of the district and locality organized a meeting with the inhabitants of neighborhood 1 where some of the peasant farmers agreed to establish a collective field on Ilha Josina Machel (later named Cooperative 25 de Setembro). This fertile and easily irrigated land, formerly owned by Régulo Adriano, was well located within meters of the Matseculi River. The members sowed three hectares of wheat, the remaining seed of the ICM, but participation was very irregular during the farming season as labor input was on a voluntary basis. No record was kept of the first year's production results, and the harvest rotted in a warehouse waiting for state transportation. The members abandoned the collective unit at the end of the season.

In the following agricultural season, 1976–1977, nine individuals (eight men and a woman) decided to form their own collective field. Seven of them had worked previously in the South African mines, the only exceptions being a Portuguese farmer who moved to the locality in 1974 and a woman peasant farmer whose migrant mine worker husband was a close friend of the other founders. Regarded by the local population as a hard worker, she was one of the few women to participate in the colonial marketing cooperative. Of the seven ex-miners, five were former members of Cooperative Moses, with two of them in leadership positions. The other two Mozambicans had worked continuously in the mines during the colonial period. All of the initial members were relatively wealthy and ambitious middle-peasant farmers, the majority having some experience as wage laborers and various sources of nonfarming earnings.

The nine individuals decided collectively that each one would contribute 4,800 escudos, totaling 43,200 escudos, to a communal fund.[27] Part of this money was to go toward paying the cooperative's expenses, and the other part was to be saved until they had sufficient cash to purchase a tractor and other mechanized equipment. Based on the experience of the colonial marketing cooperative, they selected a bookkeeper and treasurer to manage the finances and the internal organization of the collective unit. Each member was given a work card, and there was a register to monitor attendance. The collective enterprise did not inherit any infrastructure, so the members supplied the ox-plows and nearly all the seeds. The Portuguese farmer rented his tractor to plow the field and the state provided some rice seeds and a broken water pump abandoned by a colonial settler in the Manhiça District. At the time, rice, a food crop consumed largely by urban dwellers, was in short supply. The district agricultural officer, under pressure from the national government, talked the cooperative members into growing rice in spite of the disastrous experience with rice production at the colonial cooperative.

For the first agricultural campaign, the members (and their wives, who were not registered as members) planted ten hectares of rice and twenty hectares of beans and maize.[28] The production results were uneven: the rice was totally destroyed by insects, but the harvest of beans and maize was sufficient to be distributed among the members and a surplus was sold to the local population. The only expense at the end of the season was the tractor rental of 7,500 escudos. As the members explained it in retrospect, they did not reimburse the state for the rice seeds because there was no production. The balance at the end of the campaign was approximately 35,700 escudos, which the members kept as a reserve fund.

There are fewer data available on the collective field of Zonguene, neighborhood 6, which was more typical of collective fields established at that time. After a meeting with the district and local GDs, the population of Zonguene agreed to establish a collective field of four hectares on land that had been abandoned by a peasant family who moved to the town of Manhiça. According to former members of the collective (later named Cooperative Arma da Frelimo), the number of participants who worked on the field was irregular, voluntary, and basically unplanned, and there was little effort to organize or control production. During the first agricultural season, 1975–1976, they sowed four hectares of wheat from leftover seeds of the colonial cooperative. Approximately seven sacks of 100 kilograms each were harvested, or 175 kilograms per hectare, much lower than the lowest productivity per hectare at the colonial cooperative, 231.7 kilograms in 1960.[29] The members stored the crop in a warehouse in Cutane, the commercial center of the island, and over the years they lost track of it. The subsequent agricultural season, the members abandoned the collective field. At the end of 1976, there were approximately four collective fields established on Ilha Josina Machel with a total membership of 239 people and less than one hundred hectares under production.[30]

Although the experience of collective fields lasted about one year, several conclusions can be drawn. First, the cohesive membership of neighborhood 1's field, characterized by middle-peasant farmers with organizational skills and capital, facilitated its relative success compared to the experience in neighborhood 6. Unlike the majority of collective fields in Mozambique at the time, neighborhood 1 established rudimentary organizational structures based on knowledge and experience that their members acquired in the colonial cooperative. As long as the membership was limited, the cooperative's basic bookkeeping was adequate. Second, these collective fields were the terrain for discrimination on class and gender lines. Poor peasants were denied participation by the membership criterion requiring a substantial input of money and goods from each member. Women were not only denied membership but also obliged to assume the role of unpaid laborers, as wives of the members. This time, however, it was the middle peasantry, not the state, enforcing class and gender inequalities. Third, contrary to Frelimo's expectations that poor peasants would dominate the cooperative movement, it was the middle and more prosperous peasants that created them. For this wealthier stratum, cooperatives offered the possibility of capital accumulation, long denied by the colonial state. Fourth, an intractable precedent was set for relations between state and peasant farmers: farmers ignored outstanding charges to the state when production results were minimal, and the state, suffering from both paternalism and disorganization, failed to pursue the amount owed. Over time, the cooperative sector would run up an unserviceable debt to the state. Thus, despite the significant changes at the national level, the continuities of social stratification among the peasantry were entrenched. We shall see the repercussions of such an established middle peasantry later on.

## Administration of Agricultural Producer Cooperatives, 1977–1980

Following the Third Party Congress in 1977, agricultural producer cooperatives were set up in the countryside. Frelimo continued to advocate the political supremacy of poorer peasants but found itself organizationally allied to middle peasants, on whom it became dependent—with their means of production and skills—for cooperatives to work. Yet Frelimo's interventionist policies prevented the wealthier peasants from using the cooperative movement to accumulate capital, and the majority of them abandoned collective production. For the poorer peasants, Frelimo's failure to back up its rhetoric with resources and material input led to their alienation from the state as their economic base eroded. Cooperatives were not an alternative to family farming, and state farms, with their capital-intensive methods of cultivation, only provided seasonal employment. By the early 1980s, there was no social force in the countryside that supported Frelimo's socialist project. The case studies that follow are of two of the twelve cooperatives established in the Ilha Josina Machel community that I came into contact with through my work in the Ministry of Agriculture.

As had frequently occurred in its history, the Incomati River inundated Ilha Josina Machel in 1977. This time, state officials arrived and informed the inhabitants that they were to move to the communal village 3 de Fevereiro, nineteen kilometers from their community. Although some moved, most of the population resisted relocation, unwilling to give up their family farms because they knew that there was insufficient land for all of them to have farms at the communal village. Fernando Cossa, a member of the local GDs, recalled the subsequent negotiations with the government: "The people knew Josefat Machel [then director of communal villages for Maputo Province]. When he came to the island, Mr. Mombassa and I presented the problem to him. He agreed with the local population. We could stay on Ilha Josina Machel but we had to establish cooperatives."[31] In some rural communities, local political leaders who sided with the state on the question of communal villages lost the support and cooperation of the residents, fueling a growing tide of widespread political demobilization and administrative paralysis. On Ilha Josina Machel, however, in reaching a compromise on the issue of communal villages and cooperatives, the local leaders gained prestige and popular support.

Shortly afterward, Ilha Josina Machel was divided into seven neighborhoods, with each family unit entitled to a plot of forty by thirty meters around the house. These neighborhoods were established without the assistance of the Department of Communal Villages and without much skill or experience in planning. Consequently, many problems later emerged, such as the long distance between dwellings and family farms and the division of family farms into very small sections. Each neighborhood had at least one agricultural cooperative, as shown in maps 3 and 4, making a total of twelve cooperatives.[32] The exact number of hectares of each cooperative was never measured.

During the period 1977–1980, these cooperatives struggled with basic technical and organizational problems stemming from inexperience, lack of technical expertise, illiteracy, and insufficient inputs and assistance from the state. Serious deficiencies in planning, administration, and credit, combined with social and political difficulties rooted in class conflict, gender discrimination, authoritarian leadership, and limited participation, prevented the early consolidation and development of the cooperatives on Ilha Josina Machel. To illuminate some of these problems, characteristic of the cooperative movement in Mozambique, the two examples of collective production at Cooperatives 25 de Setembro and Arma da Frelimo are presented.

### Cooperative 25 de Setembro

Of the range of internal factors undermining efficient organization at Cooperative 25 de Setembro, the division of available time between the family farms and the cooperative was central. During the first year, 1977–1978, this issue was not dominant because the majority of the members were men. Of the nine founding members, eight men were heads of family households with usually two or three wives and five or more children, all of whom worked on the family farm while the men participated in collective production. Women were called in only as seasonal unpaid workers to weed and harvest the crops.

In 1978–1979, with the first increase in cooperative membership—comprised mostly of women, including the wives of the founding members—the problem of organizing labor time between the two production units came to the forefront. Following the national directive that cooperatives include poor peasants, the Frelimo district party secretary persuaded forty-eight new

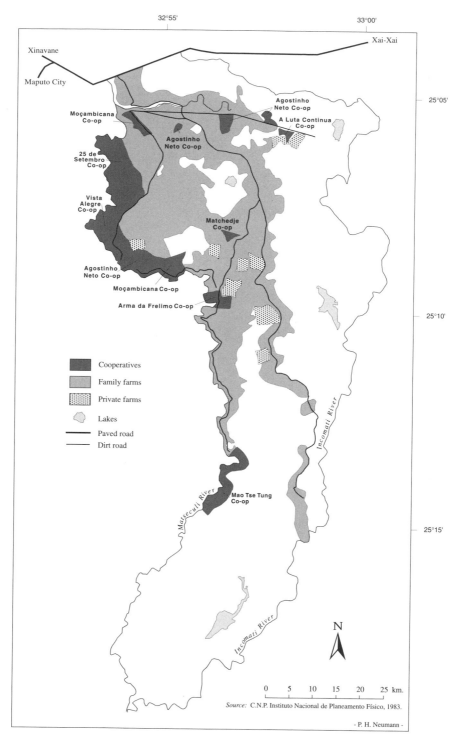

Map 3. Ilha Josina Machel: Production Units

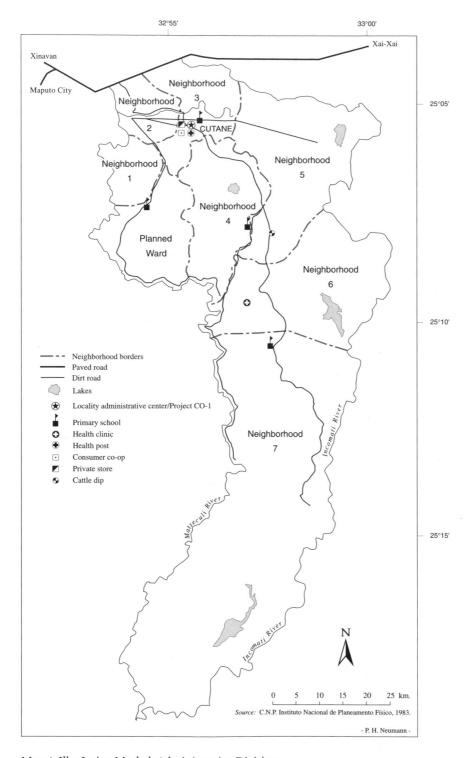

Map 4. Ilha Josina Machel: Administrative Divisions

members to join, making a total of fifty-seven co-op members. Because there was no corresponding reorganization of the crop patterns to make part of the family labor time available to the cooperative, however, peasant farmers (particularly women) first attended to the needs of the family farm, which had the same crops being grown as on the cooperative and thus coinciding with peak labor periods. Subsequently, during the 1980–1981 agricultural season, the best years of maize production on Ilha Josina Machel since independence, relatives of cooperative members weeded the maize; later, people from the Manhiça District harvested the crop. In each case, the outside workers received maize as payment for their labor, reducing the quantity to be stored for later consumption between harvests. For most co-op members, the enterprise was a new form of production where the economic results were low and insecure. While the leaders urged on members more frequent and regular attendance, the members were not prepared to balance the scale of production and participation in the cooperative with the needs of family production because the rewards were too low.

During the first agricultural season, the members did not receive monetary compensation for their work at the cooperative. One year passed before they saw their first earnings based on six months of collective work. In relation to the minimum salary of 62.50 meticais per day, four hours daily, paid to an agricultural state-farm laborer, the low earnings of 20 meticais per day, four hours daily, at the cooperative was noncompetitive.[33] Two or three months as a casual or seasonal laborer on a state farm, earning 2,100 meticais per month, provided about the same income as a whole year at the cooperative.

Yet even the first paltry earnings shared among the members precipitated internal class conflict, with five of the nine founding members leaving the cooperative. According to these individuals who left during the 1979–1980 season, their initial contribution of 4,800 escudos (this currency was replaced by the metical in 1980) to the collective should have been reimbursed before there was any distribution of funds to the new members who joined the cooperative without making a donation.[34] For the departing members, all of them wealthy middle farmers, the issue of reimbursement served as a convenient pretext for their exit from the cooperative, but their main grievance was that new members, most of them women and poor, joined the cooperative without capital or skills. The dissident members wanted the unit to remain small and homogeneous, that is, male middle peasants. By integrating poorer peasants, they saw their opportunities to use cooperatives as instruments of capital accumulation disappear. After much heated debate, they abandoned the cooperative and returned to their farms, in direct competition with surrounding cooperatives for peasant labor. The issue of repayment of the nine members' initial contribution was raised frequently over the years by those individuals who witnessed the disintegration of their economic base as their alternatives to nonfarming earnings declined.[35]

The experience of the first years of collective production at Cooperative 25 de Setembro illustrated that merely getting people to produce together did not, on its own, generate greater agricultural surpluses than family production. In cooperatives where basic cultivating practices and levels of technology were the same as on the family farm, the productivity per hectare generally fell. The reasons were many and complex. Group confidence needed time to build up and was easily fractured. New collective forms of organization were also time-consuming, involving many hours of weekly meetings to discuss work-related problems. Often the decisions reached at the general assembly meetings were not implemented, in part because members knew very little about the cooperative's financial affairs, and in part because there were gaps in the planning procedure. Despite the choice of the most effective leaders, their lack of experience and training in matters of cooperative planning and management remained serious shortcomings.

During the period 1977–1980, the cooperative had minimal contact with the state apparatus, a situation that contrasted sharply with the colonial cooperative, which was made the object of state regulation and support. The members did not recall one visit from the district agricultural officer to discuss crop planning for the agricultural season, and the few times that the District Directorate of Agriculture (DDA) was to provide seeds, there were problems of supply and late arrival. At the beginning of 1981, almost four years after the residents had initiated collective production, the Cabinet for the Organization and Development of Agricultural Cooperatives (GODCA) technicians from the Ministry of Agriculture arrived at Ilha Josina Machel to assist production planning in three selected cooperatives including Cooperative 25 de Setembro. Although these state agricultural technicians worked closely with co-op members to raise their decision-making skills, the planning session was very short. From this experience, the co-op members associated state assistance with "quick visits."

### Cooperative Arma da Frelimo

In 1981, two cooperatives in neighborhood 6, Eduardo Mondlane and Joaquim Chissano, named after the first president of Frelimo and the first minister of foreign affairs, respectively, joined together to form Arma da Frelimo. During the 1977–1980 period, as separate units, they had suffered from the same factors that determined the weak economic results of Cooperative 25 de Setembro—irregular participation, problems of internal organization, and lack of state support. These issues were accentuated as a result of power struggles between the leaders of the cooperatives, which hindered effective directorates. In contrast to the class and gender conflict that characterized Cooperative 25 de Setembro, disagreement among the leadership on issues of labor input, work methods, and planning production undermined Cooperative Eduardo Mondlane.

With much enthusiasm, the initial fourteen members, all male middle farmers, established the cooperative. Yet less than one year later, two members left to form Cooperative Joaquim Chissano. Vasco Juma Sumbana, considered an "evolved farmer" during the colonial regime, was one of the departing members. According to him, "We decided to form another cooperative because of the internal problems of Cooperative Eduardo Mondlane. We were not pleased with the direction of the cooperative. Decisions were difficult to reach. We disagreed when to plant, what to sow, and the number of hectares. We felt that the others did not work as hard as we did."[36]

The difference of opinion on these fundamental issues, which remained after the departure of the two members, affected collective participation and internal organization. The same year Cooperative Joaquim Chissano was formed, sixty new members, mostly women and poor peasants, joined Eduardo Mondlane. Although the members agreed to reorganize their labor time on the family farms to work in brigades three consecutive mornings a week, their commitment to the cooperative was very tentative. Most of them only worked the minimal amount of time, unprepared to divert their labor to a form of production that offered dubious results.

Their elected directing body—a president, secretary, production manager, bookkeeper, and social and cultural officer—did not improve internal organization. Few of the leaders knew their responsibilities and many of their tasks overlapped. They called a General Assembly meeting almost every day following the morning work in the field. The cooperative members, mostly women, who were anxious to return home to prepare the food for their families and then to tend to their own farms, resented these frequent meetings, and fewer and fewer members attended. Decisions became very difficult to reach, and often they did not reflect the view of absent members. Over time, only three of the elected directorate managed the cooperative de facto: the president, production manager, and bookkeeper.

As the years went by, the market became a serious a constraint on cooperative development. The members appeared less at the collective field during the weeding and harvesting of maize, the mono-crop of the cooperative. They first attended to their family farms, which meant that frequently the preparation, sowing, weeding, and harvesting were completed at the collective field after the optimal period, resulting in lower productivity per hectare. In turn, the low productivity combined with the low fixed wholesale price paid for maize, 6 meticais/kilo, meant that the members received little cash from its sale. These co-op members, like others across the country, were limited in their ability to respond to the market by planting the most profitable crops (e.g., vegetables), and instead, production was determined by the quantity of maize seed donated by the members from their family farms or the amount of seed saved from the previous agricultural season. Occasionally, they were given production plans that reflected the government's crop-purchase needs (e.g., rice and wheat). But the co-op members were more beholden than peasants or private farmers were to sell at official prices, a constraint that became more serious as a rural parallel market developed. As a result, they responded as if part of the state sector: by further running up debt. Measured in market prices, the state extracted surplus from cooperatives by holding down official prices.

By the 1980–1981 season, participation was so low and sporadic that the members decided to reunite Cooperatives Eduardo Mondlane and Joaquim Chissano and formed Cooperative Arma da Frelimo. The members were politically demobilized, as economic incentives were not forthcoming. For those members who continued to participate in collective production, it was part of a survival strategy. Poor peasant farmers, especially women, worked on their family plots and the collective field to spread their risks, assuming that if the family farm did not produce, there was at least a chance that something that they could consume would grow on the collective field.

These two cooperative case studies show that policies at the local level were building a political base capable of opposing the government's social objectives. Contrary to Frelimo's notion that poor peasant farmers would control cooperatives, groups of middle-peasant farmers, mostly men, saw a chance to develop cooperative farming on the basis of credit and support from the state. When state assistance was withheld and membership was expanded to include poor peasants and women without capital or skills, many of the founding middle peasants abandoned collective production. In later years, confrontations would emerge between these dissident farmers and co-op members over labor, land, and other resources.

## Conclusion

The notion of a complete break with the past and redefining society in a revolutionary context is not specific to Mozambique. Rather, the government's problem was that it expected to effect so rapid a restructuring of rural and urban life that it failed to consider the process for getting from where people were to where Frelimo hoped they could be. In each of these target areas—

local-level administration, marketing, and collective farming—Frelimo met substantial support as well as some opposition in the countryside to its new policies.

Frelimo abolished the colonial dual system of political administration and adopted a uniform system with the expectation that the political structures appropriate to urban areas would also work in the countryside, without serious thought to local realities and possible interim stages. When radical strategies did not work, Frelimo ignored the situation and allowed local compromises to determine what kind of political system really worked. Similarly, Frelimo imposed an ideal pattern of collective production without any attention to how local rural people actually organized their lives. There was no place for family or private farms in its program, for example, and middle peasants were excluded from a central role, although it was often individuals from that social stratum who formed cooperatives. When local officials intervened to expand and diversify cooperative membership, most middle peasants abandoned collective production.

In 1981, agricultural production continued to decline, and discontent among rural producers was on the rise. With the war spreading in the country and pressure from Nordic countries (major external donor to the Ministry of Agriculture) on Frelimo to support family and collective farming, the government decided to reassess its policies. Under these conditions, it decided to support two national projects designed specifically to address many of the technical, organizational, and political obstacles that hindered the cooperative movement. The next chapter examines the performance of one of these projects.

Petasse Matsolo Hobjana (in the foreground) and other members of Cooperative 25 de Setembro prepare the collective field for maize, 1982. (Photograph by Sam Barnes)

Members of Cooperative 25 de Setembro at a demonstration of the *tropicultor,* a modern, multigadget ox-drawn plow promoted by Project CO-1 and the Ministry of Agriculture in Ilha Josina Machel, 1982.

Older women of Cooperative Arma da Frelimo removing groundnut shells, 1983. (Photograph by Sam Barnes)

Women cooperative members with their children, waiting for literacy classes to begin after completing their fieldwork, 1983. (Photograph by Sam Barnes)

In 1989, Renamo launched a major attack on Ilha Josina Machel, killing residents and destroying infrastructure. The rural shop managed by Albino Bila, a long-time resident, was totally gutted, and its contents were confiscated, 1993.

During the war, transportation in the countryside was almost entirely dependent on hitching a ride. Rural people, like these women and children in Gaza Province, would wait for hours by the roadside with their bags of charcoal, rice, and maize, hoping to flag down a truck to transport them to their destinations, 1986.

At the end of the day, women cross the bridge over the Matseculi River carrying on their head piles of firewood both for family use and sale on Ilha Josina Machel, 1993.

In Chokwe, Gaza Province, women carried on their heads large tins and plastic jugs filled with water from the irrigation channels to use for drinking, cooking, and bathing, 1987.

With the end of the war in 1992, Carlos Fernando Xerindza Majonane reopened his private store on Ilha Josina Machel. The shelves were stocked with cooking oil, soap, radio batteries, *capulanas,* matches, and other consumer goods that residents were eager to buy, 1993.

Women peasant farmers weeding their maize, a food staple in southern Mozambique, on their family farm (Ilha Josina Machel), 1993.

While buses and small minivans provide transportation to urban dwellers, privately owned open trucks transport rural people and their belongings, 1993.

After the war between Frelimo and Renamo, Vasco Juma Sumbana, a private farmer, stands beside his tractor, 1993.

# 5

# Cooperative Agriculture
## Project CO-1, 1981–1983

**B**y the early 1980s the cooperative movement was in decline. Producer co-operatives that survived were almost entirely based in former settler farms, and they lost members over time. By 1982, only around 2 percent of the rural population were co-op members, and as the marginalized production units in Frelimo's socialist development strategy, cooperatives received only 2 percent of the state's agricultural investment up to 1983. Contrary to Frelimo's plan, members did not pool their individual holdings, plows, draft animals, and other resources to work together. The only exceptions were in the cooperatives surrounding major cities, where members' households had a diversified income base, and among some Frelimo veterans of the liberation war, who did most of their farming together.[1] Generally, however, cooperatives did not use their limited resources productively: they farmed collectively only a small part of the area they controlled and ran up large debts.

Three considerations influenced Frelimo's decision to provide more support to designated cooperatives in selected regions: (1) peasant farmers' increasing dissatisfaction with government policies, (2) the deteriorating economic situation and escalation of the war waged by Renamo, and (3) external pressure by donor agencies (i.e., Nordic countries) that changed their aid priorities from the state sector to the family and cooperative sectors.

In 1981, the Ministry of Agriculture launched two national projects, namely Projects CO-1 (CADECO) and CO-2 (CRED), to respond to the training and technology problems of pilot cooperatives. Project CO-1 CADECO (Center for Supporting Cooperative Development) was fostered by GODCA, financed by the Nordic countries (Finland, Sweden, Norway, Denmark, and Iceland, through MONAP), and aimed at establishing centers at the provincial level. The first was established in Namaacha (Maputo Province), covering Maputo, Gaza, and Inhambane; the second in Mutuali (Nampula Province); and the third in

Temangau (Tete Province), covering Tete, Manica, and Sofala. Later, new centers were opened in Lussanhando (Niassa Province) and Chibuto (Gaza Province). The Namaacha center had three working fronts in the districts of Manhiça-Magude, Moamba, and Namaacha-Boane. Ilha Josina Machel, one of the first areas of Project CO-1 activity, was affiliated with the Manhiça-Magude front. The objectives of the project were both technical (e.g., to introduce new techniques for harrowing, seeding, and weeding; to finance the acquisition and training of oxen for draft power; and to introduce new irrigation techniques) and political (e.g., to provide courses designed to build up co-op leaders' planning skills and to increase their understanding of the role of cooperatives within Mozambique's agricultural development strategy). In turn, Project CO-2 CRED (Regional Center for Experiment and Development) was coordinated by the Institute for Agronomic Research (INIA) and intended to set up regional centers to experiment with, and disseminate, improved agricultural technology. Besides the cooperatives, Project CO-2 was to assist the family sector and the communal villages.

Project CO-1 confronted challenges emanating both from the state and from the cooperatives themselves. As the project-assisted cooperatives became more independent and economically viable, they encountered state policies that limited their opportunities to accumulate capital. For example, cooperatives were more restricted than the family and private sectors to sell their produce at state-controlled official prices unrelated to market conditions, which became a serious constraint on cooperative development as the rural parallel market expanded. As a result, the co-op members were forced to sell their produce above the official prices but below the parallel market prices.

Another source of continuing debate between the Ministry of Agriculture and cooperative leaders was the issue of technique. When the members tried to accelerate the accumulation process by buying tractors, the government discouraged them, with senior officials explaining to co-op members that they should not become dependent on tractors and other imported machines that the state could not afford until they improved their productivity using animal traction. The project personnel were divided on this issue: those based at central headquarters in Maputo City supported the dominant forces within the bureaucracy, while those based in the countryside accepted that tractors, harvesters, and water pumps were critical to the development of the cooperative movement. For the duration of the project, the "mechanized" vs. "manual" debate was a contentious issue.

As far as Ilha peasants were concerned, Frelimo's objectives were similar to those of the colonial state: to curb market practices and restrict peasant access to mechanized equipment in order to control their wealth and independence.

Furthermore, without access to tractor services and specialized inputs, middle peasants (the stratum of the peasantry represented in cooperative leadership) recognized that they would attain much lower productivity and income in cooperatives than on their own farms. As with other aspects of Frelimo's agricultural development strategy, the peasants' reality contradicted the government's theory that economies of scale—achieved by simply bringing together scattered rural producers—would lead immediately to increases in the productivity of cooperatives relative to family farms.

Besides contradictory state actions, peasants who did not passively accept state policies but struggled to mold outcomes challenged the project. Upon the brigade's arrival at Ilha Josina Machel, the technicians were confronted by social and political problems internal to the cooperatives, such as leadership accountability, gender discrimination, and labor conflicts. They found that several co-op leaders had participated in corrupt practices (e.g., stealing the cooperative's harvest and savings for personal use), leading peasants to abandon collective production. Women, the majority of co-op members, often were sexually harassed, a problem that led to their frequent absences from the collective fields. And labor conflicts between the collective and family farms jeopardized regular participation.

Once these problems were rectified, peasant participation stabilized in the cooperatives. The middle peasants, who dominated the leadership positions, used their membership to lease their oxen and plows to the co-ops at higher prices than to the family farms, to rent the cooperative's tractor to plow their individual farms, and to enroll their children in project-sponsored courses (e.g., technical and literacy) that gave them useful skills for employment. They were more interested in obtaining the implements and inputs that were unavailable to individual producers on the local market than on the direct income earned from collective production. The poorer peasants saw collective farming as critical to their individual household survival strategies, as it offered them a way to increase their household incomes and to get food. For both strata, the primary incentive to join co-ops was access to the consumer cooperative that stocked goods unavailable in the rural areas outside the parallel circuits.

The case study was completed at the end of 1983, shortly before the war escalated in the south, but during the duration of the project, its work was increasingly affected by the war: three employees, including a Portuguese national, were killed by Renamo rebels; six project buildings with equipment were partially or totally destroyed; five transport trucks were burned; and a large number of cooperative members were killed or kidnapped. In 1984, Renamo staged the first of several attacks on Ilha Josina Machel, brutally axing several residents to death and setting fire to one of the four rural stores. By 1989, most residents were forced to sleep in the nearby town, Xinavane, returning to the island only during the day to farm their fields. As a result of growing instability and displacement, peasant farmers were unable to plan their agricultural production. It was only in April 1993, six months after Frelimo and Renamo signed the peace accord, that residents started to return to the village and rebuild their homes. But in 1981, when Project CO-1 was initiated, the situation was dramatically different and there still was high expectation that rural development was possible.

Project CO-1 had complicated relations with the Ministry of Agriculture, and the lack of clear definition of these relations was to affect its role in rural development. In the nearly one hundred pilot cooperatives that it supported, the project sought to encourage member participation, to illustrate the advantages of collective agriculture by improving the standard of living of its members, to form cooperative unions, to develop a program on the use of animal traction, and to train government officials on cooperative development.[2] From the start, there were serious misunderstandings between the CO-1 leadership and high-level bureaucrats in the Ministry of Agriculture regarding the project's objectives and capabilities, and within the project itself between the contracted foreign nationals who were based mainly in the ministry and the Mozambican technicians who worked in the cooperatives. Political, social, and ideological differences led to conflict between them and also complicated effective fieldwork.

## MONAP, Project CO-1, and the Ministry of Agriculture

Contrary to the government's propaganda that cooperatives could rely on their own internal resources, these institutions needed inputs (e.g., material resources, technical expertise, organizational support, marketing facilities, and transportation) to be successful. The cooperatives on Ilha Josina Machel owed much to the financial and technical support of the MONAP-funded projects. While northern nongovernmental support has been problematic, the organizational, financial, and technical support provided by Project CO-1 was important in sustaining and developing the cooperative movement to act as significant forces for democratization and progressive social change within Mozambique.

During the war against colonialism, Frelimo received considerable financial support from the Nordic countries. Their assistance continued after independence in the form of trained personnel and investment in Mozambique's agricultural sector to the extent that from the late 1970s to the end of the 1980s, the projects of MONAP at the Ministry of Agriculture were crucial to the country's rural development strategy. During the first phase of the MONAP programs (MONAP I), from 1978 to 1980, total Nordic allocations amounted to U.S. $50 million distributed among twenty-six projects, with the Mozambican government contributing the equivalent in local currency.[3]

The objective of MONAP I was to keep agricultural production from falling while reorganizing the colonial economy. The program gave priority to service projects (seed production, provision of spare parts, and agro-services) and direct production projects (citrus, dairy, cattle, fisheries, and forestry) of the state sector. Essentially, then, MONAP I was a massive emergency import program of spare parts, capital equipment, and vehicles, complemented with some technical assistance to meet the shortage of skilled personnel. In addition to the economic benefits from the sale of heavy equipment, the Nordic countries favored the state sector for expediency and ideological reasons. By mid-1976 food availability in the urban areas had dropped to alarmingly low levels; Nordic leaders thought the state was best equipped to reverse this trend. Moreover, those in charge of foreign aid in the Nordic countries held Frelimo's view that rural development meant investment in the "modern" state sector.

Western and Eastern donor preferences coincided. The former USSR and Eastern Europe supported Mozambique's policy to invest and increase mechanization in huge state farms because they adhered to a particular notion of socialist development that saw state farms as playing the leading role. Western countries were influenced by a concept of agricultural modernization that emphasized technical progress (the growth of output and productivity) and technical efficiency ("high input–high output" formula), as well as commodification. On the grounds of maximizing growth of output and returns to project investment, the Nordic countries supported large-scale, capital-intensive projects to "modernize" agriculture in Mozambique. It was only after an evaluation of the MONAP I program, showing its projects were not having the intended development results, that the Nordic countries shifted their allocation of resources from import supply to transforming family farming.

MONAP II covered the period 1981–1983 and consisted of twenty-three projects. Its total budget was U.S. $186 million, of which the Nordic contribution was approximately U.S. $66 million and the Mozambican portion was the equivalent of U.S. $120 million in local currency; Project CO-1 was to receive U.S. $5.6 million of this over the three years.[4] At least seven of the twenty-three projects, accounting for approximately 36 percent of the total Nordic contribution, were designed to deal with the problems of cooperatives and peasant agriculture.[5]

MONAP II officially started in January 1981, but Project CO-1 was seriously delayed because of inadequate preparation and poor management at the MONAP headquarters: there were delays in recruiting foreign personnel, serious technical mistakes in purchases resulting in high prices, and purchases of inappropriate products; and insufficient attention was paid to aspects related to maintenance and other service functions connected with imports of machinery, equipment, and vehicles. In addition, the shortage of skilled national technicians handicapped the project, and building activities were virtually paralyzed in Mozambique during 1981. A lack of imported building materials and limited management resources for construction activities within the Ministry of Agriculture resulted in costly delays. To make matters worse, the government unit responsible for Project CO-1, GODCA, was dismantled, leaving the project to assume national responsibilities for cooperative development.

Within Project CO-1, the personnel situation was a major issue. Foreign personnel were needed both for the central team based in Maputo and for work brigades in the cooperatives. The former directed subdepartments of the project—such as literacy, supplies, complementary activities, animal traction, livestock, social communications, financial administration, and planning— and frequently acted as an advisory board to the national director, while each brigade or team of technicians was supposed to have at least one foreign expert specialized in agriculture or livestock to reinforce the limited training of Mozambicans. But there was a long delay in recruiting skilled foreign technicians, and many of those contracted only arrived at the end of 1981 or the beginning of 1982.

The foreign staff differed fundamentally among themselves both in formation and in motives for working in Mozambique. Most were referred to as *cooperantes,* individuals who became Mozambican residents because they were politically committed to creating a socialist society. While some had college or university education, the Portuguese *cooperantes*—who accounted for twenty-two of the forty foreign positions—had more practical experience than formal training, reinforcing the national technicians' perception that the former were hired largely because of their friendship with the national director, a Portuguese citizen with links to Frelimo before independence. The technocrats, professionals contracted solely for their technical expertise, were in the minority.

Foreign personnel with socialist political convictions were not always beneficial. These *cooperantes* from Western countries (Portugal, Holland, Sweden, Belgium, Germany, Brazil, and Chile) were deeply divided, ranging from neo-Stalinists to social democrats, and their ideological beliefs affected their pursuant models of rural development. For example, some placed great emphasis on the development of the forces of production (mechanization and large investment) as a necessary condition for a subsequent transformation of social relations, while others saw the process as a simultaneous one. Their different views on creating rural socialism surfaced regularly at the project's regional and annual meetings.

Project CO-1 depended on the Ministry of Agriculture for the recruitment of Mozambicans trained in agriculture and livestock, but throughout its duration insufficient national agricultural technicians and inadequate training plagued the project. In February 1982, of the forty-four Mozambican technicians assigned to Project CO-1, forty-three had only a one-year agricultural training course; only one had three years of agricultural training; and no national personnel of superior level were connected to the project.[6] Furthermore, an overwhelming gender bias predominated among the Mozambican staff: all the technicians were men; women agronomists and veterinarians remained in administrative positions in Maputo. While the ministry allocated Mozambicans to the MONAP projects, the CO-1 leadership did not actively recruit women, mainly for economic reasons: it was more expensive to provide separate housing for women and men, and often, women with families needed larger accommodations and additional assistance. Thus, the project maintained the colonial established pattern of men-only state agricultural agents, most of whom preferred to work with male farmers whose confidence and organizational skills gained from experience in wage labor, as well as greater exposure to the official educational system, made them better equipped to take advantage of Project CO-1 services. The failure of the state and Project CO-1 to provide conditions for qualified women in the field had serious repercussions, especially in the south where women farmers predominated.

Given the differences in class and culture, conflict erupted between Mozambicans and foreign personnel concerning work methods. Most *cooperantes* thought of themselves as enthusiastic supporters of socialist development and were tireless in their work. But their class and cultural perspective often prevented them from engaging in democratic discussion and debate with Mozambicans, who were most affected by state policy. The situation at Ilha Josina Machel illustrated this point. For the first year and a half, the Portuguese *cooperante* made all the major decisions himself concerning the technicians and their work (setting the working and sleeping schedule, defining the tasks, choosing the working sites, and determining who received motorcycles), invoking comparison to a colonial *capataz*, an overseer of forced labor. The technicians, whose input was either not sought or ignored, began to feel as if they were working for him rather than for a development project. Their resentment was fueled by the fact that *cooperantes* signed lucrative contracts that included furnished accommodations, schools for their children, salaries paid in foreign currency, health insurance, and regular home leave—amenities that were denied to Mozambicans.

Yet these internal political problems of the project were secondary to the more immediate concern of how to provide consistent support to the cooperatives. At the project's national meeting in January 1982 the national director decided that the brigades be based permanently in the rural areas, beginning with Ilha Josina Machel. This decision meant that the technicians lived communally and sought thereby to convey to Ilha peasant farmers that the project was serious in its support of cooperative development.

The Ilha brigade consisted of a Portuguese *cooperante* and six Mozambicans, of whom two specialized in livestock and small species, and the other four majored in agriculture. The *cooperante,* a former priest, had no formal technical training but had years of work experience with peasant farmers in Brazil. Of the six Mozambicans, two were from Gaza, two were from Inhambane, one was from Sofala, and the other from Nampula, a mixture meant to facilitate the state objective of exposing its citizens to other areas in the hope of further consolidating a national sentiment. Given that the majority of rural dwellers spoke Shangaan, a dominant language in Maputo and Gaza, and not Portuguese, those technicians who were not from the south (as well as foreign personnel) confronted a language problem in assisting peasant farmers, reinforcing their preference to work with those who spoke the national language— mostly men. It also meant that at project meetings with cooperative members, the discussions were extraordinarily lengthy, as exchanges had to be translated concurrently from Shangaan to Portuguese and vice versa. For the year and a half starting in January 1982, I was affiliated with this team, assisting peasant farmers with the internal organization and management of cooperatives.

### Planning Agricultural Production for the Cooperative Sector

At the end of March 1982, the brigade was settled on Ilha Josina Machel and ready to plan the 1982–1983 campaign. The objectives for the season were to guarantee agricultural production, to provide technical and organizational support to the cooperatives, and to establish a union, with planning and organizing the production process given first priority. In previous seasons, centralized planning with overoptimistic targets, excluding the input of cooperative members, had led to poor production results. To change this trend, the planning process was opened to members' participation in every stage. Between June 15 and June 24, the first planning session on Ilha Josina Machel took place with the CO-1 team and the members of Cooperative 25 de Setembro. Together, they went through the various planning phases and discussed the problems along the way. Subsequently, each technician was assigned to assist the other eleven cooperatives, and by July 15, the cooperative plans for the

1982–1983 season were completed. Cooperative 25 de Setembro is presented below as an example of the planning process.

The directorate of the cooperative and the brigade began the first phase of the planning process with a socioeconomic survey through which they aimed to obtain the necessary social, economic, and agronomic information on the cooperative. A great deal of data was collected on its formation, its internal organization and structures, its directorate, the organization and norms of the labor force, and the history of each production season. The brigade also completed an inventory of the cooperative's resources—agricultural equipment, simple hand tools, cattle, small animals, and infrastructure. The total labor force consisted of 176 members, of which 152 (86 percent) were women and 24 (14 percent) were men. Here, like in other cooperatives in the south, the great majority of members were women, often divorced or widowed, because the men wanted steady wage work—typically nonfarming employment in Maputo and the South African mines.[7] At the end of the meetings, the co-op leaders and technicians decided that of the cooperative's 200 hectares (divided into several land parcels), approximately 150 hectares could be irrigated by water pumped from the Matseculi River and a nearby lake, leaving 50 hectares of rain-fed farmland.

With this information, together they elaborated a plan for the cooperative. Their discussions demonstrated that the members were cost- and profit-conscious. The leaders chose the food crops that were most profitable and then compared the difference between the results obtained using animal traction and tractor. For maize, beans, and groundnuts, tractor preparation would result in approximately 20 percent more kilograms per hectare than animal traction, but mechanical preparation was about twice as costly.

Such disparities between economic and production data produced considerable debate over the question of using animal traction or renting machinery. Most of the leaders believed that the cooperative could only work well with a tractor, arguing that clay soil was too heavy for the ox-plows to prepare adequately. For middle-peasant farmers, agricultural development implied the use of tractors, combine harvesters, and other motor equipment, as well as hybrid seeds; they identified agricultural modernization with mechanization, like Frelimo and donor countries. The technicians' calculations reinforced their view that when the oxen plowed the land, production was not as good as when the machines prepared the field. Thus, this group was reluctant to give up using tractors even though in the past, state-owned tractors had arrived late. A smaller number preferred animal traction because it provided an income with more flexibility and security: nearly all members of the cooperative had experience with the use of ox-plows on their family farms, and a large percentage knew how to train oxen. They reasoned that animal traction was within their control as compared to tractor rental. After some deliberation, the members concluded that they would utilize rented tractors primarily for land preparation and ox-drawn plows as backup.

This decision ran counter to one of the project's central aims: to encourage animal traction, especially the use of draft animals with new and better animal traction equipment, like the *tropicultor*. The technicians presented this "modern plow" as intermediary technology—it was capable of weeding and fertilizer application as well as plowing, and yet it was not as costly as tractor use, yet the majority of co-op leaders argued against the use of the *tropicultor*, claiming that it was a heavy piece of equipment that rapidly exhausted the oxen. These arguments held some validity: The cattle needed a better diet as the drought reduced the good pasture lands on the island. Furthermore, a 1983 report prepared by the National Directorate of Housing (DNH) estimated that approximately 70 percent of the cattle on Ilha Josina Machel suffered from tuberculosis, which affected their physical stamina. But more significant, these farmers wanted access to machinery denied to them by the Portuguese authorities.

The debate on the appropriateness of the *tropicultor* went beyond the technicians and the co-op members. At the project's training center in Namaacha and in the Ministry of Agriculture, the technicians were blamed for failing to promote it. The central team's chief technician of the animal traction division suggested that the Mozambican technicians were not doing their job: "The major problems with the *tropicultor* are the technicians, their resistance and lack of knowledge about the machine. They do not have much confidence in the machine and hence they do not sell it well."[8]

Yet the ox-drawn *tropicultors* (with healthy or tubercular oxen) were never competitive with tractors, even under ideal conditions on Ilha Josina Machel soils in trial performances. The frequent floods and large pockets of heavy clay soil dispersed throughout the island reduced their efficiency. Still, by November 1982, the cooperatives had purchased nine *tropicultors* (at a cost of 90,000 meticais each) under pressure from the project.

By the end of the planning session, the leaders had agreed to cultivate eighty hectares, about 43 percent less than the 1982–1983 state plan but approximately 21 percent more than the hectareage planned in 1981–1982. They decided to buy some seeds as well as fertilizer and pesticides from Boror, a state-owned enterprise. To avoid the outlay of great sums of money to buy fertilizers that were scarce, the leaders chose a pattern of crop rotation leaving some land fallow, and the use of animal manure. The members discussed the different land parcels and decided where they would sow the crops of the new plan. The leaders presented the proposed plan to the general assembly of Cooperative 25 de Setembro, and at the end of the meeting the members agreed to the plan.

The planning exercise was a positive step forward compared to the previous mathematical format that considered machine hours, seeds, and fertilizer but excluded the active participation of the co-op members. The project's material and methodology permitted the members to more clearly conceptualize the essentials of formulating a plan, and they were pleased that they held much of the necessary information required, yet basic improvements were needed. The calculations and costs of one hectare of each crop were still based on state norms and not the specific conditions at the cooperative. In addition, there were "gaps" in the planning method: the discussion during the planning process did not raise the issues of competing needs and labor peaks for family farms. The potential of the planning process as a method depended on resolving these issues.

## Economic Results

The economic results of the 1982–1983 season were mixed. The drought—which affected all of southern Mozambique—and insufficient quantities of seeds seriously reduced production. Sesame seed was unavailable, and seeds for other crops—maize, tomatoes, onion, garlic, cassava, and potatoes—were supplied in smaller quantities than planned. Instead, as part of the Ministry of Agriculture's emergency plan to reduce the effects of the drought, sweet potatoes were sown in large quantities in southern Mozambique. By the time the cooperatives on Ilha Josina Machel decided to sow the crop, however, the family sector had limited vine available to sell. Weeks earlier, under the direction of the Internal Commerce Ministry, Carlos Fernando Majonane's store had traded one *capulana*, a colorful cloth worn by women (worth 240 meticais), for one large bundle of sweet potato vine, about twenty kilograms (worth 500 meticais).[9] Some farmers complained about the unequal exchange: "The bundles of sweet potato weighed twenty kilos, worth 500 meticais. Yet a *capulana* was priced at 240 meticais, which meant that peasants [cooperative and non-members] of Ilha Josina Machel should have received two *capulanas* for their one bundle. We are not pleased with the situation. During colonialism, we exchanged twenty kilos for one *capulana* as they were both worth 40 escudos."[10] The policy of linkage under which goods could only be purchased in return for fixed quantities of crops made it easy for shopkeepers, sometimes acting on behalf of the state, to cheat rural producers.

Within weeks Majonane's store collected approximately thirty-five tons of sweet potato vine, which the Ministry of Internal Commerce transported to a state farm in Maputo Province for large-scale cultivation. The barter was finally stopped by the locality's administrator after many peasant farmers complained that people were stealing sweet potato vines from their farms and Majonane's clerks reported that farmers who did not plant the crop were bringing in the vine to trade.[11] Subsequently, in early April, employees from a state farm in the Magude District purchased vines from the family and cooperative sectors. As a result of these earlier transactions, the cooperatives did not sow sweet potato in large quantities. Similarly, there were problems in finding cassava tubers, another drought-resistant crop—Ilha peasant farmers did not sell the tubers to the cooperatives, as they had sufficient supplies only for their family farms.

The cultivation of fewer crops and smaller quantities than planned should have resulted in lower economic gains, but most of the crops were sold at prices higher than the official prices, with tomatoes the only exception. For example, the official wholesale price of maize was 6 meticais per kilogram, but at Cooperative 25 de Setembro, members bought twenty kilograms of maize for 500 meticais (about 25 meticais/kilogram), and nonmembers paid 750 meticais per twenty kilograms (37.50 meticais/kilogram). As maize was a staple food crop in the peasant diet, the cooperative normally sold a minimum of twenty kilograms. At another cooperative, twenty kilograms of maize sold for 1,500 meticais (75 meticais/kilogram), the same price sold by the family sector.[12] On the parallel market, maize either was sold for local consumption or found its way to the central market bazaar in Maputo.

At a meeting in early March, the co-op leaders expressed to the technicians their dissatisfaction with the official wholesale price of maize. Two points were raised: first, the seeds cost 20 meticais/kilogram, and, second, the selling price was too low to cover expenses. The leaders decided collectively to set the selling price at 500 meticais per twenty kilograms of maize for members and 750 meticais per twenty kilograms for nonmembers.[13] After the maize was harvested, some of the cooperatives raised these prices in accordance to the selling price charged by the family sector. In an attempt to control the situation, the local administrator called an emergency meeting with the co-op leadership, selected middle-peasant farmers, and private producers. He warned them that they would be guilty of speculation if they continued to sell maize at 25 meticais per kilogram and higher. Given that the decision to enforce the official price was reached after most people had already sold their crop, it only affected a few.

If Cooperative 25 de Setembro had sold its maize at the official price of 6 meticais per kilogram, the members would have earned only 164,760 meticais

(U.S. $4,119) for the 27,460 kilograms of marketed maize instead of 866,650 meticais (U.S. $21,666). The president and bookkeeper explained that "those who bought the maize at the price set by the union of cooperatives were making a contribution so that the cooperatives could pay the expenses incurred during the season."[14] Although the sale of produce above official prices enabled private traders and large-scale farmers to accumulate personal wealth—combined with their access to scarce commodities—it was essential for cooperatives to make ends meet. By 1982 official prices had been generally static for several years, while inflationary pressure had been rising. Producer prices had become unrealistically low in relation to market pressures.

At the end of the first crop period (August 1982 to January 1983) the members of Cooperative 25 de Setembro received 70 meticais per four-hour work day, slightly more than the daily wage of 62.50 meticais at the state farms for the same number of hours. Nonetheless, middle-peasant farmers earned more on their farms than at Cooperative 25 de Setembro. The example of the Cossa family represents this situation:

> In 1981–82, the family members sowed mostly maize and a small area of fresh vegetables on their farm of four hectares—in sections of one hectare each. Two adults and three teenagers constituted the labor force. An organized division of labor existed whereby the two sons and father plowed the fields and the mother and three children sowed and weeded the crops. All the family members participated in the harvest. In addition to hoes, machetes, and other agricultural tools, the family owned a team of oxen and a plow. At the end of the season, the Cossa family marketed an unknown quantity of maize and a small amount of vegetables worth 5,750 meticais. The next agricultural season, the Cossa farm increased to seven hectares. Although the total production of maize was not recorded, one of the sons estimated that at least two of the seven hectares produced 600 kilograms per hectare. They sold their maize surplus for 750 meticais per 20 kilos [37.50 meticais/kilogram]. The son estimated that the combined earnings from last year's sale of maize [1981–1982] and the current season [1982–1983] totaled 35,000 meticais. With this money, the father bought a motor bike.[15]

The organization of the production process (i.e., ensuring that each agricultural operation was performed at the optimal time); control over the labor force (immediate family members); established work norms; ownership of the means of production (i.e., hoes, ox-plow, and seeds); and experienced decision-making on production issues concerning consumption, marketing, and conservation of seeds were significant factors accounting for the superior economic results at the Cossa's family farm in comparison to Cooperative 25 de Setembro.

## Leadership, Labor Relations, and Gender Issues

In addition to planning production for the 1982–1983 season, a central concern of Project CO-1 was to create conditions that ensured the members' active participation in managing the cooperatives. This meant that the technicians first had to work with peasant farmers to resolve a series of social and political problems—for example, leadership accountability, gender discrimination, and labor conflicts. When the CO-1 technicians arrived in March 1982, most of the cooperatives suffered from corruption, mismanagement, factionalism, and absentee leaders.

During their two years on Ilha Josina Machel, the technicians worked closely with members to resolve leadership problems. In the case of Cooperative Moçambicana, the problem was not simply corruption but sexual harassment: the president had stolen most of the 1981 maize harvest for self-use and assigned leadership positions to his relatives, one of whom was constantly badgering women. Partly because of this, women frequented the collective field on an irregular basis, and, in some cases, their husbands prohibited their participation. At an open forum that included the brigade, the co-op members expelled the harassing individual and replaced the president with a popular, work-driven peasant farmer, Cecilia Fulana.

As the first and only woman president of a cooperative in the community, Cecilia Fulana experienced initial problems exerting her leadership and asserting her authority. Yet she proved to be an effective leader both in the cooperative and in the locality, benefiting from three main factors: (1) the male leadership in Cooperative Moçambicana had been sorely discredited, (2) the project technicians provided additional managerial and technical assistance to make up for her lack of experience, and (3) her own strong no-nonsense personality combined with her exemplary hard work. At one of the enlarged cooperative meetings, for example, President Fulana advised the participants that one of the elected men in the consumer cooperative's control commission, of which she was a member, had threatened to beat her because of a minor disagreement. Outraged by the threat of physical harm, she lambasted the individual and demanded that he be reprimanded for his behavior. Her male counterparts reacted similarly and, subsequently, the directorate suspended the individual from his position for six months.

The only major grievance levied by co-op members against President Fulana was her frequent absence from the cooperative due to her multiple leadership positions in the locality—deputy, OMM secretary, school board administrator, and tribunal member of the local court. While several of the other presidents also held numerous positions (and their members grumbled too), President Fulana had additional domestic responsibilities that her male counterparts did not. The paucity of women co-op presidents (as with other leadership positions in the public sphere) had less to do with widespread discrimination and more to do with women's own resistance to add other tasks to their daily productive labor in the countryside, which included family farming, collective production, carrying firewood, caring for children, cooking, and providing health care.

From the CO-1 central team's point of view, most of the cooperatives' internal difficulties were directly linked to misunderstandings of elected officials' responsibilities and the governing structures of the cooperative. To overcome these problems, the Ilha brigade met weekly with the leaders until they understood their obligations as elected officials and the function of the general assembly and administrative bodies, and they also participated in the cooperatives' general assembly meetings. At Cooperative 25 de Setembro, for example, a technician regularly attended these monthly sessions and would initiate discussions of absenteeism, membership, work brigades, timetables, and labor organization if the members or leaders did not raise the issues themselves. In an attempt to build group confidence, members were encouraged to discuss the problems of the collective. Given that before independence rural women rarely spoke in public, it was common that men—armed with the self-confidence gained from experience in the wage economy—were more articulate than women in expressing and defending their interests.

One of the issues raised by an elderly man at a general assembly meeting was the need for a division of labor between the young and the old members. According to the individual, the daily agricultural work was too arduous for old people, "especially those of us who are sick and suffering from tuberculosis (common among ex-miners) and other ailments."[16] The members reached a consensus: they would try a more complex division of labor that took into consideration generational differences. An entry from my daily journal describes the form that this new division of labor took:

At 6:30 A.M., in front of the cooperative warehouse, the members of brigade A, who were beginning their three-day shift, received instructions from the production manager. The brigade was subdivided into two groups and each one was assigned a leader. These subgroups were divided according to age: One group consisting of young women was to open the irrigation channels for the potatoes. Some of the old women and men in the other group were going to till a section of the field, and others were to transport sweet potato vine to another area where it would be transplanted.[17]

In this case, young women performed the heavy agricultural work of opening the irrigation canals, and old persons carried out the lighter tasks of tilling the field and transporting plants, yet the gender division of labor remained intact: women performed the manual agricultural tasks (weeding and hoeing), and able-bodied men, who had spent years in charge of water pumps and pipes on the colonial plantations or in South African mines, remained responsible for the irrigation system and machinery maintenance. When they were not working with equipment in the field, men did nonagricultural jobs, such as cutting and transporting thatch and wooden posts to build the cooperative's warehouse and other infrastructure, as well as masonry work. In their opinion, they deserved to be paid more for their labor, which required skills, than women, who simply used hoes. To establish a more equitable sexual division of labor and a differentiated wage scale based on expertise, the cooperative had to overcome the legacy of Portuguese colonial and South African hiring practices. In particular, women needed access to training to make up for the disadvantages of their previous relative exclusion from formal-sector employment, a role in which the state and donor projects could play.

The other cooperatives in the community were less organized than Cooperative 25 de Setembro. Leaders at Cooperative Arma da Frelimo called daily meetings after the morning's work in the field, meetings that were characterized by little input from the members for two major reasons: first, they were too frequent, and, second, several of the men intimidated the women. After the CO-1 technician participated in a number of these sessions, he raised the issue of their frequency and pointed out that fewer and fewer women attended because they wanted to tend to their domestic tasks and family plots.[18] In response to member discussions of the first issue, meetings were eventually reduced to one per week. Nobody questioned the nature of women's work, although it was a central problem of collectivization of peasant farms—the male technicians and co-op leaders assumed that women would provide subsistence from family plots, care for children, cook, fetch water and firewood, and somehow also work in cooperatives. At another session, the technician questioned the methods of some of the men who shrieked at the women members to participate in the discussions. In the months that followed, the number of women who spoke at the general assembly meetings increased only slightly, but more of them approached the technician on an individual basis to discuss labor problems and other issues.

Redistribution of power, whether in gender or class terms, was not something that could be decreed by leaders or brought about by enlightened state technicians; it was a long process. Yet because initial contact and methods left lasting impressions and often set the terrain for state-peasantry relations, the technicians made a conscious effort to let co-op members set their own agenda at meetings. At the first enlarged general meeting of the twelve cooperatives, held in a converted warehouse, for example, the technicians asked residents to outline the problems they confronted as co-op members and farmers instead of the typical procedure whereby state officials controlled what was (or was not) discussed. The meeting, which went on nonstop for more than eight hours, was lively, characterized by frank criticism of the government and its failure to support peasant farmers. Later, one woman commented to me:

> I know you probably are very tired as the meeting went on for some time without a break. But you must understand that this was one of the first opportunities that we have had to meet and discuss our problems openly. In the colonial era, we were not permitted to hold meetings. Now, we can discuss the important issues in detail. We often repeat what someone else has just said to ensure that we understand the main points, as we are responsible for recounting what has taken place to those individuals in our neighborhood who were not able to attend this meeting.[19]

The majority of participants had to remember the main issues since illiteracy meant that note-taking was not an option.

Although literacy classes were not part of the project's official program, the central team gradually adopted the position that co-op members could only take effective control of their enterprises if they knew Portuguese (the language used with the government) and had basic numeracy skills. Given the colonial legacy, which particularly disadvantaged women—in terms of the education, skills, experience, and self-confidence to enable them to be full participants in cooperatives—literacy was also a gender issue on Ilha Josina Machel. It was all too easy for a few men with the knowledge of Portuguese and other skills to replace the state as dominant in making decisions for "inefficient" women co-op farmers.

Project CO-1, in collaboration with the Ministry of Education, organized a forty-five–day training course for literacy instructors on Ilha Josina Machel in December 1982. The cooperatives were requested by the technicians to select as attendees children of members, eighteen years and older, who had completed the minimum of grade four. Most of these children came from middle-peasant households where the parents saw the course as an opportunity to improve the status and income of the family. A group of twenty literacy-instructor candidates participated, of whom eleven passed. Five of them were young women. That the project paid the individuals during the course and then provided a monthly subsidy to those who passed gave added importance to the literacy activities. The instructors felt the project employed them, and the tendency of young men, in particular, to seek wage employment outside Ilha was slightly reduced.

The literacy program then began with the participation of 698 cooperative members, of whom the majority were women. Of the 433 members who took the examination in November 1983, 332 passed. In other words, over 60 percent of the members originally enrolled finished the course, and almost 50 percent passed. In terms of those who took the final examination, 77 percent were successful, surpassing the national outcome of 67 percent. The results in some cooperatives were even higher: In Cooperative Agostinho Neto, 46 of the 50 members enrolled took the final test, and all of them passed. In Cooperative Vista Alegre, of the 60 members enrolled, 58 (or 97 percent) took the test and 50 (or 86 percent) passed.[20]

An investigation team from the National Directorate of Adult Education (DNEA) attributed the favorable literacy results of Ilha Josina Machel to three factors: (1) conducive social climate, (2) socioeconomic development, and (3) enthusiastic literacy instructors. Of these three, the residents were most animated by a climate of social transformation: "The atmosphere on Ilha was one of movement—with bicycles, motor bikes, land cruisers, lorries, *tropicultors,* tractors. It was an atmosphere of visits, focused on the ever-growing participation of cooperative members in the management of their own cooperatives. There was a great deal of awareness among brigade members with regard to questions of mobilization and participation. The cooperative members felt this concern about their own participation and began to believe that they were people with valuable ideas and experiences instead of simply objects, exploited and marginalized peasants."[21] In other words, during 1983, literacy classes were introduced in a situation that was conducive to learning because of much hard work already realized by the project.

Second was the relationship between the process of socioeconomic development in the community and the new demands to become fluent in the Portuguese language—to read, write, and count. An example taken from my daily journal illustrates this effort: In the process of planning the 1982–1983 agricultural campaign at Cooperative 25 de Setembro, I needed to consult the archives of Mecanagro in the Palmeira to calculate the cost of their services for the previous year. I went, found many anomalies, and informed the management commission of the cooperative, creating a huge commotion. The members considered themselves to be at fault, a reflection of their own lack of control in negotiations with clients like Mecanagro. President Chavango exploded angrily, "We are tired of being abused and treated like ignorant peasants. We have to learn Portuguese."[22] Next in contributing to the success of the literacy program was the team of instructors who integrated themselves into the daily activities of the cooperative. According to the DNEA investigation team, "The majority of literacy instructors treated their work very seriously and were very dedicated, the impact of which was clear in the high results on the final exam. In a climate in which there was a positive expectation for social changes, the instructor was important."[23]

From 1981 to 1983, more than 850 co-op members participated in the project's training activities.[24] Of this total, most were male middle peasants, even in the south where women outnumbered men. Part of the reason for the disproportional activity by men was that the location and duration of the training courses discouraged women's attendance. Constrained by family responsibilities and by societal norms, women could not attend the two- to six-week courses held at the Namaacha Center. When training activities and dissemination of new technology took place in the community (scheduled to accommodate family and collective production), women were more likely to participate.

Yet the type of training also mattered. For example, most cooperatives sent some women to the three-day animal traction demonstrations held in the collective's own field. These women usually had learned how to plow as the daughters or wives in cattle-owning families and had more experience in this traditionally male sphere than most men, whose primary work experience was in the urban areas and mines. When it came to individuals to attend the project's complementary training activities (construction, water-rising equipment, upkeep of pumps, and diesel mechanics), however, and the tractor driving and maintenance course, only men were selected. In comparison to the state farms—where women gradually were being trained to use and maintain agricultural equipment and machinery, and the number of women tractor drivers was increasing—the project trailed behind. The leaders of the cooperative union (mainly men)—assisted by the all-male brigade—who selected the participants at the project's courses were heavily influenced by a gendered division of labor that associated men with machinery and women with manual equipment. In contrast the state had a mandate to challenge this situation.

## Union of Cooperatives: Strength in Unity

One of the principal objectives of Project CO-1 was to assist the cooperatives in establishing a union that would handle those tasks in which cooperation presented real advantages: accounting, marketing, purchasing supplies, contracting specialist technicians, and so on. But the building of a union of cooperatives proved to be a slow process. Government policy and state bureaucrats at the Ministry of Agriculture hindered the co-op members' attempt to use the union as a way of improving their economic and social position.

The leaders of the twelve cooperatives formed the union of cooperatives on Ilha Josina Machel in September 1982. The union's mandate was threefold: (1) to improve work relations with Mecanagro, the state-run machinery park; (2) to get support from state agencies and foreign NGOs; and (3) to open a consumer cooperative. Of these three tasks, Project CO-1 played a most active role as a liaison to improve the relations between Mecanagro and the cooperatives. The numerous meetings held between the co-op members and Mecanagro personnel at the local level provided a forum for both sides to articulate their problems and expectations for the season. Under pressure from the project, Mecanagro sent two additional tractors to Ilha Josina Machel, thereby providing more machinery to attend to the cooperative, family, and private sectors. As a result, the state-owned tractors plowed more hectares in the collective fields than the previous years.[25] Furthermore, many of the middle-peasant farmers, who were given priority as co-op members, rented these tractors for use on their own individual farms. While the number of tractors was insufficient to meet the rental demand, middle-peasant leaders began to feel that cooperative membership brought them tangible benefits.

The CO-1 technicians also assisted the union in contacting professionals and donor agencies. In early 1982, for example, the project paid 65,000 meticais to the provincial directorate of public works and housing to build a bridge at the entrance of Ilha so the community was not isolated during floods. A team of technicians from the DNH also designed a detailed map of Ilha, indicating the neighborhoods and the cooperative, family, and private farms, to facilitate a rational division of agricultural areas for the various sectors, and the brigade accommodated a team of agricultural technicians from the INIA to design soil maps of the island. The CO-1 brigade also initiated visits and accommodated foreign delegations to visit Ilha with the objective of raising material assistance for the union. The World Federation of Lutheran Churches, for example, provided them with a tractor, pulverizers, and a water pump. An ex-miner was trained to drive and maintain the tractor, which was used on both collective and family farms. As news of the success of these pilot cooperatives circulated in Maputo City, film crews from Canada, Denmark, and the United States came to the villages and made video recordings and films that were used to rally more financial support for the cooperatives.

Of the three tasks, the establishment of a consumer cooperative was paramount. It would provide the material incentive (e.g., flour, sugar, rice, salt, oil, matches, soap, and other commodities) for members to increase production and help to stabilize a permanent labor force in the producer cooperatives. Without being guaranteed the basic necessities through such a cooperative, the members had few material incentives to engage in collective work and to produce a surplus. Often, many were absent from the collective fields, some in search of food and other basic requirements, while others learned that it was easier to get what they needed in the parallel market. When the local stores had products to sell, the residents were forced to line up overnight, and then they still were not guaranteed purchases, as there were never sufficient quantities to distribute.

The private rural store owners were in a very powerful position, as they determined the quantity of goods to be distributed, but the norm depended on the quantity of goods at the district warehouse. In each district, a private trader was nominated as district wholesaler to receive the district's consumer goods ration (e.g., oil, sugar, soap, and textiles) and to distribute it to the retail traders. Of the four stores on Ilha, two received minimal supplies from a warehouse in Xinavane and the other two received their goods from an outlet in Manhiça. These warehouses distributed their goods according to the number of private stores and consumer cooperatives under their jurisdiction. Consequently, the four stores did not receive goods on the same day or in identical quantities, which made it difficult to coordinate or monitor their sale and provided fertile ground for speculative activities. One merchant in particular was well-known to residents for hoarding products to sell later to friends and others at higher than official prices. Although residents condemned his activities, they lacked the evidence to bring charges of speculation before the local tribunal.

In May 1983, the consumer cooperative opened on Ilha Josina Machel, with membership numbering more than 970 peasant farmers. In the brigade's monthly report, it was estimated that the consumer cooperative would benefit around 4,500 individuals, more than two-thirds of the island's population.[26] The membership criteria, established by the directorate of the union, required regular attendance at an agricultural cooperative and a membership fee of six hundred meticais in accordance with the law. To have access to the products, each member bought a ration card at the agricultural cooperatives and then had it signed by the president each month to indicate regular attendance. The first products distributed to each of the members were rice, flour, and sugar. Over the next few months, other basic rations included oil, salt, maize, butter, and matches. The store also sold other products—glass lanterns, dishes, glasses, cutlery, crockery, shoes, cookies, radio batteries, and machetes—but not in sufficient quantities for all its members.

The consumer cooperative, like the earlier people's shop, confronted the problems of inexperienced personnel, insufficient quantities of appropriate goods, and competition for products with private stores, which were favored by the district wholesaler. The warehouse managers preferred to sell goods (and in greater quantities) to private stores for reasons including monopoly of resources (i.e., transportation vehicles, storage facilities, and experienced personnel) and knowledge of the marketing and distribution process, security of payment, friendship, and bribes. These managers also used coercive power to force the inexperienced cooperative personnel to buy undesirable goods. Given these operative factors, the state could have enforced allocation priorities at district and national levels, but despite official rhetoric, Frelimo did not give consumer cooperatives more consideration than private stores in the Manhiça District or elsewhere in the countryside.

Some of the problems that emerged at the consumer cooperative, especially the distribution of scarce commodities, had no easy solutions. Members of its administrative bodies tried to develop a democratic system of distribution to determine how and to whom the limited supplies would be sold. In the case of batteries, for example, the store manager divided the total quantity between the number of cooperatives, and within each cooperative, the batteries were sold only to members who owned radios. As a result, the system controlled the circulation of batteries, a popular consumer item in the parallel market. In contrast, the eighty-two pairs of shoes were sold on a first-come, first-served basis, which was an unsatisfactory system for the members, especially for those who lived farthest from the shop. The directorate of the union was aware that scarcity was the breeding ground of inequality and of conflicts of interest between classes and between areas, but they could not increase quantities of supplies because the goods did not exist at the national level; however, they took steps to avoid a system that favored the leaders.

## The Demise of Project CO-1

Following the Fourth Party Congress in 1983, the cooperative movement did not receive the promised resources and assistance from the state. Instead, with the growing food shortages worsened by drought and war, Frelimo increased its authoritarian tendencies. Shortly after the appointment of the deputy minister of the family and cooperative sector, the ministry sent instructions to rural technicians to draw up the agricultural plans for cooperatives and inform the members of the crops and the hectares to plant, an act that indicated a return to the old, failed planning methods characteristic of the pre-1981 period. These directives had a particularly demoralizing impact in those communities supported by the cooperative projects. After a visit from the deputy minister to Ilha Josina Machel, one of the project technicians summarized the official position: "The deputy minister said it was obligatory for each cooperative to grow cassava and sweet potato. At the same time, he was not concerned with the planning process that Project CO-1 had developed. For the deputy minister, there were too many sheets. He was interested in one sheet entitled, 'Consolidation of areas, gross values of production, costs, and results.' And on that sheet, he was only interested in a few columns: crops and activities, hectares, and net income."[27] For nearly two years, state technicians had worked closely with residents to promote members' participation in the development and planning of collective production. By learning to plan, peasant farmers developed an understanding of and capacity to fight for local basic needs. These efforts were now undermined by the central government.

Besides these difficulties, Frelimo's forced urban removal program, known as Operation Production, created turmoil in the cooperatives. District administrators, accompanied by presidents of local assemblies and other local state representatives, organized meetings at cooperatives and threatened to send so-called unemployed individuals to work on both state and private farms. Their methods, characteristic of the colonial authorities, only served to undermine their legitimacy among the rural population. On Ilha Josina Machel, co-op membership expanded dramatically as small-scale farmers and nonfarming individuals (i.e., traders, fishermen, and artisans) joined to avoid possible deportation to the northern provinces. For those who entered the cooperatives at this time, membership was part of an interim domestic survival strategy in the face of political and economic adversity. Although many of these persons were undesirable members (known to the locals as lazy and quarrelsome), government officials forced the co-op to accept them. By determining cooperative membership in this fashion, Frelimo undermined the members' control over their own units of production, thereby leading to internal conflict and demobilization. Furthermore, involuntary membership intensified the growing adversary relationship between the peasantry and the state.

In 1984, the two cooperative projects were integrated in the new National Directorate of Rural Development (DNDR) at the Ministry of Agriculture. While it was mandated to serve the needs both of the cooperative and family sectors, DNDR favored individual producers. The rural brigades were recalled and the Mozambican technicians were either reassigned to other areas or to other agricultural tasks.

Although the project-supported cooperatives lasted only three years initially, with a one-year extension, several conclusions can be drawn. First, the need for Project CO-1 illustrated the difficulty, under Mozambican conditions, of "counting on one's own resources," a phrase Frelimo frequently used to express the need to solve problems based on self-reliance. Rather, collective agriculture required services, supplies of inputs, and technical assistance, and it was only once the project provided the necessary resources to the cooperatives that peasant participation stabilized. Second, Ilha farmers joined the cooperatives to get access to tractors, tools, and seeds for use on their family farms as well as scarce consumer goods. Middle farmers came to see their participation in cooperatives as a way to improve their family households, and poor peasants came to rely on cooperatives for food and as a source of income. Thus, the Ilha Josina Machel cooperatives were successful not because they collectivized family farms, as Frelimo intended, but because of the tangible benefits they provided their members. Third, cooperatives had to be integrated into the regional economy so members could market their crops at fair prices and purchase consumer and producer goods in exchange. While the consumer cooperative provided its members with access to valuable state-supplied goods, this was not sufficient: the weakened state distribution system could not substitute for an active local population whose actions create thriving markets and material exchange. Low prices, the nonavailability of basic commodities, and disruption in the marketing system caused most peasant farmers to reduce marketed production. But these were not the only reasons. In the next chapter, peasant farmers describe some of the other factors that accounted for the decline in crops sold.

# 6

# Peasant Farmers and Household Survival Strategies

**T**he government's rural development strategy was flawed not only because it pursued policies inimical to the peasantry but also because it tried to force an ideal pattern on rural society without any attention to how rural people actually organized their lives. In Mozambique, as in many other countries attempting to improve agriculture, leaders imposed a uniform strategy of national development upon a regionally diverse and socially differentiated rural society, and they failed to consider peasant realities. Furthermore, Frelimo's confidence in the support that it had from the peasantry was used to justify programs of rapid political and economic change. When radical programs did not work, the government claimed it was due to peasant resistance to change or backward attitudes—recurrent themes in the literature on the state and peasantry—rather than to inherent problems in its own policies.[1] For the peasantry, willingness to participate in collective agriculture was part of a risk-spreading strategy rather than a commitment to socialism. As agricultural producers characterized by diverse rural livelihoods and by class stratification, they had very well-conceived survival strategies. This chapter extends our analysis beyond national policy errors to local considerations—individual household survival strategies and historically rooted socioeconomic links between villages—that affected cooperatives.

Labor organization at the cooperatives on Ilha Josina Machel was affected by the members' individual household strategies of integrating cooperative activity with other economic activities. The members had a number of economic recourses—wage labor, hunting, fishing, small artisan activities, and petty trade—in addition to family farming and collective production, and the dominant pattern was that they combined cooperative agriculture with one or more of these activities. For the majority of peasant farmers, the cooperative sector was an appendage to family farming: with one foot in the cooperative's

153

collective field and the other on the family farm, they assumed that if the latter did not produce, there was at least a chance that something would grow on the former.

Given the uncertain rewards of collectivization, it was impossible for peasant farmers to abandon family production or wage employment, which meant that in terms of policy the cooperatives had to accommodate the family sector and wage labor. On Ilha Josina Machel, Project CO-1 technicians and cooperative leaders employed a gradual and flexible strategy toward peasant participation in collective agriculture—regular attendance was required, but if a member was unable to work, a household substitute replaced her or him to get the work card punched. They allowed local compromises to determine what kind of system best suited the members.

The case studies provide insights into the debate on agricultural production decline in Africa since independence. International agencies and individual scholars have attributed declining agricultural production to government policies that discourage or inhibit agricultural growth.[2] They argue that the policies of African states have been systematically biased against the agricultural sector, giving priority to industrial development, pacifying urban wage earners and the unemployed, and enlarging the patronage available to state officials. Depressed crop prices have been the major disincentive, resulting in lower output. Yet, according to Mozambican farmers, state control of prices was only one factor (and not the most significant one) behind their reduced productivity. After all, peasant farmers were dissatisfied with low fixed prices in the colonial period but continued to grow crops and market surpluses. In the interviews, peasants explained how postcolonial agricultural policies made inputs (e.g., seeds, hoes, and other hand tools) difficult to obtain and consumer goods scarce. While they all attributed decline in productivity to Frelimo's accession to power, the precise factors varied for different households. For example, since independence, some households have cultivated smaller fields or had less labor to work their fields because of shortages in cash and food to pay workers. For others, it was more a question of inadequate access to seeds and other inputs, consumer goods, and markets, in addition to low prices. Local evidence suggests that merely freeing up prices for inputs or "getting the price right" for crops (the World Bank's prescriptions) will not necessarily lead to sustainable increases in agricultural production.

## Cooperative Labor Force Profiles and Family Household Categories

Of the 6,971 Ilha Josina Machel residents, which included both adults and children, 1,306 individuals were cooperative members in 1982.[3] The data below are based on my interviews of 270 members (21 percent), conducted at Cooperatives 25 de Setembro and Arma da Frelimo. Of the 176 members at Cooperative 25 de Setembro, there were 152 women (86 percent) and 24 men (14 percent). The distribution of members by gender and age is presented in table 6.1. The dominant age group was sixty years and older, consisting of 10 men (42 percent) and 57 women (38 percent), yet there were nearly as many women in the thirty to forty-four age-group. Overall, members tended to be elderly, although middle-aged women participated in significant numbers. The 176 members came from a total of 94 households (i.e., immediate family aggregate) of which 52 had 1 household member at the cooperative, 30 had 2 members, 9 had 3 members, and only 3 households had 4 or more members.[4] It was typical for only 1 household member to be a cooperative participant, although with the opening of the consumer store, a growing number of households had at least 2 members. This was because of the fact that while 1 person was enough for the household to have access to the consumer store, distribution of goods was organized on an individual basis: the more household members registered, the more goods made available.

Of the 94 members at Cooperative Arma da Frelimo, there were 75 women

Table 6.1 Distribution of cooperative members by gender and age, 1982–1983

| Age Group of Member | Men | Percentage | Women | Percentage | Total | Percentage |
|---|---|---|---|---|---|---|
| Cooperative 25 de Setembro: 176 members | | | | | | |
| 15–29 years | 4 | 17 | 15 | 10 | 19 | 11 |
| 30–44 years | 3 | 13 | 50 | 33 | 53 | 30 |
| 45–59 years | 7 | 29 | 30 | 20 | 37 | 21 |
| ≥60 years | 10 | 42 | 57 | 38 | 67 | 38 |
| Total* | 24 | 100 | 152 | 100 | 176 | 100 |
| Cooperative Arma da Frelimo: 94 members | | | | | | |
| 15–29 years | 0 | 0 | 7 | 9 | 7 | 7 |
| 30–44 years | 2 | 11 | 20 | 27 | 22 | 23 |
| 45–59 years | 7 | 37 | 17 | 23 | 24 | 26 |
| ≥60 years | 10 | 53 | 31 | 41 | 41 | 44 |
| Total* | 19 | 100 | 75 | 100 | 94 | 100 |

Source: Projecto CO-1, "Plano anual 1982–83. Cooperative 25 de Setembro," 1983, p. 5 (photocopy), and "Plano anual 1982–83. Cooperative Arma da Frelimo," 1983, p. 5 (photocopy).
*Total percentages reflect sum of unrounded numbers.

(80 percent) and 19 men (20 percent). This cooperative had a membership older than that of Cooperative 25 de Setembro: 69 percent of its members were over forty-four years, compared to 59 percent at the latter. More than 40 percent of the women's labor force were sixty years and older, and the majority were widows. The 94 members came from a total of 76 households of which 59 had 1 member at the cooperative, 16 had 2 members, and only 1 household had 3 members.

Regular attendance at the cooperatives depended on the household's available surplus labor power, income, and sources of income. According to the individuals interviewed, whose earnings varied significantly, they did not have adequate money to meet their immediate family's needs. The situation for the poor peasants was clear: Their homes needed repairs, they owned no furniture (borrowing a neighbor's bench or chair for me to sit on during the interview), and they slept on thin mats. Broken pots and old utensils were visible. Normally, they dressed in old and torn clothes. In contrast, the middle-peasant farmers' income was insufficient in comparison to the money they earned during the colonial period.

Of the 270 interviews, 7 case studies are presented below, each typical of the diverse peasant farmer households on Ilha Josina Machel. Their varied combinations of economic activities are organized in three broad groups, with examples for each, illustrating the role that cooperatives played in their household survival strategies. Middle-peasant households who had a solid base in small-scale farming and a regular wage income characterize the first group. They usually had a full-time wage earner (usually a husband or son) employed in South Africa, Maputo City, or at a nearby state enterprise. Those households with migrant wages earned in South Africa fared better economically than those with a relative working at a state farm.

Peasant households with migrant workers still in South Africa had advantages in hiring seasonal laborers. They often received consumer goods, including food, and South Africa's currency, the rand. Most of the goods were for the miner's own household—goods that his immediate family needed from day to day to survive, such as agricultural hand tools and zinc sheets to repair roofs, as well as soap, salt, sugar, flour, paraffin, and clothing—but in a few cases, households set aside a part of these goods to exchange for farm labor. Consumer goods like sacks of maize and flour were given a production use by exchanging them for labor. Because payment was nearly always in kind (e.g., five kilos of maize per day per worker), the households could not afford to hire workers for more than a few days at a time; thus, seasonal laborers (consisting of one to two persons) usually were part-time, working only two to three days consecutively. These farm laborers were often poor peasants in the community, but occasionally they were individuals who left drought-stricken areas in Maputo and Gaza Provinces in search of food for immediate family consumption and maize seed for the next planting season.

Households with a member employed full-time at a state enterprise used the wages to invest in agriculture (hiring draft animals and plows and buying seeds) and to pay for general household expenses. Often, the wage earner was a wife or daughter working as an unskilled agricultural laborer in the sugar plantations, earning the minimum wage of 1,800 meticais a month. Although most households had been used to selling surplus crops in the colonial era, peasant farmers claimed that in the last few years they only produced sufficient crops for self-consumption. Several factors accounted for their low productivity, including alternate years of floods and drought and lack of funds to replace their means of production. Many peasant farmers attributed the decline in productivity to Frelimo's accession to power: peasants explained that since independence they (1) farmed smaller fields, (2) had less labor to work their fields, (3) lacked cash to replace their old draft animals (which were sick more often under Frelimo because there were not sufficient veterinary services available), (4) had inadequate access to seeds and other inputs, and (5) had less access to transportation facilities and markets. These factors varied with a different mix for different households. Typically, these households had to integrate nonagricultural activities with wage labor and family farming to make ends meet. Group 1 represented about 20 percent of those interviewed.

The second and most numerous group consisted of middle-peasant households that had a base in small-scale farming combined with commodity production within the local community (i.e., plowing the farms of other households with their oxen in exchange for payment, engaging in petty trade, or undertaking various crafts such as house construction, brick making, carpentry, and tailoring). Most households were not willing to disclose all their activities. For example, manufacturers of alcoholic beverages and *curandeiros* usually refrained from describing their activities directly or in detail; that information came from others in the locality. Usually this group depended solely on family labor, using both immediate and extended relatives on their farms with payment in kind. When it was necessary, they sold a small agricultural surplus or a few chickens, ducks, or goats between harvests. Many claimed that they consumed all their crops, unlike during the colonial era, when they produced for the market. They explained that the bumper maize harvest in early 1983, which enabled them to hire outside workers to harvest their crop in return for maize and to use barter in other transactions (i.e., maize for fish or sugar), was an exception. Group 2 represented about 45 percent of those interviewed.

The third group included a significant number of poor peasant households —usually consisting of single mothers, widows, and the elderly—who did not have sufficient land to cultivate or who were too old to farm. An increasing number of households were too poor to farm: they were able to keep farming only if they spent much of their time as temporary agricultural laborers for middle-peasant and private farmers in the community. In return for their labor, they received flour, sugar, soap, and other scarce commodities. These households failed to produce sufficient food crops on their farms because they did not have a sufficient labor force and they lacked the means of production, in particular draft animals and plows at critical periods in the agricultural season. Their fields were plowed late, if at all, and many were forced to prepare their farms with a hoe, compromising agricultural production. In a few cases, they exchanged two or three weeks' labor for three to four days' use of draft animals to plow their fields. Most of these households were engaged in pottery making, mat weaving, alcohol brewing, and thatch cutting—the simpler and less profitable crafts—and had cheap tools of production. Although an immediate family member or members might have worked seasonally or part-time in the wage economy, the cash contribution to household expenses was very little in relation to the high costs of consumer goods and speculative prices in the parallel market. These poor peasant households did not have food reserves or cash accumulated. Group 3 represented about 35 percent of those interviewed.

The expenditures of the seven households are not presented in a tabular form because the data were fragmentary. The capital outflows for oxen, plows, and agricultural tools, for example, were not known. The information I collected during the interviews, however, suggests that the major expenditures were food, clothing, and land preparation for the family farm (i.e., tractor or ox-plow rental). Other specific expenditures incurred by some members included: school expenses for the children (i.e., uniforms and matriculation costs), medical treatment paid either to traditional healers or for services provided in Swaziland, construction of houses (made from local materials or bricks), and the purchase of small animals (chickens and ducks).

## Case Studies: Family Life and Work Histories

*Group 1*

OLINDA FULANA: MIDDLE-PEASANT HOUSEHOLD

Olinda Fulana, fifty-seven years old, was born in Bilene, Gaza Province.[5] She was the oldest girl and the third born of nine children, of whom three died at birth or shortly afterward. Like most young girls in her village, she never attended school and still could not speak Portuguese, although she was fluent in Shangaan. As far as she could remember, her father always worked in the South

African mines, and eventually her three brothers had become migrant workers too. With his wages, her father invested in the family farm, purchasing cattle (which he later reproduced), plows, and other equipment. As a daughter of a livestock-owning family, she learned how to plow the fields.

Olinda moved to Ilha Josina Machel after she married her husband, also a native of Gaza. She was the first and eldest wife of Tomé Manhiça, one of the founders of Cooperative 25 de Setembro. They had seven children together, of whom four were dependent on them: two young girls, eleven and thirteen years old, who attended primary school, and two male teenagers, sixteen and seventeen years old, who studied at technical colleges in Xinavane (Maputo Province) and Chimoio (Manica Province). The other three children, all women, were grown and married. Two of them settled with their families on Ilha Josina Machel, living in different neighborhoods than their parents, and were members of Cooperative Vista Alegre.

Tomé Manhiça, in his mid-sixties, always worked in South Africa. He was a miner until several years ago when poor health forced him to change his job and he was hired as a cook for the Eastern Rand Company. With the money he earned in South Africa, the family bought and raised cattle, so that in 1983 they owned more than fifty-two heads. During these years, he returned with a sewing machine, a bicycle, a radio, chairs, tables, *capulanas,* and other clothing for Olinda and their children. Manhiça paid three local artisans to build four cement houses for his immediate family: one for each of his wives, for whom he paid *lobolo,* and one for his children.

Although Olinda was evasive about the total number of hectares the household cultivated in the colonial era, she repeated how "it was always sufficient to grow food crops for consumption and sale, as well as wheat." In those days, Olinda explained, "there was no difficulty in selling products. I transported and sold some crops to local store owners. It was common for residents to buy my maize from my field, which was not far from the main walking path." She was one of a handful of women registered as a member of the colonial wheat-marketing cooperative. Unlike the men who often joined Cooperative Moses to avoid forced labor, she grew wheat to have access to services (tractor and other machinery rental) and supplies of inputs (seeds and fertilizers) provided by the ICM. Their landholding also had a few banana and papaya trees as well as sugarcane.

While the principal source of labor was the household, occasionally Olinda hired temporary agricultural workers from the community to assist in the maize harvest. They were paid in kind, generally food. In addition, Tomé Manhiça employed a young man to look after his cattle herd, a common practice in migrant laborers' households in southern Mozambique. In 1970 he hired Agostinho Hobjana, a sixteen-year-old youth who lived with his mother in the same neighborhood as the Manhiça household. Over the years, Hobjana was not only paid but also given clothing as well as other consumer goods from South Africa. In 1982, Manhiça gave Hobjana an ox for taking care of his cattle. According to Olinda, Hobjana sometimes used their draft animals to prepare his mother's farm.

With independence, the household reduced the number of hectares cultivated, although Olinda did not specify by how much. She still farmed her own two-hectare landholding, usually plowed by the oldest son of the second wife, using two teams of oxen owned by her husband. Despite her easy access to ox-plows, she preferred her farm to be prepared by tractor and opted for Mecanagro services whenever they were available. In 1982, for example, she paid 2,100 meticais for a state-owned tractor to plow her land. Olinda and her two girls then sowed maize, cassava, sweet potatoes, beans, and cabbage. Of the total agricultural production, she sold an estimated 50 kilograms of cassava (to a neighbor who lost most of her maize to the drought) and conserved the rest. The household also raised chickens, goats, and ducks for their own consumption. Her means of production included two plows, two hoes, a machete, and an ax.

Olinda and her husband were part of the original founders of the first collective on Ilha Josina Machel. In 1976, Tomé Manhiça contributed 4,800 meticais to be used as start-up capital. Even though it was Olinda who actually worked in the field, she did not become an official member until the following year. Later, when the collective was transformed to a cooperative, she joined and paid 600 meticais. According to Olinda, she enrolled in cooperative agriculture because "Frelimo came to the island and told people they should work together to increase production. I joined because it was important to support the new government." In 1980, her husband's two younger wives—who lived in the same compound as Olinda—enrolled as members. They worked in different brigades so that there was always one adult overseeing the family farms. Olinda and the other two wives had regular attendance during the 1982–1983 season and participated in the literacy classes, primarily because participation was mandatory. For Olinda, the benefits of learning Portuguese were not evident, as she used Shangaan in her daily affairs; the main reason she continued to be a member was to purchase the crops produced at the cooperative.

Although the three wives lived in the same compound, they kept their incomes separate. Olinda did not know her husband's salary, but in 1982 he sent her 9,000 meticais, and when he returned he gave her another 15,000 meticais. According to Olinda, her husband always sent the same amount of money from South Africa. She also earned 10,920 meticais at the cooperative and another 20,000 meticais from the sale of two heads of cattle slaughtered for a celebratory festival organized by and for cooperative members. The estimated household income for the 1982–1983 season was thus 54,920 meticais, but this amount was probably a low assessment since Olinda was not willing to reveal entirely her sources or amounts of income.

She did not know the total expenses of the season because her husband paid all the bills, including their children's school expenses, and purchased all the family's clothing in South Africa. The family did not spend a major portion of their money on food, as their farm produced sufficient crops for their own consumption. With the money from the cooperative, Olinda bought rice from the stores and tomatoes, maize, beans, and potatoes from the cooperative. She also paid 600 meticais to join the consumer cooperative. In the past, she had used her earnings to pay for traditional medical treatment. According to Olinda, she had sufficient money, as evidenced by the ongoing construction of a new six-room brick house in the courtyard. While the total cost of the house was unknown, one of the three local builders informed me that there was still a shipment of bricks in Maputo, valued at 27,000 meticais, waiting to be transported to the village. Given the general economic crisis in rural Mozambique, the building of a new brick home indicated the family's wealth.

## Josef Tlemo: Ex-Miner/Middle-Peasant Household

Josef Tlemo, sixty-nine years old, was the head of a household consisting of a wife and two teenage sons, sixteen and seventeen years old, who attended school on Ilha Josina Machel.[6] He also had four married children from his other two wives, both of whom died prior to 1980. Rita Chauque, his third and only living wife, was the thirty-nine-year-old daughter of Johanne Chauque, a prominent farmer in the community. According to local residents, Chauque did not have to join the colonial cooperative to avoid *chibalo* in the colonial era; the Portuguese authorities had let him alone because he was a very hard-working and successful farmer who produced large quantities of maize, beans, and other food crops for sale to local stores. By marrying Rita, a woman nearly half his age, Tlemo not only had someone to care for him in his old age but also became integrated into an influential family. In addition to his immediate family, he was responsible for two nephews, sons of his deceased older brother. Although their mother was alive, she was too poor to provide them with basic necessities. The two boys, eleven and thirteen years old, ate lunch daily in Tlemo's house, and he also paid for their school uniforms and books.

As a young man, Josef Tlemo was employed as a laborer on a Portuguese settler's farm in Maputo. After one year he left because he was paid very little. He returned to his parent's home in Magude and worked a year at the Incomati Sugar Estates before he migrated to South Africa. At the Incomati, he learned how to use the irrigation equipment and watered the sugarcane. But like his father, Malunguana Tlemo, he went to work in the mines at the first opportunity. As a miner in South Africa from 1928 to 1938, he completed a total of five contracts. He worked mostly in the West Rand Mines, which because of the high number of accidents that took place underground was considered by experienced miners to be one of the most dangerous and unpopular mines in Johannesburg.[7] Subsequently, from 1939 to 1947, he was employed at a factory where the workers made iron pipes and zinc sheets. He earned about 1,200 escudos or 24 rand per month. While in South Africa, Tlemo also attended school and completed grade four in Shangaan.

In 1947 he returned to Mozambique and moved to Ilha Josina Machel. He had heard that the land was fertile and approached Régulo Panguene Timana, who gave him nine hectares. With the money he earned in South Africa, he bought his first ox-plow and formally established himself on his farm. He also purchased equipment (hoes, machetes, axes, sickles) and some small animals (chickens, ducks, and goats) and paid *lobolo* for three wives. According to Tlemo, "the *régulo* gave me land because I had a plow and oxen. Also, at that time, few people lived on Ilha Mariana [the colonial name for Ilha Josina Machel] and fertile land was abundant. When I moved here with my wives and children, there were still buffalo roaming." He quickly established himself as a *machambeiro*, a peasant farmer who owned sufficient means of production (a team of oxen and a plow) to produce surplus crops for market. He often employed nonfamily members as temporary workers to perform seasonal tasks (i.e., weeding and harvesting), paying them in kind.

In 1953, he joined the colonial cooperative and sowed one hectare of wheat on his landholding. Initially in charge of a group, he trained apprentices and later became the president of Cooperative Moses, representing all members of the community. As president, he sought to improve wheat production through increased mechanization, but the Portuguese opposed this idea primarily because they wanted to control the growth of Mozambican middle farmers to ensure that the latter did not threaten the state-subsidized economic position of settler farmers. Tlemo was forced to return to the mines in 1960 after the colonial authorities threatened to jail him as one of the instigators behind the membership's decision to purchase a tractor and other machinery. For the next two years he worked underground at Western Holdings Mines.

In 1962, tired and sick from mine labor, Tlemo returned permanently to Mozambique and found employment at the Incomati Sugar Estates, where he maintained and repaired machinery and equipment, as well as supervised the irrigation of sugarcane. His starting salary was about seven hundred escudos monthly, and when he left he was earning about twelve hundred escudos. Over the years his health deteriorated, and in 1973 he quit his job, making him ineligible for a pension. Shortly afterward, Tlemo began treatment for tuberculosis, an infectious disease associated with the mining industry.

With independence, Tlemo gave his married son, Simião, 3 hectares of his landholding. On his remaining 6 hectares, he cultivated maize, beans, cassava, and sweet potatoes for home consumption. A few banana and tangerine trees around the house provided his permanent crops. In 1982, Tlemo's means of production were a team of working oxen, a plow, two machetes, two axes, and a sickle, nearly all purchased with his earnings from South Africa. He also owned a cow and fewer than a dozen chickens. The labor force consisted of his immediate family—a wife and two teenage sons. Simião also helped his father a great deal (he built a large new granary) even though he had a wife and six young children. While Tlemo usually prepared his field with animal traction, he paid Mecanagro for tractor service when it was available. For example, in 1981 he paid 768 meticais for a Mecanagro tractor to plow 4.5 hectares, and in 1982 he paid 2,100 meticais for it to plow and grade 2 hectares. According to Tlemo, he had sufficient money to hire a tractor for all 6 hectares: "The problem was not a lack of money but a widespread demand for a few tractors. There were more peasant and private farmers requesting tractor service than there were available machines." To transport the maize and other crops from the field, he often borrowed his father-in-law's wagon. Since independence Tlemo generally has conserved his maize production for family consumption. In 1983, however, following a bumper harvest, he exchanged three hundred kilos of maize (worth 6 meticais/kilo at the official price) for one hundred kilos of sugar (worth 16.50 meticais/kilo) at Majonane's store.

In 1976 when Frelimo cadres arrived in the community to persuade residents to form a collective, Tlemo saw it as an opportunity to reap the economic benefits denied to Mozambican middle farmers in the colonial era. He joined with eight progressive farmers to form a collective, each contributing 4,800 meticais as start-up capital. While half of them left once cooperative membership expanded in 1977, Tlemo stayed for two reasons: his age and lack of alternatives, especially given his poor health. Over the years, as his family's standard of living deteriorated, he demanded that the cooperative reimburse him for his initial contribution. To avoid confrontation, the cooperative returned most of it in installments: 200 meticais to pay for his travel expenses to Swaziland, 1,200 meticais to join the consumer cooperative, and 800 meticais for a new plow handle. Tlemo's main tasks at the cooperative were to train workers and supervise irrigation. From 1977 to 1983, Josef Tlemo was secretary on the cooperative's directorate, a leadership position, and assistant to the party secretary of the neighborhood.

Since 1978 his son Eduardo has worked at the cooperative with the family ox-plow using Tlemo's work card. In 1983, he received his own work card and

Denise, the youngest son, took over the ox-plow registered under Tlemo's name. With the opening of the consumer cooperative, however, Tlemo was anxious that Denise obtain his own work card. According to him, "all the children of Fernando Chavango [the president of the cooperative] had their own card, and hence, access to the products at the consumer shop. All cooperative members' children should have their own cards so everyone can benefit equally." His other son, Simião, who joined the cooperative in 1977, acquired skills at project-funded courses. In 1981, for example, he was taught better planting techniques by agricultural technicians at the Namaacha center, and the following year he participated in a two-week course on better plowing techniques. When the World Federation of Lutheran Churches donated a new tractor to the cooperative union and the directorate selected individuals to learn how to drive and maintain it, Simião was chosen for training as a tractor driver in Tete (June 1983).

Since 1973, the year Tlemo left Incomati, his wife has worked as an agricultural laborer at the sugar plantation. The company chose to replace sick or old workers with members of the same household to reduce recruitment costs. Peasant households thus internalized the recruiting system because they feared losing a steady income. The work shift, from 5:00 A.M. to 2:00 P.M., six days per week, allowed her to till the family farm in the afternoon. With full-time employment at Incomati, the household was guaranteed a steady source of income and five kilos of sugar per month. In addition to Rita's salary and cooperative earnings, Tlemo made and sold mats, which served as mattresses, at 300 meticais each. For the 1982–1983 agricultural season, the family income consisted of cooperative earnings (20,160 meticais), ox-plow rental to the cooperative (14,000 meticais), Rita's salary (25,200 meticais), and the sale of small-scale crafts (2,400 meticais), totaling 61,760 meticais. The major family expense for 1983 were food, tractor rental, seeds for the family farm, two trips per year to Swaziland for medical treatment, school expenses, and clothes.

*Group 2*

FERNANDO CHAVANGO: EX-MINER/MIDDLE PEASANT/LARGE HOUSEHOLD

At sixty-two years old, Fernando Chavango headed a large household consisting of three wives and twelve children, which included two young adults, five children at primary school, and five children under eight years old.[8] Another five children lived outside the household—two married daughters, a son studying at the agricultural school in Namaacha, a daughter attending middle school in Manhiça, and a daughter attending high school in Maputo. While colonialism had deprived Chavango of an education in Mozambique, he made sacrifices to ensure that his children studied beyond secondary school, because he understood that in a postindependent Mozambique only those children who were educated would be able to lead a better life. His first opportunity to study was as a migrant laborer in South Africa, where he passed level six in Shangaan. Later in independent Mozambique, he went to adult literacy classes and completed level four in Portuguese. A native of Ilha Josina Machel, Chavango had one brother and two sisters who lived nearby and a very large extended family in 1982.

At eighteen, Chavango's first job was at the Incomati Sugar Estates, where he worked for three years as an agricultural laborer in the sugarcane fields. Subsequently, he was employed for five years as a cook at Rossio Garcia, a labor depot near the South African and Mozambican borders, for Mozambicans on their way to the mines. Chavango left that job in 1946 to work as a cook in South Africa, where he stayed until 1949. When he returned to Mozambique, he already had arranged his first mine contract to begin in 1950 at State Mines, Number 4. He did two contracts there, sixteen months and twenty months, respectively, and after each period he came home to help his immediate family with the farm. Subsequently, he completed two contracts at the Orange Free State Mine, of which the last one ended in 1958. As an aide to an electrician, his last contract paid about thirty-six cents a day. As a migrant worker, he always sent money home to his immediate family in Mozambique. Chavango elaborated: "For example, when I was at the Orange Free State, I sent 2,000 meticais with a *ghayisa*, a returning migrant, for my family. More or less I sent home 2,000 meticais each time, although I sometimes worried if the money would reach them. And I always returned with goods from South Africa." From the wages he earned in the mines, Chavango bought a plow, two oxen, chickens, ducks, and a bicycle, and he paid *lobolo* (bride payment of 2,800 escudos) for his first wife.

In 1958 Chavango returned to Ilha Josina Machel to farm his sixteen hectares with his newly purchased oxen and plow. More than half of his land was located within two hundred meters of the river, and the remainder was higher dry land. The family farm, consequently, produced crops even during periods of severe drought. While Chavango did not elaborate on his relationship with the *régulo* who was responsible for land distribution, other residents commented. According to one long-time resident, Chavango received better-irrigated and more fertile land than most farmers because, "he was in charge of the *régulo*'s local alcoholic brew. Timana (the *régulo*) sold part of his alcohol to the local inhabitants and kept the rest for his own consumption. For this reason, Chavango occupied good land."[9]

During the colonial period, Chavango marketed large quantities of maize, beans, and groundnuts to a local store owner who had shops in Xinavane and on Ilha Josina Machel. According to Chavango, "the people were limited to selling their products to the same store owners. They set the price for the produce and then paid both in cash and in kind. We never received just cash for our produce. They then sold the products outside." The sale of his crops enabled him to pay *lobolo* for his second and third wives and buy three more teams of oxen, another plow, goats, a machine to husk maize, and a radio. He also paid for the construction of a masonry house. In 1958 he joined the colonial cooperative after a brief apprenticeship and quickly established himself as a group leader. As an active member of Cooperative Moses, Chavango grew wheat and was guaranteed a regular income from its sale, even though the set price was lower than that paid to Portuguese farmers.

After independence, he found it difficult to buy sufficient quantities of seed, especially maize, to cultivate his sixteen hectares. Gradually, he left about ten hectares fallow, which later were divided among Cooperatives 25 de Setembro, Vista Alegre, and Moçambicana, a donation that insured Chavango's eventual leadership position. On his remaining six hectares, he and his immediate family produced maize, beans, groundnuts, cassava, and sweet potatoes for home consumption. The sole source of labor was the household. In 1982, his means of production were four teams of oxen, two cows, sixteen sickles, seven hoes, two axes, and a machete.

One of the original founders of the collective field, Chavango became the president of Cooperative 25 de Setembro in 1977. Since then he worked every morning at the cooperative, although he was paid just for three days per week. Between 1977 and 1981, he and his three wives regularly participated in cooperative agriculture to have access to the produce. In most years his farm grew sufficient food for family consumption, but since the end of the 1970s, his fields were inundated periodically by drainage from the Incomati Sugar Estates, which flowed into the Incomati River and then flooded sections of the island. Thus, cooperative production compensated for crops lost on the family farm.

In 1981, Chavango decided that two of his children should join the cooperative, as there were possibilities to develop skills. In December of that year, his sixteen-year-old daughter, Molina, entered the cooperative, and the following February, she attended a seven-month dressmaking course paid for by the cooperative, which planned that she would repair and sew clothes for the members who depended on the community's private tailors. After she completed the course, the cooperative was unable to purchase a sewing machine, so her training went unused. In 1982, she attended a three-week management course paid by Project CO-1 and became the cashier at the consumer store. Chavango's eighteen-year-old son also joined the cooperative in December 1981. One of the few people on the island with grade seven education, he assisted the bookkeeper and occasionally worked with the family's ox-plows at the collective field. In 1982 he participated in the forty-five-day literacy course sponsored by Project CO-1 and became one of the three teaching instructors at the cooperative. Chavango's younger son joined the cooperative in August 1982 and took over the responsibility of working with the family's ox-plow. By 1982, seven members of the Chavango family were official cooperative members. The division of the household between the two brigades permitted them to balance family production with collective activity. At any given morning, half the household members worked at the cooperative and the other half at the family farm.

During the 1982–1983 season, the household income was dependent on breeding and selling animals, earnings from collective production, and ox-plow rental to the cooperative; these activities rendered 2,125 meticais, 71,820 meticais, and 14,800 meticais, respectively. Molina's earnings, 9,000 meticais based on three months at the consumer store, and Euzebio's salary, 7,500 meticais based on five months work as a literacy instructor, gave the household an additional 16,500 meticais, for an estimated annual income of 105,245 meticais; it probably was substantially higher because ox-plow rental to neighborhood residents was not included in the total (the going rate was 300 meticais per day, and it usually took three to four days to prepare 0.5 hectares; although Chavango would not speculate on his income from animal traction, several cooperative members indicated that they rented from him). School expenses, food, and clothing were the major household expenditures. According to Chavango, his household lacked a sufficient income.

In 1982, Fernando Chavango was the president of Cooperative 25 de Setembro, president of the association of twelve cooperatives on the island, a member of the directorate of the Union of Cooperatives, the secretary of the consumer cooperative, a member of the locality's Commission of Supplies, the Frelimo party secretary of the neighborhood, and a deputy of the locality.

## TALITA MUCAVETE: PETTY TRADE/ARTISAN/MIDDLE-PEASANT HOUSEHOLD

Talita Mucavete was a forty-eight-year-old married cooperative member.[10] She was born in Manhiça and moved to Ilha Josina Machel after she married Paulo Chauque, a nephew of Johanne Chauque (see case study 2). They had four children—three daughters and one son. Her son, Alexandre Paulo, was married and worked in Maputo, and the other three children lived at home. The son's two wives, Rita Cutana and Isobel Cuna, and his three young children lived with Talita. The daughters-in-law were both members of the cooperative. Unlike most women, Talita spoke Portuguese, although she communicated mostly in Shangaan. She explained that as a young girl she learned Portuguese in a Manhiça primary school run by missionaries, but she was unable to attend secondary school because her parents could not afford the fees. Before her marriage, Talita never worked outside the household.

Talita's husband, who was in his mid-fifties, had completed about four contracts in the South African mines, beginning when he was only eighteen years old. Paulo Chauque returned to Mozambique in 1953 and worked at the Incomati Sugar Estates until 1980. During his last few years of employment there, he earned about 1,980 meticais per month. At the beginning of 1980, he quit his job because "there were no products to purchase at the company's store and the salary was too low to buy many of the goods that were only available on the parallel market." He turned to small artisan activities on Ilha Josina Machel, building houses made from local materials, selling fish, and renting his two teams of oxen and plows to peasant farmers. Around the same time, Alexandre Paulo, who usually forwarded money to his mother, began to send sugar, soap, and other basic commodities that were scarce in the rural areas. Most of the products came from his workplace, the Hong Kong restaurant in Maputo City, where he was a cook. He lived on his monthly ration supplies, available only to those who lived in the cities.

The household's main source of goods and cash came from Talita's traditional medicine practice. Following independence she earned most of her income from the treatment and training of others. Highly respected by local residents, Talita had a waiting list of persons who wanted to be her apprentices. Since 1981, her business had increased in part because of the lack of supplies at the rural health clinic and in part because of the high turnover of health workers employed there. As residents grew more discontent with the poor services offered at the clinic, they turned to Talita's services and to the growing number of other *curandeiros,* traditional healers, in the community. Contrary to Christian Geffray's argument that Frelimo prohibited rural people from practicing their cultural traditions, state officials never intervened in the *curandeiro*'s business in Ilha Josina Machel. According to one husband who sent his wife to Talita for a three-year training program in 1981, he paid 6,000 meticais in kind (sugar, pineapple, chickens, and goats) and 15,000 meticais in cash. With some of the sugar and pineapple, Talita made an alcoholic beverage and sold it to locals at 10 meticais a liter. Talita also received small animals for her services. In 1982 she owned more than thirty chickens, three goats, numerous ducks, and approximately forty guinea pigs. Other gifts from her students and patients included *capulanas* and soap from South Africa.

Often the women who trained under Talita worked as unpaid agricultural laborers on her family farm of two hectares. In June 1982, for example, her husband's ox-drawn plows prepared the land, and five women apprentices weeded and harvested sweet potato, maize, and cassava. It was "part of their duty to work in the fields while under training." The use of extrafamilial labor was more than simply the use of traditional forms of labor recruitment (e.g., *tsima,* communal work with other women) or part of an individual household survival strategy: it was also part of an accumulation strategy. These unpaid women laborers grew food crops on Talita's farm for consumption and market, and freed her labor to expand nonagricultural economic activities. According to Talita, and confirmed by neighbors, her students did not farm the combined three hectares of Rita and Isobel.

In 1978, the two daughters-in-law joined the cooperative, and in 1981 Talita enrolled, registering as a member to have access to cooperative production, yet cooperative agriculture was never a priority. During the 1982–1983 season, she had difficulties balancing her nonagricultural activities and family farming with collective production, and she frequently sent her oldest daughter, fifteen years old, as a replacement. In June 1982, however, Talita's daughter had a baby and consequently remained away from the cooperative for two months, meaning that Talita was recorded as absent for the months of June and July and was unable to purchase goods at the consumer shop. Yet even this was not critical for the household, as evidenced by a luncheon they organized for me.

As a gesture of friendship, Talita invited me and my two colleagues to a multicourse meal at her home on July 14, 1982. Once in the well-kept compound, we were escorted to a very large thatch-roofed hut that Paulo Chauque had recently built. There were five other structures, including a small locked hut in the corner where Talita kept her plant roots, herbs, and other medicinal supplies. As we waited to be served, Talita entered the hut wearing a South African kerchief and a new *capulana* as well as several silver bracelets on her arm. After the common greetings and exchanges took place, she offered us a warm bucket of water and South African laundry soap to clean our hands in preparation for the meal. She and her daughters-in-law served her husband and us. Given the cool winter temperature, we began with tea, condensed milk, and a choice of white or brown sugar. Tea was followed by a fresh salad consisting of lettuce, tomatoes, and onions served with vinegar and oil dressing and salt. There were two large plates of local fresh bread, which were refilled several times during the meal. The entrée included rice, potatoes fried in oil, and grilled chicken, which she killed for the occasion. In between each dish, Talita brought in warm water and soap to clean our hands, although we were using individual plates, forks, and knives. She also offered us the choice of Mozambican beer or a fruit concentrate to mix with water. It was an exceptional meal, unusual to find in a Maputo restaurant and even more so in a rural community. At other cooperative households, we sometimes were offered cassava or maize porridge, hardly equivalent to Talita's elaborate luncheon.

The sources of income for the 1982–1983 season were cooperative production (20,790 meticais), traditional medicine practice (60,000 meticais), ox-plow rental (15,000 meticais), house construction (10,000 meticais), fishing (24,000 meticais), and a contribution from Alexandre Paulo (12,000 meticais). The estimated income of the household was 141,790 meticais.

*Group 3*

MARIA MACAMO: WIDOW/POOR PEASANT HOUSEHOLD

Maria Macamo, fifty-nine years old, was a widow.[11] Her husband, Rafael Tovela, a former miner in South Africa, died before independence shortly after returning to Mozambique, sick, from South Africa. He had worked a considerable number of contracts, but there had been only enough money to live on at that time. They had three children: Rosalina, a married daughter living in Xinavane; António, a son working in Maputo; and Leonora, a daughter who lived with Maria along with her two young children, five years and two months. Leonora's children had different fathers, neither of whom supported his child. Maria struggled with her daughter to provide the children with food and clothing.

Maria was born in Bilene, Gaza Province, to Madinda Macamo and Lotasse Bila. Her family was poor and she never attended school. Her first wage employment was at the Incomati Sugar Estates, where she began as a seasonal laborer and eventually was hired full-time to weed and cut sugarcane, despite the physical hardship of the work. (This is an example of the phenomenon discussed in chapter 3 whereby the proletarianization of women was used by the colonial system to extract more labor from the peasant economy.) According to Maria, she had to work because her husband did not make enough money to buy food and clothing for her and the children. After working for more than twenty-five years, she left the Incomati in 1978 because of poor health.

In 1982, Maria and Leonora cultivated a two-hectare family farm, the same landholding that Maria had farmed during colonialism. They rented an ox-plow from Pedro Novela, a cooperative member, for two days to prepare the land, paying him six hundred meticais. They did not rent from the same person each year but always had their land prepared by an ox-drawn plow, even if it was poorly done. Maria and Leonora ordinarily planted maize, beans, and sweet potatoes on their two hectares. In the garden around the house they sowed a small quantity of cassava, sweet potatoes, and sugarcane, and they also planted a small area of lettuce, tomatoes, and cabbage. Ilha peasant farmers did not normally cultivate these crops for two reasons: (1) the seeds were difficult to arrange, and (2) few peasants knew much about horticulture techniques. Leonora, who bought the seeds in Xinavane, claimed that she learned about horticulture from a farmer in the district. In 1983, Maria and Leonora sold a small quantity of lettuce and cabbage to local residents. Their only means of production were two hoes, an ax, and a machete. More important than income from crops was the sale of chickens—Maria explained that they raised chickens "to pay for their bills." From January to April 1983, she sold more than twenty chickens at two hundred meticais each.

The household compound, with two huts and an elevated chicken coop, was very clean. At the beginning of 1982, Maria hired a local artisan to build her house. He constructed the frame, and the two women applied the clay mud to the walls. Since Maria supplied the wooden posts for the frame, she only had to pay him five hundred meticais, half the price that Leonora paid for her new house. Maria explained that they had to move their residence in 1979 because the community needed her land to create neighborhoods. Although the village residents were not forced to relocate to communal villages, the creation of neighborhoods displaced some persons—usually poor households like Maria's that lacked political power.

She joined the cooperative in 1978, the same year she quit her job at the Incomati Sugar Estates, because she wanted to have access to cooperative production. At that time everyone was asked to contribute three hundred meticais to the cooperative's general fund. At the cooperative, she usually worked with a hoe; she did not know how to use animal traction. Leonora became a member in 1982. Mother and daughter requested different brigades so that one of them could work at the family farm each morning, and both had regular attendance at the cooperative in 1982–1983 except for Leonora's two months' pregnancy leave. Since the all-male leadership did not consider pregnancy leave as legitimate time off, Leonora was unable to purchase products at the cooperative during her absence. Once she returned, Leonora was eligible for all the benefits that the other cooperative members enjoyed, including a six hundred–metical loan from the general fund to cover her membership fee at the consumer cooperative. Neither Maria nor Leonora held official positions in the cooperative or in the local administration.

The earnings of the cooperative, the proceeds from the sale of marketed crops and chickens, and the money sent from António in Maputo were the major sources of the household income in 1982–1983. These activities rendered 17,570 meticais, 4,000 meticais, and 6,000 meticais, respectively, totaling 27,570 meticais. António's cash contribution went toward the construction of his mother's new house, ox-plow rental to prepare the family farm, clothes, and food. Maria felt that her immediate family's income was not adequate: in addition to a shortage of cash, they needed *capulanas* and more maize for consumption. Their major expenses were food, ox-plow rental, and clothes. Maria noted that in 1983 ox-plow rental increased to four hundred meticais per day, meaning that it was going to cost about twelve hundred meticais for three days' work on her land, double the amount she paid in 1982 but still inadequate to properly prepare her entire farm.

## PETASSE MATSOLO HOBJANA: WIDOW/POOR PEASANT HOUSEHOLD

Petasse Matsolo Hobjana, a native of Ilha Josina Machel, was a sixty-four-year-old widow.[12] Her husband, Fabião Hobjana, a former miner in South Africa, died in 1972. Despite his many years of service in South Africa, he never bought cattle or invested in the family farm, instead spending most of his money on food and alcohol in South Africa, and when he returned to Mozambique he entertained his drinking friends at Majonane's, the local licensed restaurant. Occasionally, he returned with clothing for the children, but Petasse did not depend on his contributions. Before independence she began to work at the Incomati Sugar Estates as a temporary laborer, becoming full-time in 1970. Like Maria Macamo, she was too poor to simply farm and so became part of the Incomati's proletarianized women's force for the next five years. Petasse explained that she worked at Incomati "so that the family would have money if we encountered something we needed." She gave some of her earnings to her husband and kept the rest for family needs.

Petasse and her husband had four children. In 1982, the eldest son, Francisco, worked in South Africa (as he had done since before independence) and returned to Mozambique only between contracts to visit his wife, Heliza Ngoenha, who lived with Petasse. They had had two children, but both died shortly after birth. Petasse also had two married daughters: one lived on Ilha, and the other lived in the district of Magude. Her seventeen-year-old son, Armando, was unemployed and lived at home. His last job was at the Incomati Sugar Estates, where he had worked for two months by using a friend's card and earned about 1,735 meticais a month. Previously, Armando was an agricultural worker on a vegetable garden in the Manhiça District, but he left the job because the salary was low and he had the opportunity to work two months at the Incomati. Like many young men, he did not consider the cooperative as an alternative to wage labor because the earnings were too low and irregular.

During colonialism, Petasse grew maize, sweet potatoes, beans, and cassava on the 2-hectare family farm, divided into two parcels—1.5 hectares and .5 hectares—that were separated by about two kilometers. She sold large quantities of maize to the Portuguese store owners and sweet potatoes to residents. In 1975, she left the Incomati Sugar Estates and returned to family farming combined with small artisan activities. According to Petasse she made and sold crockery because she was poor: "I learned to make clay pots because I was poor. It was important to eat and make an income." Petasse explained that "the [family] farm has not produced much because of a shortage of seed." She charged ten meticais for small pots, forty meticais for the medium size, and one hundred meticais for the large ones. Although she sold many of them, they brought in only small sums of money. With some of these earnings, though, Petasse rented an ox-plow to prepare her fields for the 1982–1983 season, paying the owner nine hundred meticais for three-days' work. Petasse and Heliza then sowed maize, cassava, and a little area of beans. Armando helped with the weeding on an irregular basis. The household's only means of production were two hoes, two machetes, and an ax.

In 1980, Petasse and her daughter-in-law joined the cooperative "because of the benefits. At the cooperative they produced maize and other crops. The family farm did not produce enough and I wanted access to the cooperative's production." As a new member, she contributed three hundred meticais to the general fund. At the cooperative she and Heliza usually worked with a hoe. In mid-1982, however, the household was short of money because Petasse's son was not sending it home regularly, so Heliza left the cooperative in July to work at the Incomati Sugar Estates so that they could buy food. With a borrowed work card from a friend, she worked there as an agricultural laborer for five months. At the end of December 1982, she returned to the cooperative, where the bookkeeper put her on probation for six months (February to July) because of her absences. During that period her attendance was regular, and she was readmitted as a member of the cooperative in August 1983. In the same six-month period, Petasse expanded her trading activities to make money to buy food. She paid a forty-metical return bus fare to Macia in Gaza Province and bought a quantity of tobacco for five hundred meticais from a private farmer. At home, she processed it and then sold small quantities to local residents, earning one thousand meticais. The sale of snuff became part of her regular income-generating activities.

For the 1982–1983 year, the main sources of income were Petasse's earnings from the cooperative (10,570 meticais), small artisan and trade activities (11,000 meticais), Heliza's five-month salary (9,000 meticais), Armando's contribution (1,735 meticais), and money sent from Francisco in South Africa (2,000 meticais). The total estimated household income was 34,305 meticais. Petasse spent most of her cooperative cash on food, clothing (two *capulanas*), and medical treatment from a *curandeiro*. She also invested some of it in her tobacco trade.

ERNESTO COSSA: EX-MINER/POOR PEASANT HOUSEHOLD

Ernesto Cossa, fifty-eight years old, lived alone with his wife, Amelia Ndava.[13] They had one son, António, who was seventeen years old. In 1982, António left home in an unsuccessful search for a job in Gaza Province; by mid-1983, he still was unemployed and his parents did not know how he managed to live. Ernesto Cossa never attended school and did not speak Portuguese, although at one time he attended the literacy classes at the cooperative. He had no formal training of any kind.

For his first job, Cossa worked as an agricultural laborer at a Portuguese-owned vegetable garden in Maputo. In 1945 he traveled to South Africa, where he worked approximately fifteen contracts, mostly at the Western Deep Level Mines Limited. He finished his last contract in 1975. Despite his extensive experience in the mines, Cossa never succeeded in earning more than the minimum wage. He began as an unskilled surface laborer and ended as a semiskilled feeder boy (a mechanic's aide). His starting salary was about 2 shillings a day in 1941, and his last contract paid 2.71 rand a day. Over the years, with the money he earned from South Africa, Cossa paid *lobolo* for his wife and bought food, clothes, and cattle.

In 1947, Cossa moved with his wife from Xinavane, his birthplace, to Ilha Josina Machel. The *régulo* gave him a large farm on which his wife cultivated maize, beans, and wheat. After each mine contract, he was obliged to pay 100 escudos to the *régulo,* in addition to a portion of his crop as tribute in kind. They also sold surpluses of maize and beans to the local store owners. In the 1950s, he joined the colonial cooperative so that during his seven-month residence in Mozambique between mining contracts he would not be rounded up for *chibalo,* forced labor. Cossa elaborated: "As migrant workers we were supposed to be exempt from *chibalo.* Yet there were many cases where men were rounded up in the middle of the night, especially if they failed to pay the *régulo* the expected 100 escudos upon return. Even though I paid a cash tribute to Timana [the *régulo*], I joined the cooperative to further reduce my chances of doing forced labor."

When Cossa returned from South Africa in 1975, he tried unsuccessfully to find employment in the capital, Maputo. In his words, "I looked for work in Maputo but I could not find anything. There were great line-ups for employment. People needed a family connection to get a good job." He resettled in Ilha and assisted his wife in plowing their family farm with draft animals and other seasonal duties. After his oxen died in 1977 and he was unable to replace them, Cossa gave a section of his landholding to a friend; he no longer had the means of production to cultivate a large farm. By 1982 his family farm was only one hectare and he owned two hoes, a machete, and an ax. Cossa and Amelia also raised a few chickens and ducks, which they bought with the money earned from her monthly wages at the Incomati Sugar Estates.

For the 1981–1982 season, they did not have sufficient money to rent an ox-plow, so, for the first time, Cossa and Amelia had to prepare their family farm by hoe. Given the heavy clay loam soils, which could not be cultivated easily by hoe, productivity was very low. For the following season, Cossa decided to exchange his labor for draft animal use to prepare his field. He hired himself out to Pedro Novela, a cooperative member and a farmer with oxen and a plow, to form a production team. He then worked full-time plowing the fields of Novela as well as the landholdings of other peasant farmers who hired Novela's animals, and in return, Cossa was allowed to plow his own farm. On their own farm, Cossa and Amelia sowed maize, cassava, sweet potatoes, beans, and cabbage for family consumption.

As soon as the cooperative opened its membership to all residents, he joined because he had no possibilities of wage employment and was used to working continuously, although not in agriculture. According to him "it was the only way to arrange food. The cooperative worked because it had a water pump, the land was better, and there were more people." Given his reliance on cash from mine labor, Cossa was anxious that the cooperative begin paying "monthly wages" as soon as possible. In the 1980s, however, as it became difficult to find food to purchase on the market even when one had cash, Cossa came to appreciate the cooperative's distribution system: part of the harvest initially was distributed to all members and the remainder was sold in small quantities throughout the season. During his three-day shift in the cooperative, Cossa's job was to train individuals in animal traction and to supervise their work in the fields.

Cossa's wife began to work at the Incomati Sugar Estates in 1973. Like most women employed there, Amelia's task was to weed and cut the sugarcane. In 1982 she was paid 65 meticais per day; this daily wage increased to 100 meticais per day when the cane had to be cut and harvested. Her shift was in the morning, which enabled her to till the family farm in the afternoon. Amelia's other daily household duties included collecting firewood, fetching water from a neighbor's well, and cooking the meals. When there were products at the stores, she stood in the line, often returning without purchases. According to Cossa, the money from Incomati paid for the food, and the earnings from the cooperative covered their clothing expenses. During the 1982–1983 season, the opening of the consumer store accounted for his almost perfect attendance at the producer cooperative. His earnings (11,760 meticais), combined with his wife's salary (18,000 meticais), gave them a total income of 29,760 meticais for the year, barely sufficient to sustain the household.

## Reflections on the Case Studies

These case studies and other interviews with peasant farmers show that cooperative participation meant different things for different classes and social groups. For groups 1 and 2, consisting of middle-peasant households, the cooperative provided an opportunity for upward mobility (i.e., to develop skills through training courses). These peasant farmers rapidly adapted their economic activities to the market situation, as cooperative participation brought valuable access to membership in a consumer cooperative and to inputs that could also be used on their family farms. Their benefits increased with the arrival of Project CO-1, which provided seeds, fertilizer, agricultural hand tools, and equipment for sale, as well as family extension services. For those with access to South African wages, however, the incentive to join was less than for those who depended on cash from a monthly paycheck in Mozambique. Women whose husbands or sons regularly sent them cash and goods from South Africa usually were not interested in joining cooperatives, or they gave collective work a low priority. Households with regular access to cash were able to hire part-time laborers, usually women, to do the most difficult work on their fields and had little interest in adding collective labor to their activities. In the minority were women like Olinda Fulana who not only worked in cooperative agriculture out of a sense of duty to the government but also understood that government policy could change suddenly against smallholders, making it wise to belong to the collective.

For group 3, comprised of poor and vulnerable people, it was politically astute to belong to a cooperative because it was a state policy. For the very poor, especially those not strong enough to farm a landholding on their own, the small amount of cash and produce distributed by the cooperative was vital. Access to food was the most important incentive: working at producer cooperatives enabled people to join the consumer cooperative and to buy scarce food and other commodities at official prices. In addition, cooperative produce was on sale in small quantities to members. Individuals in this group often joined the cooperative to make up for land and equipment shortages. The low productivity of the family farms and the problems of replacing their means of production also meant that the cooperative was one way of spreading their risks.

Beyond these differences, the cooperative sector played a useful role in household economic strategies for all these groups. The examples given illustrate that peasant farmers' reproductive base relied on a complex interdependence between family farm production and wage labor, and to a lesser extent on cooperative production.

Another aspect revealed in the interviews was gender-differentiated attitudes to subsistence and commodity production within cooperatives. Those men who joined cooperatives gave a high priority to producing for sale and preferred a regular monthly salary. For women, the main advantage of cooperative membership was not cash distribution but access to the consumer cooperative and the possibility of taking a loan if there was food at the local stores at a time when the crops in their fields were not yet ready. Direct distribution and sale of cooperative produce to members were also more important for women than men. When men earned cash their job was done, whereas women still had to walk and wait in line to procure food.

This is not to say that women were not also interested in cash distribution, as there was ample indication that they were indeed; rather, the priorities of men and women for the "mix" of cash, kind, and shopping facilities were different. In a 1983 random sample of ninety-five Ilha cooperative members, consisting of sixty-eight women and twenty-seven men, about 68 percent of the women said they joined the cooperative for access to products (food, seeds, and consumer goods) compared to 32 percent who belonged for the products and cash. None of them joined for the money only. In comparison, approximately 18 percent of the men said they enrolled for the products only, 78 percent joined for the products and cash, and only 4 percent cited money as the main incentive.

Cooperative agriculture was attractive to, and advantageous for, those people for whom kin and marriage relations did not form a reliable source of economic, social, and emotional support. In addition to its role as an economic enterprise, the cooperative was a social body that functioned in an emotionally supportive way. For example, the group was concerned with visiting the sick and elderly and dealing with personal problems. The cooperative also helped poor individuals build or repair their homes and lent members money to deal with household crises such as funeral expenses.

It was widows and widowers, women whose husbands or sons gave them no financial help, and others without familial support networks who were most committed to the cooperative movement. This phenomena was not restricted to Ilha Josina Machel; in cooperatives in the periurban areas, known as the Green Zones, and elsewhere in southern Mozambique, research has found that members tended to be "the single and the elderly."[14] For those for whom the family or kinship system was not a reliable source of support, the cooperative became an important alternative based on working together and meeting regularly to solve common problems. The rising number of female-headed households not only indicated the growing crisis in gender relations but also contributed to the realization that for many women the traditional kinship system no longer provided a minimum of economic security (i.e., access to food and means of production). Through cooperating along nonkin lines within cooperatives, such women could replace or supplement mutual aid based on kinship and marriage.

## The Impact of Village Relations on Collective Farming

The control and regulation of the labor force in the cooperatives was affected by traditional customs of the area in addition to individual household strategies. For example, the participation of nonmembers in the maize harvest during the month of March played havoc with collective organization. Cooperative 25 de Setembro, as well as other cooperatives and family farms, employed outside labor to collect their maize. People from the Magude and Manhiça Districts of Maputo and from districts in Gaza arrived on the island to participate in *corimela*, a traditional custom practiced in southern Mozambique during periods of natural disasters; these individuals were traveling from an area affected by drought or flood to other areas in search of seed to sow the following agricultural season. They offered their labor to farmers in return for a determined amount of seed. By 1983 the custom had changed; the seeker of seed not only harvested the crop but also paid in cash for the seed.

At Cooperative 25 de Setembro, a total of sixty-five nonmembers harvested maize. Individuals worked one day in the field and collected the crop, and afterward they bought twenty kilos of maize at a cost of 750 meticais. These nonresidents of the island consisted of two different groups. First, there were those from Mapulanguene, a locality in the district of Magude, adjacent to the Transvaal in South Africa. The exchange had gone the other way in 1977, with the flooding of the Incomati and Limpopo Valleys, when residents from the village, including the president and the bookkeeper of Cooperative 25 de Setembro, went to Mapulanguene and offered their labor to peasant farmers in return for seeds. Pedro Novela, the bookkeeper, described his search:

> In January 1977, I left with Simião Tlemo [another cooperative member] and Fernando Chavango [president] in search of seeds. At first I went from house to house looking for maize, sleeping anywhere. We finally found work at Mapulanguene. Chavango returned to Ilha after fifteen days. Simião returned in February. I stayed away until March as the island was flooded and I could not swim. Simião and I managed to return with three sacks of maize each [about 270 kilos]. The population of Ilha has not participated in *corimela*, at least in large numbers, outside of the island since 1977. It is because of the past relationship with those of Mapulanguene that the president and the cooperative members do not refuse to sell at least twenty kilos of maize to each of them.[15]

The second group was comprised of individuals from districts in Gaza Province who were severely affected by the drought. Most of these people were women in search of seeds. Cooperative 25 de Setembro directed the majority of these individuals to other cooperatives or family farms in neighborhoods 4, 5, 6, and 7, which were less affected by the drought than neighborhoods 1, 2, and 3. These neighborhoods are illustrated in map 4. One of the four women who spent a night at the brigade's house, Marta Tivana of Macia, Gaza Province, described her efforts to acquire seeds:

> I live in the communal village of Agostinho Neto in Macia. I have three chil-
> dren, two of whom I left at home [she was nursing a child under one year].
> My husband used to work in Maputo and then South Africa but he does not
> work now. We heard that Ilha Josina Machel had maize through others that
> returned with twenty kilos. I came with a friend from the village, prepared to
> buy maize with money. Our husbands did not oppose our leaving as we are
> all looking for food. We left Macia yesterday. We took a bus to Magude and
> slept there last night. This morning we took another bus to the intersection
> and walked here. We passed through neighborhoods 4 to 7 and managed to
> buy maize from peasants' fields. Each of us bought twenty kilos at six hun-
> dred meticais (thirty meticais/kilo). We will return to our homes tomorrow
> using the same transportation route. We plan to sow the maize seed in our
> fields.[16]

These women did not work for the maize. In contrast, some of the women from Gaza were transported in 1.5-ton trucks owned by Mozambican miners who worked in South Africa and were on six months leave between contracts. These men charged the women for transportation costs to Ilha Josina Machel and often offered their services to the cooperatives.

At Cooperative 25 de Setembro, two men from Gaza transported the maize in their truck from the cooperative's field to the warehouse alongside women who carried maize on their heads and the cooperative's ox-carts pulled by *trop-icultors*. By the end of the morning, the truck had made five trips from the field to the warehouse, transporting a total of fifteen hundred kilos. The owner of the truck explained his presence on the island: "I arrived on Ilha yesterday with my cousin from Xai-Xai [the capital of Gaza]. We were told by Pedro Novela to return today. Since we had a truck it was no problem. When we returned today, we brought three people in the back; each paid the equivalent of the bus fare from Xai-Xai to Ilha Josina Machel. Both my cousin and I are going to receive sixty kilos of maize each for our services. I plan to eat forty kilos with my fam-ily and sow the other twenty kilos."[17]

He went on to explain that it was the first time he had provided this type of service as he had just recently bought the truck: "My cousin and I both work in the Kloof mines in South Africa. We are between contracts and plan to return together in July. Before independence, we both worked in South Africa. I have worked six contracts. I do not want the road closed to the mines because there is food and water in South Africa. With the money I earned in the mines I bought this truck, which I will leave with my family in Gaza, for one thousand rand. [He earned one hundred rand a month.] When I return to South Africa I want to buy another truck."[18] For their services, Cooperative 25 de Setembro sold each of them sixty kilos of maize, approximately forty kilos more than the norm for outsiders.

At Cooperative 25 de Setembro, the leaders were careful to ensure that the members were the first to purchase forty kilos of maize and that only a limited number of nonmembers participated in the harvest. The bookkeeper and the production manager established a system of stamped cards that were distributed to nonmembers, and they then recorded the number of people in an exercise book.[19] The other cooperatives were more disorganized. Cooperative Agostinho Neto, for example, which had serious problems of labor organization, uneven participation, and a frequently absent president, sold maize to nonresidents of Ilha before it sold to its members. According to the literacy instructor at the cooperative:

> The production manager agreed to let outsiders pick the maize from the field. The agreement was that they could buy 40 kilos of maize for fifteen hundred meticais. These outsiders from Ilha began to work in the cooperative yesterday. No record was kept of the number of people but based on the 480 kilos sold, it is possible to calculate that twelve nonmembers collected maize from the field. Today more people arrived. In the morning, I counted a total of thirty-eight people: eight from Incoluane, seven from Chihenhice, ten from Xinavane, seven from Macia and six from Chibuto (districts of Maputo and Gaza Provinces). By the afternoon, more people arrived. They came because they heard that Ilha had maize. Tomorrow, those people will work in the fields. On Sunday (four days later) the cooperative will sell maize to the members at a price of five hundred meticais per 20 kilos.[20]

The situation at Ilha Josina Machel became so chaotic with the influx of nonresidents that the administrator called a meeting with the inhabitants. He encouraged individuals to conserve their maize, and cooperatives were advised to store their production to avoid starvation during the months between the two harvests.[21] According to the president, "the members of Cooperative 25 de Setembro deposited sufficient maize in the warehouse to last until September when the second harvest will be ready. Cooperative Agostinho Neto [in comparison] only has sufficient maize to sell to its members until May because the leaders sold too much to outsiders."[22]

One of the technicians who assisted the cooperatives in neighborhoods 4 and 5 described the situation of the family sector for cooperative members and nonmembers: "Peasants are walking to Xinavane and Manhiça transporting maize on their heads. They go with their children and other relatives. Others sell on the island but not for meticais. They exchange the maize for fish or for sugar. The sugar comes from the Incomati or Maragra plantations."[23] These peasant farmers produced a greater maize surplus on their farms than previous years, and they were determined to market their production. Given the collapse of the market and the devaluation of the metical, they resorted to barter relationships, which were widely practiced by both the government and ordinary citizens in the early 1980s.

During the maize harvest, the technicians explained to the cooperative leaders that the participation of nonmembers affected the planning and organization of labor. The response of the leaders of Cooperative 25 de Setembro was that natural disasters were not predictable and floods might send those of Ilha Josina Machel to the same villages of the peasant farmers who harvested their maize.[24] This decision was understandable, in a situation of high insecurity and uncertainty, to maintain such "safety links" even at the cost of some disorganization of the labor process.

## Conclusion

Small-scale agricultural producers combined diverse economic activities to ensure the survival and reproduction of their households and community. At Ilha Josina Machel, their strategies of integrating cooperative production with other economic activities varied depending on factors including their household size and availability of labor power, monthly earnings, and the sources of income. The different socioeconomic conditions and income-generating options meant that a single blueprint for cooperative development was simply impossible.

Ilha peasant farmers, like agricultural producers in the rest of the country, marketed less crops after independence than before. Middle and wealthier peasant farmers described how they were unable to market their produce and buy goods after the Portuguese shopkeepers and settler farmers departed, but they also explained how Frelimo's agricultural policies made inputs difficult to obtain and consumer goods scarce. Centralized policies, including low producer prices set by the state, undermined incentives for crop marketing.

In 1983, both the village cooperatives and family farms harvested a bumper maize crop. This bountiful harvest was more a result of increased services and inputs supplied to peasant farmers than a vagary of the weather: Project CO-1 technicians had ensured that co-op members had seeds, hand tools, plows, and in some cases, tractors, at the optimal time to prepare the collective and individual fields. They also had provided technical assistance and extension services to the cooperatives and family farms. The consumer cooperative, stocked with increasingly scarce consumer goods at official prices, was another incentive for peasants to increase their production. After the farmers harvested their crop, they created a thriving local market, selling their maize above the fixed state price. The 1983 bumper crop showed that Mozambican farmers, like agricultural producers elsewhere in Africa, generally respond to market incentives.

While Ilha peasant farmers were interested in earning cash, they were more than just profit-maximizing petty commodity producers looking to augment income without having to measure impact upon family or community.[25] Given southern Mozambique's history of recurrent natural disasters, combined with state indifference or neglect, they took a wider view of their self-interest. After the maize harvest, for example, cooperative members chose to store less food stocks in order to maintain relations with farmers in Mapulanguene. Peasants based their decision more on rational long-term planning—that is, it was part of their safety net—than on a desire to exit beyond state control or to escape the demands of socialism. The maize surplus was invested in protecting their continual access to a reciprocal village "survival strategy." But as the war spread throughout the countryside, it jeopardized these individual and community survival strategies.

**Part 3**

# The Transition from Socialism to Capitalism

# 7

# Postsocialist Mozambique and Land Reform, 1984–1993

**In the post-1983 period,** external factors and the war against Renamo assured the failure of Mozambique's socialist experiment. The two main constraints were the lack of foreign exchange and the destruction of productive capacity and human capital, leaving Frelimo confronting two unpalatable alternatives: continue to pursue a failing socialism, or open its economy to capitalism. The leadership chose the latter. From the mid-1980s on, the state continued with policies that were antithetical to peasant farmers' interests but now in the name of capitalism and with the approval of international finance. This chapter examines Mozambique's transition from socialism to capitalism, with an emphasis on the dramatic shift in state power and class alliances.

In 1984 Mozambique joined the IMF and the World Bank. Subsequently, in 1987, the government agreed to an orthodox structural adjustment program, the Economic Rehabilitation Program (PRE), which marked a sharp reversal of Frelimo's past economic policies and rhetoric. This program, renamed the Economic and Social Rehabilitation Program (PRES) in 1991, represented a move away from the centralized socialist planning of the early 1980s toward a much greater reliance on market forces.

While the PRE facilitated the renegotiation of Mozambique's debt and access to desperately needed foreign aid and credit, the political price for economic relief was high: it led to the weakening of state autonomy as Western international financial institutions, aided by a variety of other agencies and organizations, took over the economy and the direction of the country's development. The reforms called for by Mozambique's austerity program also reshaped the power and privileges of the government and others directly dependent upon the state. As the state reduced its economic role, notably through privatizing those enterprises that were nationalized following independence, many individuals in the state apparatus lost their positions, including directors of large-scale farms and factories as well as heads of operational divisions in the Ministries of Agriculture and Planning. The dominant internal political force shifted from the modernizing state bureaucracy to the private sector, largely dependent upon the resources made available by external forces: the World Bank, multinational enterprises, regional development banks, and NGOs. Privatization of state assets also had an impact on rural households. While some state farms and factories were sold to foreign and national investors, transferred to their former owners, or became joint venture companies (JVCs, enterprises owned jointly by the state and by domestic or foreign capital), others went bankrupt and closed, resulting in urban as well as rural unemployment. Many rural households no longer had access to a regular wage income, jeopardizing their subsistence and reproduction.

At the same time, the war, coupled with the hardship of the economic recovery program, affected party coherence and party domination of the state. The once unified Frelimo became fragmented and incapable of providing a consistent set of policies that could form the basis for a national development strategy. The leadership disagreed on the pace and means for reaching its goal of a capitalist market economy as well as the role of the central regime during the transition period. Since the mid-1980s, then, the party ceased to be a unifying force, and ordinary citizens started to question its legitimacy.

These political and economic changes also incited intense competition over resources, especially land. While private property still was not legal, an intensive struggle for land emerged. In the periurban areas, peasant farmers (i.e., small-scale farmers who own or at least have access to plows and oxen, rely on family labor, and market a small proportion of their crops) and cooperatives fought to keep their fields from private farmers (i.e., capitalist producers who own their means of production, often mechanized equipment, employ full-time wage labor, and market a significant proportion of their agricultural production), many of them well-positioned senior government officials, ministers, and veterans from the independence war. In the rural areas, peasant farmers and cooperatives battled private farmers, both Mozambicans and expatriates, and foreign-owned multinational corporations.[1] Given its financial constraints, Frelimo aligned with private capital (foreign and domestic) and large-scale private farmers.

In this period, the setting was prepared for a postwar Mozambique in which the country would assume its pre-1975 status as a provider of services (e.g., transport and tourism) and labor for South Africa. International capital (especially South African and British) and its corresponding financial institutions reasserted their dominance, while the restricted Mozambican economy was firmly reintegrated into the South African economy. The country's resubordination to South Africa, however, was only one aspect of its transition from socialism to capitalism. International finance institutions came to dictate economic policy-making while Western NGOs substituted themselves for state agencies, especially in the countryside. In addition, private foreign firms set up agricultural enterprises employing quasi–forced labor methods and forced cultivation practices. Even Frelimo itself contributed to the reinstatement of both colonial labor policies (by enforcing cotton production) and colonial administration (by restoring the system of indirect rule). In some rural areas, for example, there was a return to chiefly authority, in which rehabilitated traditional chiefs were mandated to govern rural populations and to collect taxes on behalf of the government.

Given that Mozambique did embrace capitalism, a current debate among scholars pertains to the nature of capitalist development in the country. On the one hand, critics of privatization have argued that what has been happening in Mozambique is tantamount to recolonization—that is, a return to the colonial period of foreign monopolies and super profits, forced labor and forced cash-crop production, and Portuguese and Asian control of rural trading networks.[2] Kenneth Hermele predicted that the combination of two features—the lack of an autonomous base in a national class alliance and the increasing dominant economic and political role of South Africa in the region—will lead to a weak, dependent form of capitalism in Mozambique that will serve the South African economy with labor, transport routes, markets, and raw materials. Similarly, John S. Saul emphasized Mozambique's "resubordination to South African and global capitalist dictate."[3] Other scholars, like David N. Plank, focused on how the country's unmanageable debt and dependence on aid had seriously eroded Mozambique's sovereignty. Consequently, donor agencies and northern NGOs, or the "new missionaries," as Joseph Hanlon labeled them, had indirectly recolonized the country by taking over many of the social and economic functions formerly performed by the state.[4] Going beyond Hanlon's use of recolonization as a metaphor, Plank employed the concept to suggest that in Mozambique, "the most likely successor to post-colonial sovereignty will be neo-colonial vassalage, in which Western powers assume direct and open-ended control over the administration, security and economic policies of 'deteriorated' states under the banner of the U.N. and various donors."[5] Despite the varied emphases among these scholars, their writings share a focus on the extent to which policy has been dictated from outside. Three main points emerged in the recolonization literature: (1) the Mozambican state had become dependent on the World Bank, IMF, and the external aid community; (2) the indigenous capitalists lacked their own capital and owed their existence to external investment; and (3) the privatization of Mozambique's industrial and agricultural giants had severely weakened the ability of the state to exercise strategic guidance over the economy.

On the other hand, new research has suggested a more complex view of what has been taking place in Mozambique. In her article on capitalist development in Nampula and Cabo Delgado, M. Anne Pitcher argued that through privatization the state has tried to reconstruct its authority and reconsolidate itself. While privatization constrained the government's capacity to shape the economy, it also offered opportunities for Frelimo to seek political legitimacy at the national and local levels. The state supported many Mozambican entrepreneurs, enabling them to buy companies and land—thus creating clientele and patronage networks. In this way, Frelimo successfully cultivated a new constituency. While Pitcher's research challenges those who classify Mozambique's ongoing privatization as recolonization, we must have studies in other areas and sectors before we can draw more general conclusions.

My conclusions based on research in rural southern Mozambique have stressed that those who have benefited the most from the government's land reforms (e.g., selling of state farms and granting of land concessions) have been foreign-owned multinational corporations, foreign private capital, and Frelimo party members and supporters.[6] Indeed, as Pitcher conceded, foreign investors from Great Britain, Portugal, and South Africa have been the principal beneficiaries of the divestiture of large state farms and industries. As of 1993, forty thousand hectares belonging to the state-farm sector were divested, mostly to large, non-Mozambican capital interests.[7] Moreover, Frelimo had taken advantage of privatization by allocating land and agribusinesses to government members, local party officials, administrators, and other supporters, especially in Maputo, Gaza, Nampula, and Sofala.[8] In most cases, peasants were largely excluded from the process.

Much of the foreign investment (and divestment struggles) in the countryside has been in strategic areas where there already existed some infrastructure, markets, and transportation (roads, railways, and ports). In its early attempts to implement a policy of rapid development, Frelimo concentrated its resources in the same areas where colonial capital had invested, namely, commercial land, or "land with access to water for irrigation or year round cultivation, land which is located close to major transport circuits or in peri-urban areas with good access to markets, land which is sufficiently fertile for demanding commercial crops such as cotton, land planted in permanent crops, and grazing land with easy access to watering points for cattle."[9] Not only was the south given preference over other regions, but even within regions, certain districts received more support than others because of preexisting conditions. In the 1990s, Portuguese, British, and South African private capital also has shown a decided preference for these same areas, thereby further deepening the uneven development of Mozambique.

## Undermining the State: War, Structural Adjustment, and NGOs

In 1984 Frelimo still was capable of policy innovation. In response to the Fourth Party Congress decisions, the government tried to reverse economic decline by implementing a series of reforms predicated on four main policy and institutional changes: (1) regional prioritization, (2) administrative decentralization, (3) liberalization of commercial activity, and (4) allocation of resources on the basis of economic pragmatism rather than ideology.

In spite of these changes in policy, South African destabilization campaigns undermined Frelimo's efforts to implement its land and agrarian reforms. Pretoria continued to support Renamo, although the 1984 Nkomati Accord required the governments of both South Africa and Mozambique to prevent their territories from being used as bases for attacks on the other. By 1986 the war threatened the subsistence and security of millions of Mozambicans. More than 2.9 million rural dwellers were forced off their land; of these, 1.7 million were displaced inside the country, while the remainder fled across the borders. The government estimated that the number of those in need of emergency aid was 4.5 million, or about one-third of the entire population.[10] Given the context—a devastating war and growing foreign exchange shortage—Mozambique adopted its first structural adjustment program in 1987.

The Mozambican PRE contained the typical salient features of other IMF austerity programs, including the expansion of market forces; easy access to capital for the private sector; dramatic devaluations of the national currency; emphasis on fiscal responsibility; cuts in the civil service, government subsidies, and social services; and the sale of state-owned enterprises. Despite the additional protection for the social sectors (health and education) in 1991, the overall objectives of the program have remained fundamentally the same since its initiation: to reverse the decline in production and restore a minimum level of consumption and income for all the population, particularly in the rural areas; to reduce substantially the domestic financial imbalances and strengthen the external accounts and reserves; to enhance efficiency and establish the conditions for a return to higher levels of economic growth once the security situation and other exogenous constraints eased; to reintegrate official and parallel markets; and to restore orderly financial relationships with trading partners and creditors.

The results of Mozambique's structural adjustment program for the six-year period 1987–1993 were uneven. In the first three years, the PRE reversed the economic decline that had characterized the pre-1987 period. Thus, in spite of the war, the Mozambican economy experienced some growth under the program. The gross domestic product (GDP)—a key indicator for those measuring the effectiveness of structural adjustment programs—increased by 4 percent in 1987 and by 4.5 percent both in 1988 and 1989.[11] The PRE also was successful in undercutting the parallel economy. At the end of 1989, the currency and prices had real value, markets were unified, declining levels of production were reversed, and market agricultural production had increased.

But those positive trends did not last. In 1990, the economy experienced the lowest annual rate of increase since the program was introduced. The GDP only grew by an estimated 1 percent, the balance of trade deteriorated by about 15 percent, and the overall balance of payments declined by about 4 percent. Exports rose by an estimated 4 percent, failing to meet the 9 percent target. Inflation, which had run at 30 percent in 1989, rose to 40 percent in 1990 and climbed to 55 percent in 1992. During the year 1990–1991, growth rates again slowed to less than 2 percent due to the worsening war situation, poor rains, and a lag in foreign aid disbursements. The regional drought in southern Africa reduced Mozambique's GDP still further, by 1.4 percent, in 1992.[12] For three consecutive years, then, the GDP declined. Although the war was a major factor in the country's continuing economic crisis, the economic slowdown also was attributed to the serious inadequacies of the recovery program itself.

Not all sectors, regions, or social classes benefited or suffered equally under Mozambique's austerity program. Agriculture's share of the capital budget decreased from an average 24 percent in the 1975–1986 period to 10 percent in 1989–1990, even though this sector was supposed to be key to the rehabilitation strategy.[13] And the content of state expenditures changed little in the adjustment period. Planned expenditures gave priority to a few large-scale, capital-intensive export crop projects in Maputo and Gaza Provinces and the Beira corridor in Sofala, deepening the pattern of regional imbalance.[14] According to the Ministry of Agriculture's three-year investment program for 1991–1993, approximately eleven of its one hundred projects accounted for half of total agricultural investments, with most of the funds earmarked for irrigation projects on state and commercial farms. Only one of the eleven projects—basic seed production—was aimed primarily at supporting the peasant sector. The agricultural investment budget thus reinforced the state's ongoing neglect of and indifference to peasant agriculture.

Just as rural areas were not uniform beneficiaries of PRE reforms, not all agricultural producers have gained from the liberalization of prices for crops and from the renewed functioning of official market channels. Data for 1987 to 1989 show that the initial incentive of available goods did not sustain surplus production: a substantial rise of 79 percent in crops sold by peasant farmers in

1987 was followed by smaller increases of 16 percent in 1988 and 17 percent in 1989.[15] Marketed agricultural production for 1990 showed a decline of over 20 percent, the first time that an increase had not been recorded since 1985.[16] It was negative for 1992 as a result of the worsening drought but increased in 1993 as a result of heavy rainfall at the right time and the peace accord between Frelimo and Renamo.[17]

Although the war and climatic conditions accounted for some of the fluctuation in agricultural production during this period, structural problems were also significant. Farmers and traders confronted difficulties in marketing agricultural surpluses and getting access to required credits for inputs. In 1987, for example, Ilha Josina Machel farmers and cooperatives harvested their second consecutive year of bumper crops, including large surpluses of maize, beans, squash, and other vegetables.[18] But they were unable to sell most of their produce due to marketing and transport problems. The government structure responsible for commercial agriculture in Maputo Province, DIPROM, did not provide the local stores with even basic goods, so there were no incentives for Ilha residents to market their surpluses. Indeed, according to a Maputo journalist visiting the island, "the stores only have empty shelves and the employees have nothing to sell." Consequently the local population was forced to engage in barter, often accepting the first offer. They exchanged maize for cattle, kerosene, and sugar as well as other products not produced locally. Individuals who sought food—in some cases for their own consumption, and in other cases for resale in large urban centers or other places where these crops were scarce—brought these items to the community. On behalf of the residents, the local administrator, Matata Bombarda Tembe, explained that, "We are not hungry for food but for manufactured goods. Given the problems that emerge in the absence of an organized commercial trading network, peasants are forced to sell their surpluses in the parallel market, not in the normal channels, and in some cases, the peasants do not feel motivated to increase their production because of the risk of not being able to sell it." The cooperatives' main problem was the lack of transportation to sell their crops outside the community. Fernando Chavango, president of Cooperative 25 de Setembro, lamented that they were forced to feed most of their carrots to the pigs that the cooperative raised because they had no transport. Similarly, the preceding year, they had harvested sixty tons of squash and fed it to the cooperative's animals for the same reason.[19]

In addition to these structural problems, other reasons help account for production decline in the 1987–1993 period. The peasantry's terms of trade had deteriorated since 1986, and, consequently, some peasants had reduced their marketed output. Crop price increases simply did not match the high prices for tools and consumer goods. In Nampula Province, for example, peasant producers in 1986 (i.e., before the PRE) had to sell 10.4 kilos of rice to buy one meter of cloth (at official prices), whereas in 1988 they had to sell 33 kilos, and in 1990 the exchange had risen to more than 80 kilos of rice for the same meter of cloth.[20] Official government figures and independent sources showed that a similar imbalance in terms of trade came to exist for other crops as well.[21] Referring to the reduced purchasing power of the peasantry on Ilha Josina Machel, Administrator Tembe declared that, "the official prices of agricultural products do not compensate for the current prices of manufactured goods."[22]

Price increases for consumer and capital goods sharply limited effective demand and thus the growth of domestic markets for both agricultural and industrial production. In the case of agriculture, crops frequently ended up being stored in warehouses and eventually rotting, as consumer demand fell and market outlets simply could not be found. In 1993, for example, surplus crops produced by peasant farmers in Nampula, Tete, and Gaza decayed because there was no local market for them. The hungry people in these provinces, of whom there were plenty, did not have the money to buy the surpluses, and the foreign donors of food aid preferred to ship their own grain from the other side of the world rather than to buy locally.[23] Thus, more than twenty thousand tons of surplus from the 1993 harvest, mainly grain, remained in the hands of Nampula peasants. Prior to the war, Nampula had supplied food for the thousands of workers on the state-owned tea estates in the neighboring province of Zambézia, but Renamo burned down many of the processing plants during the war, and the tea industry was decimated. Meanwhile, the state marketing board, Agricom, was unable to buy the peasant surpluses because IMF-imposed credit ceilings did not allow it to borrow sufficient money from the banks.

The IMF's and World Bank's fixation with "getting the price right" for farmers' crops, inputs, and supplies neglected other critical features required for successful rural production. These organizations assumed rural producers were ready to increase production rapidly just in response to incentives of prices and consumer goods. Yet, as we have seen, Mozambicans had reduced their marketed production because of numerous factors in addition to low prices, such as the collapse of services and supplies, lack of consumption goods, and poor terms of trade. By focusing narrowly on price, these institutions abstracted one activity—exchange—from the totality of relations of production and power. In many areas of the African countryside, for example, decontrol of prices has done little to help peasant farmers because traders, often collaborating with local officials, were able to exercise monopsonistic control (especially where the roads were in need of repair) and thus maintained unfavorable terms of trade for small-scale producers, who often received only a fraction of the selling price in urban areas.[24]

In addition, the World Bank and IMF failed to take into account three significant factors: (1) an ongoing war, (2) a historically weak infrastructure and marketing network, and (3) a poorly developed agricultural extension service. During this period the war remained the major obstacle to economic recovery. By disrupting production and transport over wide areas of the country, the war cut off large numbers of people from any direct contact with the domestic market and effectively prevented the PRE from operating in many parts of the country. Where peasants remained on the land, Renamo's disruption of rural commercial networks effectively prevented many agricultural producers from marketing their crops, causing many to give up producing surpluses altogether. A large part of the commercial activity that did take place in rural Mozambique did so under the protection of the military, by means of slow-moving military convoys and centralized stockpiling of agricultural produce and manufactured goods in defensible district capitals. The war imposed this cumbersome way of organizing commerce and caused a bottleneck in terms of commercial expansion and productive growth.

On Ilha Josina Machel commercial activity came to a halt in 1989. That year Renamo attacked the locality and totally destroyed the two best-managed private rural shops—one owned by Carlos Majonane and the other run by Albino Bila. According to Majonane, among the items destroyed in his shop were food crops and such educational material as books and pencils stocked in preparation for the start of the school year.[25] Without these shops in operation, Ilha residents had even fewer outlets to market their crops and to buy the goods they needed. Between 1990 and 1992, Renamo stepped up its armed activities in Ilha Josina Machel, killing many residents, destroying infrastructure (including the warehouses at Cooperative 25 de Setembro), and planting land mines, preventing families from cultivating a large portion of the available land.[26] While most residents were eventually forced to seek refuge in the nearby towns, cooperative leader Fernando Chavango recounted that, "some people who slept in Xinavane returned during the day and worked two hours on their farms and even in the cooperatives, including Cooperative 25 de Setembro, in order to grow food for themselves and their families."[27]

Second, Mozambique's weak infrastructure and marketing network further constrained agricultural production. The lack of roads, bridges, shops, warehouses, and means of transport was a major hindrance to commercial activity and economic growth. The enormous destruction caused by the war to this already meager infrastructure only exacerbated the problems. Some private traders took advantage of the situation and levied a "war tax"—that is, sold consumer goods at higher prices to peasants and bought their surpluses below regular prices—in areas where rural producers had no alternatives and where the war entailed enormous risks.[28] But more frequently, the private sector was reluctant to assume the responsibility for regions of the country where security problems were frequent, where the marketed quantities were limited, or where products marketed were of low commercial value. Moreover, private traders were restricted by a lack of capital and credit for the purchase of trucks, building of warehouses, and purchase of crops. In the early 1990s, they were more active in rural areas than they had been a few years earlier, but there still was virtually no competition among them. As elsewhere in Africa, this contributed to deterioration in the peasantry's terms of trade.[29] Meanwhile, the role of Agricom was scaled down to a buyer of last resort, but insufficient resources prevented it from acting in this capacity.

Third, Mozambique's agricultural extension service remained relatively small and lacking in technical and material support, which made it difficult to sustain increased agricultural production. Extension was oriented primarily toward certain agricultural priority areas and was overwhelmingly gender biased. In the Chokwe irrigation scheme in Gaza, for example, the middle and wealthier peasants, primarily men, were the major recipients of the family sector's extension services. The extension agents (all men) preferred to work with male farmers who owned their means of production and showed initiative, and, therefore, were easier to assist, even though most peasant farmers were women. Because agricultural extension was nearly nonexistent for the peasantry in the colonial era (except for cotton), the World Bank did not consider it essential to restore rural production.[30]

Meanwhile, the situation in the towns and cities deteriorated. Poverty increased for most urban dwellers, while a small minority (e.g., the private commercial sector) accumulated a large share of wealth. In 1989 the government documented that two-thirds of the population—approximately ten million people—were living in conditions of absolute poverty. The World Bank's compensatory social programs in 1991 only targeted the "vulnerable groups," defined as the poorest 10 percent, thereby excluding the great majority of Mozambicans who lived in precarious conditions.[31]

The living standards of urban wage earners deteriorated because of soaring prices, the removal of food and housing subsidies, and fees for social services like health and education. The decline in living standards also led to a reduction of real purchasing power and a rise in malnutrition.[32] Periodic increments to the minimum wage rate did not keep pace with higher living costs. Atalia Macamo, a cleaner in the sales department at Matola Industrial Company, a major food complex on the outskirts of Maputo, underscored the situation of countless urban dwellers who found themselves caught in the squeeze between wages and rising prices: "Life is better now. There are lots of things to buy. There are clothes. There is everything. You don't have to go to Swaziland to buy things. But there is no money."[33]

The plight of the urban poor was worsened by the flood of displaced persons from the rural areas who tried to escape the war as well as by the unexpected return in 1991 of about fourteen thousand Mozambican migrants who had been working in the German Democratic Republic (GDR) until the fall of the old Eastern European regimes.[34] As a result of unification with the Federal Republic of Germany, the former GDR abruptly repatriated Mozambicans—and many other foreign workers—from their relatively stable existence to a war-torn country that could not use their skills and where unemployment was rampant, thus adding to political and social instability.

Workers vented their mounting frustration through increased labor militancy. The 1990s ushered in a wave of unprecedented strikes, mostly in the public sector, and an independent trade union movement emerged in the wake of the country's new constitution. Concurrently, the urban crime rate rapidly rose. In a 1991 Mozambican magazine, the editor suggested that the surge of mob violence reflected that "the majority of the urban population had finally reached the "riot threshold," a concept used by the World Bank and IMF bureaucrats to indicate the state at which their structural adjustment measures have finally pushed a country too hard."[35]

During this period Mozambique's merchant stratum was the principal beneficiary of the PRE. The opening to the market fostered a rapid growth in its economic power and political influence. The PRE enabled the private commercial sector to displace the state from both retail and wholesale commerce and to generally increase its economic role and control of the country's economy. The private sector came to control the bulk of all domestic commercial activity—with the state limited to monitoring its activities—with much of the wholesale activity increasingly concentrated in the hands of a relatively small number of large (mostly Asian) trading houses.[36] Other Mozambicans who have prospered since the introduction of the PRE were individuals engaged in speculative activities, especially trade and transport. For example, one Nampula trader with a trucking fleet that traveled regularly between Mozambique, Swaziland, and South Africa admitted that he had made more money in the first two years of the PRE than in the entire previous decade.[37]

In the face of the PRE and economic and military destabilization in the 1980s, the government reduced its spending for social services. Education and health budgets, which stood at 17 and 7 percent, respectively, of the state's budget in 1986, accounted for only 3.2 percent combined in 1991.[38] Unable to fund equal and general access to social services, Frelimo decided in 1989 that the private sector could also provide housing and education, and later, in 1992, health facilities as well.

More consequential than lifting the state monopoly on key social services was the subsequent proliferation of donor agencies that effectively took a large share of the control over public expenditures away from the state. In health care, for example, the national health system came under attack with the proliferation of selective provisioning. Public health was disaggregated into separate, uncoordinated, competing programs for immunization, essential drugs, and diarrheal disease control—each managed independently with its own financial resources.[39] Thus agencies effectively fragmented integrated programs.

The state was further weakened by a growing "brain drain"—the flight of highly trained Mozambican employees from the public sector to donor agencies and the private sector. The majority of skilled professionals preferred working for donor agencies because of better income prospects—salaries were paid in dollars and therefore remained insulated against exchange-rate devaluation—and because they were so much better equipped in terms of services and supplies. These incentives outweighed increasing Mozambican complaints that their salaries were lower than those paid to expatriates with allegedly equivalent skills, and that they were excluded from the highest managerial positions.

The expanding market for employment of local professionals by donor agencies resulted in a tendency for the latter to refrain from supporting state administration and developing the state's managerial capabilities. Instead they favored support to specific programs, often ones requiring their own institutional setup and management, thereby creating almost autonomous entities. In 1980 there were only 7 foreign organizations operating in the country; by 1991 there were 180 foreign NGOs, most of them with their own explicit agenda—without reference to the government, its plans, or the structures in place to implement those plans.

The proliferation of NGOs in Mozambique, as elsewhere in Africa, initiated a debate about their role in promoting (or hindering) development.[40] On the one hand, some people are highly critical of international NGOs, denouncing them as an important instrument of the "new imperialism of low-intensity management at grassroots level."[41] In the most comprehensive study of NGOs in Mozambique, Hanlon argued that the influx of NGOs in the 1980s played a uniformly suspect role in undermining the credibility of the Mozambican government by insisting that foreign representatives control the entire operations. While manifesting the "human face" of structural adjustment, through food aid and other programs, aid agencies like World Vision and CARE pursued their own policy agenda of undermining the state and hastening the pace of market-driven privatization. Hanlon provides numerous examples to show that such agencies had the effect of disrupting, undermining, and even destroying the economy rather than strengthening it. In Inhambane Province, for example, donors were reluctant to buy locally and sometimes swamped the market with cheap foreign inputs, which put local firms out of business.[42] Those critical of NGOs do not underestimate the difficulties of working with a weak and increasingly corrupt state, but they do argue that to bypass the state and create a parallel state apparatus at best maintains a weak and inefficient state, and at worst deepens problems of coordination and efficiency. It is unlikely that Mozambique, or any country, can work its way out of underdevelopment with weak government. Donors should engage and negotiate with the state, critics argue, not circumvent it.

On the other hand, some perceive NGOs as contributing to economic development, promoting a democratic culture, and strengthening civil society in Africa.[43] In Mozambique, former NGO personnel have argued that these organizations must be seen as diverse entities with different objectives and manifold operations.[44] They claim that to portray northern NGOs simply as villains ignores many more powerful players, Mozambican and foreign, that bear responsibility for the ongoing suffering of millions throughout the country. Furthermore, given Frelimo's antipeasant bias and its financial constraints, some analysts have argued that NGOs have a strategic development role to play in Mozambique, especially in supporting the cooperative sector.[45] While both groups raise pertinent issues, ultimately assessing the role of foreign-based NGOs and their effectiveness in attaining stated goals is an empirical activity.

## The State, Party, and Private Capital

For nearly fifteen years, scholars have portrayed Mozambique as a unified, cohesive, single-party state led by Frelimo, a united party that was reasonably popular and that had proven its capacity for self-criticism and self-renewal.[46] Even after the death of Mozambique's first president, Samora Moises Machel, in a mysterious plane crash in South Africa in October 1986, the party maintained its unity and showed its strength as a collegial body; its leaders unanimously elected Joaquim Alberto Chissano as Machel's successor. The war and the impact of PRE, however, took a heavy toll on the Mozambican leadership. By the late 1980s, the political dissatisfaction with Frelimo had heightened, and its internal cohesion had disintegrated. Two of the major issues were corruption among party and government officials and the role of the state in economic development.

The PRE's austerity measures and its legitimation of the pursuit of individual profit made it very difficult for Frelimo officials at all levels to live on their regular salaries. Although parallel economic activities had been a part of an essential survival strategy for many lower-ranked cadres, just as for the majority of Mozambican wage earners and civil servants, they enabled more influential cadres to acquire considerable private wealth. Thus, the public became aware of senior party members, bureaucrats, and military officers who used their political positions to acquire land, build comfortable homes, and purchase expensive imported luxury goods. The possibility for further capital accumulation was extended in 1989 by the Fifth Party Congress, which decided to remove all restrictions limiting investment and the number of workers that party members could employ on their farms and in other enterprises. Since the congress, many Frelimo members have emerged as "born again private sector entrepreneurs," reaping the benefits of their political positions to get access to coveted scarce resources.[47] Moreover, the congress resolution solidified a client-patronage network, giving the state the license to reward supporters with land and companies.

The opening of entrepreneurial activities to public officials combined with the PRE's liberalization reforms gave greater impetus to a rapidly growing class alliance between private and state bureaucratic interests. This public-private alliance is based on the exchange of scarce resources controlled by each group. In the countryside, for example, state-employed district administrators establish local alliances with traders and private farmers, exchanging services of mutual benefit. In such local alliances, the administrator may offer a trader or a private farmer the possibility of acquiring a tractor or a truck, and in exchange he would receive assistance to build a house in Maputo or to establish himself in business or agriculture, at times in joint ventures or partnerships with the same private traders and farmers.[48] Thus, the administrators who used to be the local representatives of Frelimo's national project have taken on a much more individualistic and opportunistic ideological outlook.

While government corruption was prevalent but petty in the past, the advent of a capitalist market economy gave it new scope. Two major investigations in Mozambique since 1989 implicated civil servants and party members in a multimillion-dollar bank scandal as well as in the misappropriation of international emergency aid. On several occasions, members of the People's Assembly openly discussed the growing seriousness of corruption, especially by party and government officials. In December 1989, for example, assembly member Sergio Vieira warned against the appearance of new "Nkavandames," in reference to a crisis that wracked Frelimo in the late 1960s. The general secretary of the Mozambican Women's Organization, Salomé Moiane, warned of the ramifications of unabated corruption, referring to the mass demonstrations that led to the changes in Eastern Europe: "We will be confronted with the same sort of thing if we carry on like this. And all our necks will be on the block because of half a dozen crooks. I am prepared to lose my head for what I have done, but not for what others have committed."[49] The number of corrupted officials was far more widespread than Moiane cared to admit. Periodic administrative interventions and disciplinary measures were not sufficient to curb the increase of crimes.

As we have seen, Frelimo in the late 1980s erased from its agenda a socialist development strategy to provide basic services and a minimum standard of living to all Mozambicans. Since then, party members have held strongly divergent views on the methods and timing for adopting free-market policies to deal with the country's development problems as well as the role of the state in the transition process. In the early 1990s, there seemed to be two salient positions. The most prominent was held by those primarily concerned with the creation of a national bourgeoisie and the interests of private capital, with a very strong commitment to modern-sector growth and direct foreign investment. They leaned toward the rapid withdrawal of the state and disinvestment in social services, in the name of efficient market solutions. The minister for economic and social affairs, Eneias Comiche, endorsed this view: "We think that privatization is part of the government's defined policy for conferring greater efficiency on our companies. The state's role is to regulate the system. The state should not be managing companies."[50] A smaller and less powerful group within Frelimo continued to emphasize the need for investment and regulating critical markets as well as intervening to strengthen a number of areas to help revive peasant agriculture. While supportive of private investment, they were critical of the speedy and unchecked penetration of foreign capital, which they saw as leading to what Jorge Rebelo, one of the early Frelimo leaders, termed the "capitalism of the jungle."[51]

Crucial shifts of policy might have been forced on the government, but clearly all its members did not see them as unmitigated tragedies. Since the introduction of the PRE, many members supported capitalism with the same dogmatism and rigidity as they had upheld socialism in the preceding years. For example, at an international conference in 1990, the minister of transport and communications, Armando Guebuza, remarked that although structural adjustment had brought many hardships to the Mozambican people—not least because the market economy exacerbated social class differentiation and contributed to more social injustices—these were the prices to be paid for "progress."[52] The changes in government policy may have originated outside, but the changing balance of class forces within Frelimo and their alignment with external forces facilitated the domination of private capital and foreign investment.

Frelimo's earlier decision to change from a Marxist-Leninist party to a party for all Mozambicans at the Fifth Party Congress in July 1989 had raised questions about its priorities. Membership was extended to all citizens, including property owners and religious believers, transforming the party into a conglomeration of different class positions and projects. Although some analysts interpreted it as an attempt to return to a broad nationalist strategy for ending the long war against Renamo, others argued that Frelimo had decided to break its alliance with peasants, workers, and other social groups that lost ground in the era of war and PRE, in favor of the propertied classes, national and foreign.[53] Yet this alliance had been based more on myth than on reality. Since coming to power, the Frelimo state had pursued policies that were antagonistic to the peasantry. The party's abandonment of Marxism-Leninism only ended its "official" alliance with peasants and workers. In practice, this alliance had been fraudulent for decades.

The pervasive influence of external forces was apparent in 1990, when Frelimo adopted a multiparty system even though the majority of those taking part in the debate on the new constitution, particularly in rural areas, were in favor of maintaining the one-party state. In December 1990, the National Assembly adopted a new multiparty constitution, which allowed for direct elections for the president; complete separation between the party and the government (i.e., no longer would the president of Frelimo automatically be president of the country); and freedom of the press, the judiciary, and religious expression. The introduction of free-market capitalism and political pluralism combined with the expansion of fundamental individual and collective rights and freedoms guaranteed in the new constitution were supposed to allow Mozambicans to play more active roles in their own governance. Since then, however, there have been discouraging signs that formal representation may only alienate the majority of impoverished Mozambicans from the democratic process. In effect, "politics" has become the exclusive domain of professional politicians representing privileged social groups in the urban areas—businessmen, lawyers, and bureaucrats. As of December 1993, there were at least thirteen opposition parties officially registered, many of them overtly racist and regionalist. The perplexing array of acronyms, multiple press conferences, and apparent activity obscured the fact that few of these parties had a coherent ideology, political platform, or development strategy to rebuild Mozambique. Furthermore, given the country's realities, it is probable that when it comes to economic policy, the leaders elected under the country's pluralist system will find themselves at least equally accountable to foreign donors and private capital.

Meanwhile, Mozambican capitalists found that an open market economy was not the hoped-for panacea. Their grievances included the preferential treatment given to non-Mozambicans as well as the influx of foreign products. Even before a new national policy for tourism had been created, local traders and hoteliers had objected that the best opportunities had gone to foreigners. Concerned about cheap imports flooding the market, manufacturers protested that they could not compete with the industries of neighboring countries—on average, those in Mozambique worked at only 30 to 40 percent of their installed capacities in 1991. National companies moaned that liberal reforms served mainly outside interests, as foreign products sold at lower prices than those locally produced, crowding them out of a market that they contended they had a right to exploit. The problem was made worse by illegal imports and by tied-aid (aid tied to purchases in the donor country or linked to a particular development project) from international donors. They provided 80 percent of Mozambique's GNP but often insisted on importing their own goods for distribution, even when some of equivalent quality was available locally.[54]

Despite the high profile given to capital inflow and investment, the domestic economy did not benefit as expected. In 1991, outside agribusiness, industrial foreign-investment projects were worth less than $8 million, and national companies had little capacity to reinvest. According to the government, the lack of capital markets, a cumbersome bureaucracy, the lack of incentives to invest, poor infrastructure, and unclear laws on land discouraged investors.

## Conclusion

By the 1990s, the Mozambican state had been undermined and transformed by more than a decade of political destabilization, economic decline, and structural adjustment. Frelimo had abandoned its socialist principles and embraced capitalist development sponsored by the World Bank and IMF institutions. This transition to capitalism was accompanied by a dramatic erosion of domestic authority, as international finance institutions and NGOs took over the direction and content of economic and social policy in addition to other responsibilities previously reserved for the state. External dependency had limited the prospects of strong and autonomous national development.

Is the conclusion, then, that outside forces were responsible for undermining the country's sovereignty? Certainly external demands and aid conditions have been overwhelming. Yet to portray Mozambique simply as the victim ignores critical internal forces. After all, not all Mozambicans have suffered equally under externally imposed conditions. The government's move to a capitalist-oriented market, combined with the removal of investment and accumulation restrictions on Frelimo members, unleashed new class interests in the state apparatus that readily aligned with private and international capital. Meanwhile, the country's structural adjustment program has increased the hardships of ordinary Mozambicans at least as much as it has resulted in economic advance. In the urban areas, a dramatic fall in living standards has led to increased political instability. In the countryside, peasant farmers have not benefited from price liberalization due to continuing poor terms of trade for their produce, rising inflation, and declining purchasing power, among other reasons.

Evidence on rural differentiation under structural adjustment in Mozambique has been very limited, although rural misery has increased notably. However, the form of land privatization and divestiture of state enterprises that has taken place has not primarily benefited peasant farmers or even other Mozambican agriculturists. On the contrary, it has been associated with government officials from provincial governors to local administrators, Frelimo party members and their supporters, former state-farm managers, and military veterans, as well as with a reassertion of foreign firms.

For more than seventeen years the war between Frelimo and Renamo prevented Mozambican farmers from producing at capacity. Since 1992, peace has brought the prospect of increased privatization and foreign control of the land that they used to cultivate. In the months leading up to the country's first multiparty elections in 1994, both Frelimo and Renamo came out in support of privatization. None of Mozambique's political parties, however, seized upon the land issue by presenting a coherent vision of a new policy. Indeed, they made little effort to actively mobilize rural dwellers as serious constituencies. The exclusion of the rural population from the political discourse cast doubt on whether Mozambican leaders will seriously address their various concerns in the future.

# Conclusion
## Past and Present Policies

**F**rom the 1950s to the 1990s, Mozambican peasants have endured extraordinary hardships. Agricultural policy turned from colonial intervention and restriction of peasant farming to state control and promotion of rural socialism and finally to open markets and private farming. Each phase was marked by changes that encroached upon peasants' livelihoods and production in the form of forced cash-cropping, collective farms, and land grabbing, respectively. Despite regime changes, both the colonial and postcolonial Mozambican state pursued policies inimical to the peasantry with the same results: increased peasant dissatisfaction and alienation from the state.

For most of the colonial period, Mozambican peasants were subjected to forced labor on public works and private enterprises and to forced cash-crop cultivation; they supplied labor to the foreign-owned plantations and to settler farms. Peasants also became migrant laborers for the mines in South Africa and Rhodesia and for the plantations in Malawi and Tanganyika. The state discriminated against the middle and wealthier peasants in particular by limiting the amount of land that they could have and by prohibiting their employment of labor in order to check African accumulation. As in other African settler colonies, the Portuguese wanted to prevent the development of an economically strong African class of agrarian capitalists that would compete with settler farms and plantations for land and labor.[1] In this context, the colonial state subsidized and consolidated settler farming by providing cheap credit, building the transport infrastructure, coordinating marketing facilities, and maintaining extension services. The state intervened in the labor market, through the creation of labor codes and internal migrant labor, to ensure that plantations, like settler farms, had sufficient labor supply. Without state intervention and assistance (e.g., distribution of inputs, credit, transport, marketing facilities, and labor supply) settler farms and plantations could not have overcome and eliminated African competition.

But beginning in the late 1940s with cotton production and then increasing in the 1950s, Portugal was obliged to make concessions in the colonies, fostering a process of commodification and differentiation among African producers. The reasons for these shifts in state agrarian policy were both economic and political, ranging from the declining competitiveness of colonial exports to emerging African nationalism. On the one hand were increasing economic problems in Mozambique, including rural unemployment, the subsequent influx of rural men into the cities, and a dependence on imports of maize, wheat, rice, and other staples that negatively affected the balance of payments.[2] Additionally, the quality and price of colonial cotton were no longer competitive on the world market.[3] On the other hand, with the rise of nationalism in the 1950s and the onset of the liberation wars in the Portuguese colonies in the early 1960s, it was politically expedient to develop a Mozambican stratum of commercial agricultural producers that would align with Portuguese rule. The colonial state decided to give some assistance to an upper stratum of peasants, hoping that they could contain any popular movement for independence.

This new colonial economic and political strategy enabled the better-off Mozambican peasantry (e.g., *assimilados,* traditional chiefs, *régulos,* and middle-peasant farmers) to strengthen its position and improve its socioeconomic status. These wealthier farmers received technical assistance and regular inputs such as seeds, fertilizers, and oxen. Furthermore, they were exempted from forced labor and allowed to hire workers. Over time, these farmers, like the settlers and plantation owners, became dependent on the state for inputs, services, and credit. Colonial marketing cooperatives were part of the strategy, too: middle-peasant farmers established cotton cooperatives in the north and wheat cooperatives in the south. Although development was always a controlled process, some rural communities—like Ilha Josina Machel—flourished. Yet African producers remained frustrated by discriminatory colonial policies that hindered their opportunities to accumulate (e.g., rigid limitations on land acquisition, restricted marketing practices, and set prices considerably lower than those for European farmers). Discrepancies emerged between official policy and practice as the colonial state tried to balance its agenda of protecting settler agriculture—its first priority—and promoting certain kinds of African agriculture.

Agricultural production, wage labor, and other off-farm employment were all part of the mix for the livelihood and reproduction of Mozambique's differentiated peasantry on the eve of independence. Rural off-farm employment included casual wage labor and nonagricultural self-employment within rural communities as well as permanent wage work and migration. Building on Bridget O'Laughlin's theoretical analysis of the political significance of rural social differentiation in Mozambique, the individual case studies in preceding chapters reflect a broad diversification of rural livelihoods.[4] These ranged from rural families that cultivated small subsistence plots and depended on monthly earnings from the Incomati Sugar Estates to purchase much of their food to households that grew most of their own food but also regularly marketed surpluses of wheat, maize, sweet potatoes, and other crops. With independence, then, the question of agrarian transformation should have included a debate that was open enough to shape arguments for alternative policies toward a regionally diverse and differentiated rural society.

But once in power, Frelimo leaders discouraged discussion of this issue and remained predisposed to socialism in the countryside. According to their imagined rural society, there was an economically weak and politically compromised embryonic petty bourgeoisie who would dissipate with the exodus of Portuguese settlers and traders. Furthermore, by withholding state assistance, Frelimo would squeeze the private and middle peasants, the groups it had come to distrust during the war of national liberation, thus leaving a homogeneous class of peasants. In planning their development strategy, the new leaders embraced a simplistic vision of agrarian class structure based on a dualist model of a traditional subsistence-oriented peasantry opposed to a modern large-scale commercial sector. In agriculture, this strategy involved moving the dispersed rural population to communal villages; concentrating investment in large, mechanized agro-industrial state enterprises; encouraging immediate cooperativization of peasant farming; and restricting private markets. Frelimo transformed abandoned settler farms and plantations into state farms and, to a lesser extent, cooperatives. There was no land reform—that is, the state did not return to the peasantry land that the Portuguese had confiscated. The result for Mozambican agricultural producers was that independence was not the hoped-for panacea.

Frelimo's policies—for example, the incorporation of some peasant farms into state enterprises, the disproportionate channeling of resources to the state farms, forced villagization, and the widespread coercion of peasants into "voluntary seasonal laborers" on state farms—created extreme tensions in the rural areas between state farms and peasant farming, alienating wide sectors of Frelimo's original support base. By concentrating investment in public-sector enterprises, Frelimo's strategy of rapid accumulation resulted in a shortage of producer supplies and consumer goods such as sugar, oil, and soap in the countryside and unfavorable terms of trade for the peasantry. With low prices for crops and few commodities to buy, peasants had little commercial incentive to engage in surplus production of food or export crops, so they reduced their farming areas under cultivation and productivity.

Meanwhile, despite Frelimo's intent, cooperatives were not an alternative to family farming. According to official discourse, the middle peasants would pool their resources (draft animals, plows, hoes, and seed) with poor peasants and collectivize their individual farms to work together. But contradictions emerged that undermined Frelimo's plan, and, consequently, the leadership retreated from this aspect of its cooperativization program. These contradictions stemmed from the diverse ways that the rural population responded and came to shape cooperatives on the ground. In cases where middle peasants determined co-op membership, for example, they used their own draft animals, plows, seed, and other means of production on the collective fields. But once local authorities, under central state directives, intervened in a haphazard way to expand and diversify membership to include poor peasants, the wealthier ones deserted the cooperatives, taking their animals and equipment with them. Without state investment, better-off peasants knew that cooperatives would be less efficient and productive than their own family farms. Eventually, this group of middle and wealthier peasants came to compete with cooperatives for poor peasant labor and other resources.

In other cases where some middle peasants remained in cooperatives, they came to lead and manage these units of production. Even when poor peasants were the numerical majority in cooperatives, the leadership positions were held by middle peasants, mostly older, prosperous men. Young men did not participate in the cooperatives because the income was irregular and insufficient for them to establish independent rural households; instead, they sought full-time wage employment. The majority of cooperative members were women, especially in the south. Within the cooperatives they did the manual fieldwork—seeding, weeding, and hoeing—while men did the skilled jobs—irrigation, animal traction, construction of silos and other infrastructure—reproducing the gender division of labor on the family farms. Thus, contrary to intent, Frelimo's cooperative policy sharpened rather than repressed both class and gender divisions in the countryside.

Although cooperatives are no longer central to Frelimo's agrarian policy, the experience is relevant to current and future debates on agricultural development and land reform. Three main points emerge from the cooperative experience in Mozambique. First, given the members' diverse rural livelihoods and different economic strata, a single strategy of cooperativization for all the peasantry would not be successful. People joined cooperatives for different reasons, as we have seen. Some needed a small, monthly cash income, while others wanted to supplement their food supply. Prosperous male farmers joined to get access to implements and inputs unavailable to individual producers on the local market. Membership also entitled them to state resources that they used to enhance their positions. Widows, older women with few children to care for, and women whose independent production was very insecure relied on cooperatives for their food. For them, it was their only chance to avoid starvation. In other cases, women joined because extra quotas of staples and consumer goods were sold at official prices or because of patronage ties to the prosperous peasant farmers who dominated the leadership of the cooperative.[5] Grouping people of different social strata who organized their livelihoods in unique ways worked only in the context of extreme shortages of goods. But even then cooperatives did not integrate the broad mass of rural people.

Second, where producer cooperatives did function, like the Project CO-1–supported ones on Ilha Josina Machel, it was because they provided access to consumer items, inputs, and food, whether it was seed, fertilizer, and machinery for members' own family farms; technical assistance and extension services provided by project personnel; or quotas of staples and consumer goods sold at official prices in the cooperative store. Yet even these successful cooperatives did not collectivize individual plots to form cooperatives as Frelimo intended.

Third, contrary to the critics of Frelimo's socialist strategy, who denounce Mozambique's leaders for alienating the peasantry from its land and cultural traditions, cooperatives did not fail because they were part of a state-imposed project foreign to traditional peasant culture. Rather, this study found an alternative explanation for the failure of Mozambique's socialist experiment. From the peasantry's perspective, despite Frelimo's perception, willingness to participate in collective production was part of a risk-spreading strategy rather than a commitment to socialism. In Mozambique as in many countries attempting to transform agriculture, leaders imposed a uniform strategy of national development upon a regionally diverse and socially differentiated rural society rather than considering peasant realities.

Frelimo was forced to retreat from its central goal of rapid collectivization of peasant production in part because of the way that rural people responded to its programs and in part because of the weakness of the central state. The predominant theoretical tendency in accounts of third-world agrarian politics assumes that the state is an omnipotent, single, monolithic structure. Indeed, Christian Geffray and other scholars have depicted the postindependent Mozambican state as a hegemonic, authoritarian, and alien force intent on imposing its modernizing policies on a traditional rural population.[6] In contrast, my study challenges these interpretations, revealing the often-competing agendas between the central state and local state functionaries around agrarian policy, which resulted in contradictions at the local level.

The issue of technique is illustrative. While senior officials at the Ministry of Agriculture promoted animal traction in the cooperatives, the Project CO-1 technicians, in alliance with the co-op members, pushed for tractors and other imported equipment usually channeled to state farms. In the end, the cooperatives bought several multigadget plows promoted by the ministry, but the technicians also worked with cooperative leaders to elaborate a schedule with Mecanagro, the state machinery park, to increase tractor rental in both the co-operatives and family farms. Furthermore, the technicians in liaison with NGOs had tractors and other mechanized equipment donated to the Ilha Josina Machel union of cooperatives and then paid for two individuals to at-tend a training course on tractor maintenance. Senior ministerial officials and the project's central team based in Maputo City reprimanded the technicians for their actions, but the technicians, who worked on a daily basis with peasant farmers in the field, sided with the cooperatives that wanted access to modern equipment to increase their productivity. Because their credibility was contin-gent upon making cooperatives work by getting the services and goods needed, these state technicians took a different view of cooperative development from the state bureaucrats at the ministry. But the divisions were not simply be-tween the central state and field-based technicians; there were also fundamen-tal differences between the technicians and local administrators over labor organization in the cooperatives and casual labor for state farms. Although these two groups both represented the state, they held competing opinions on how to pursue official government policy. These and other examples force us to give more attention to the complex and changing relationships between state officials and the peasantry as well as among state officials at various lev-els — an issue neglected in the literature.

Over time Frelimo adopted a gradual and vacillating approach to coopera-tivization. Despite ad hoc agrarian reforms in the mid-1980s — the products of foreign donor pressure, self-criticism, and necessity — Frelimo agreed to a structural adjustment program in 1987, a break with the previous socialist strategy in that the new policies are supported by international finance capital. Given its economic constraints, Frelimo had little choice but to align with pri-vate (foreign and domestic) and international capital (World Bank and IMF). The simultaneous divestment of state farms, a key component of the country's program, did not primarily benefit peasant farmers, or indeed, other Mozam-bican agricultural producers. Those peasants who received small plots — usu-ally on the most marginal land — in the initial distribution of state farmland have struggled to keep them from large private farmers. In addition, many state workers whose salaries were critical to the subsistence and reproduction of rural households lost their jobs when the state farms were sold or closed down. Rather than peasant farmers, the main beneficiaries of large state-farm and industrial divestiture have been British, Portuguese, and South African foreign investors. At the same time, however, the state has guaranteed that some Mozambicans have profited from the transition to capitalism by al-locating land and agribusiness to government officials, ministers, Frelimo vet-erans, and ex–state-farm managers. In facilitating their takeover of small and middle-sized state enterprises, Frelimo has created a patron-client relationship with these new indigenous private owners who owe their existence to the government.

Mozambique's transition to capitalism in the late 1980s did not improve the lives of ordinary rural producers because of rising inflation, declining purchasing power, and continuing poor terms of trade. Often, farmers that produced surpluses were unable to sell their crops because of marketing and transport problems. In several provinces, Mozambican peasants were pressured to grow cotton and other cash crops in resurrected colonial-style plantations, often under terms and conditions that had prevailed in the colonial period. For these reasons, peasants considered changes in regimes, "as so many storms in the political sky while the hard realities on the ground remained unchanged."[7]

The conflict over redistribution of state farmland was only one aspect of the ongoing land struggle in Mozambique. Small-scale agricultural producers have protested land-grabbing by party members, Frelimo supporters, and other individuals in the periurban areas and the countryside. In recent debates much attention has focused on land tenure as a means to provide security to peasant farmers and a new land law. Government officials have discussed whether the development of smallholder production would be best achieved by instituting a system of individual land titles or by returning to communal tenure under the *régulos*. Researchers associated with the Land Tenure Center (LTC) at the University of Wisconsin have contributed to the debate largely through voluminous reports, products of their well-funded USAID research projects.[8] In brief, LTC proposals for agrarian reform have promoted the smallholder model of development; called for the restoration of tradition and the defense of the peasantry within an indigenous capitalist development strategy; and recommended an immediate halt to large-scale concessions of land, the general reform of Mozambican law to assure greater stability in land ownership, and the reinstitution of the *regulado* system.[9]

While the LTC researchers have highlighted the need for land reform, there are serious weaknesses in their approach and prescriptions for agrarian reconstruction in Mozambique. Critics of this scholarship have correctly pointed out that it has reproduced the dualist model in the countryside, with the smallholder sector—a euphemism for peasants—standing in homogeneous opposition to large-scale commercial enterprises. By failing to recognize a differentiated peasantry with diverse rural livelihoods, this smallholder model is likely to repeat many of the same errors as Frelimo's flawed socialist strategy.

The central weakness of this scholarship, however, is that it addresses only one aspect of the agrarian question in Mozambique. By narrowly focusing on land ownership, these researchers have ignored the importance of wage labor and off-farm employment for rural livelihoods—a criticism O'Laughlin made and that my interviews with peasants support. The new ownership of previously state-run farms is not only significant because large, foreign companies now control the land, but because rural men and women have fewer chances of finding off-farm employment. Moreover, the problem has been exacerbated with the downsizing of rural government under Mozambique's structural adjustment program. Although need for wage employment continues to be more marked in the southern provinces, it is still important in the center and north of the country, where commercial agriculture predominates. In Nampula in the 1990s, for example, many rural households have continued to rely on off-farm work, as they did in the late-colonial period, with men hired as seasonal workers for cotton companies, full-time employees at service jobs, and factory workers in the city of Nampula and in smaller towns.[10]

The war between Frelimo and Renamo failed to erase class stratification or reduce rural livelihoods to homogeneous subsistence production. Indeed, on a return trip to Ilha Josina Machel in 1993, I found off-farm income still essential in reestablishing rural households and investing in agricultural production. The private farmer and store owner Vasco Juma Sumbana had bought another tractor with his savings from commercial trade and hired full-time workers for his farm.[11] Middle peasants who still had relatives working in South Africa during the war had purchased draft animals from the Incomati Sugar Estates in order to prepare their fields. Co-op members, however, expressed concern that they had lost nearly all of their cattle during the war. Cooperative leader Fernando Chavango explained that they had requested that the provincial director of agriculture provide them with a set of work oxen for animal traction and reproduction.[12] Contrary to the depiction of a rigid modernizing institution imposing its foreign policies, these peasants expected state intervention in the production process. Yet, given the political and economic constraints existing in Mozambique and the multiplicity of demands on the postwar government, the chances of state assistance were slim. As in the past, agricultural producers will need to reorganize themselves to assert and protect their rights to land, "the terrain of democratic struggles in Africa."[13] Equally as critical, they will need to demand the development of rural industries and a modern infrastructure in order to live and prosper in the twenty-first century.

# Glossary

*agricultor* African "evolved" farmer who had capital resources, cultivated large areas, made regular use of wage labor on a permanent or seasonal basis, and marketed most of his/her production

*aldeamento piloto* colonial government strategic hamlet

*aldeia comunal* communal village

*assimilados* assimilated Africans whom the Portuguese state considered to have mastered the Portuguese culture and language

*cabos* junior chiefs

*cantineiros* rural shopkeepers

*capataz* African overseer of forced labor

*capulana* colorful piece of cloth worn around the waist by Mozambican women

*chefe do posto* lowest-level Portuguese rural subadministrator

*chibalo* forced labor

*circumscrição* circumscription; rural administrative subdistrict

*colonato* irrigated settlement scheme of small farms

*colono* a member of a *Colonato*

*conselho* council; unit of local government in twentieth-century Mozambique

*cooperantes* foreign volunteer workers

*corimela* traditional labor custom practiced in southern Mozambique

*curandeiros* traditional healers

*ghayisa* a Mozambican migrant laborer employed in the South African mines

*grupos dinamizadores* dynamizing groups; politically organized mass-based groups formed in the immediate postindependence years

*indígenas* natives or unassimilated Africans

*indota* subordinate to the chief who was responsible for collecting taxes *lobolo* bride price

*lojas do povo* people's shops run by the Frelimo state

**machambeiro** middle peasant in southern Mozambique, whose resources included at minimum a plow and several draft animals and who cultivated three to twenty hectares (relying primarily on household labor) and marketed a significant proportion of produce

**metical (pl. meticais)** unit of currency in independent Mozambique

*palmatoria* wooden pronged instrument used for beating the hands

*proviso* provision; formally stated condition or stipulation

*regedoria* (also *regulado*) chieftainship or territory assigned to the régulo

*régulos* African political authorities or chiefs invested by the colonial state

*sipais* sepoys; African armed policemen in the service of the Portuguese colonial state

**Sul do Save** region south of the Save River

*tropicultor* modern, multigadget ox-drawn plow

*ujamaa* communal village in Tanzania

# Notes

The following abbreviations are used in the notes and bibliography:

AIM   *Agência de Informação de Moçambique*
BGU   *Boletim de Agência Geral do Ultramar*
CEA   Centro de Estudos Africanos
DNH   Direcção Nacional de Habitação
ICM   Instituto dos Cereais de Moçambique
JEC   Junta de Exportação dos Cereais
MOA   Ministry of Agriculture, Mozambique
MONAP   Mozambique Nordic Agricultural Program
NPC   National Planning Commission
SAR   *Southern African Report*
SARB   *Southern African Review of Books*

## Introduction

1. Isaacman, *Cotton Is the Mother of Poverty*; Newitt, *History of Mozambique*; Vail and White, *Capitalism and Colonialism*; Wuyts, *Peasants*.

2. Egerö, *Mozambique*; Hanlon, *Mozambique: Revolution under Fire*; Isaacman and Isaacman, *Mozambique*; Munslow, *Mozambique*; Saul, *State and Revolution*; Saul, *Difficult Road*.

3. Vail and White, *Capitalism and Colonialism*; Head, "State, Capital and Migrant Labour"; Cross, "O capitalismo colonial."

4. First, *Black Gold*. The debate is covered in the booklet by Neocosmos, *Agrarian Question*, 24–69.

5. Hermele, *Contemporary Land Struggles*, 3–8.

6. Mackintosh, "Agricultural Marketing and Socialist Accumulation," 246.

7. CEA, *Famílias camponesas da Angonia*, 14.

8. Pitcher, "Coercion to Incentives," 135–42.

9. Hermele, *Land Struggles and Social Differentiation*.

10. Like every guerrilla movement, Frelimo resorted to some coercion, so the question is how much. The early literature on the war made the argument that Frelimo enjoyed a massive base of popular support in the immediate pre- and

postindependence period. For example, Davidson, "Politics of Armed Struggle"; Davidson, *People's Cause;* Saul, *State and Revolution;* Isaacman, *A Luta Continua;* Isaacman and Isaacman, *Mozambique.* In contrast, Henriksen argued that Frelimo resorted to coercion to mobilize peasant support *(Revolution and Counterrevolution).* None of these sources constitutes well-documented research on peasant views in this period. No research speaks to the question at all in terms of detailed empirical material, such as Kriger's study on Zimbabwe, *Zimbabwe's Guerrilla War.*

11. O'Laughlin, "Through a Divided Glass."

12. Frelimo, *Report to the Third Congress;* Isaacman and Isaacman, *Mozambique,* 96–99; Munslow, *Mozambique,* 105–12.

13. O'Meara, "Collapse of Mozambican Socialism," 92; Isaacman and Isaacman, *Mozambique;* Munslow, *Mozambique.*

14. Frelimo, *Report to the Third Congress.*

15. Vail and White, *Capitalism and Colonialism;* Hermele, *Land Struggles and Social Differentiation.*

16. Saul, "Rethinking the Frelimo State," 151.

17. CEA, *Mozambican Miner,* 152.

18. On the question of "class suicide" it should be pointed out that in its original Cabralian formulation, it had more to do with individuals rather than entire classes. For example, it is out of the question that the middle peasantry as a distinct group or stratum would commit class suicide. Cabral, "Social Structure in Guinea."

19. Salomão Moyana, "Produzir algodão e castanha de cajú não é favor, é ordem do estado," *Tempo,* 19 Oct. 1986, 12–15.

20. Saul, *Difficult Road;* Hanlon, *Mozambique: Revolution under Fire;* Hanlon, *Mozambique: Who Calls the Shots?* (quote in next paragraph from p. 6).

21. Roesch, "Peasants and Collective Agriculture"; Roesch, "Socialism and Rural Development"; Roesch, "Rural Mozambique and FRELIMO's Fourth Congress"; Roesch, "Renamo and Peasantry."

22. Hermele, *Land Struggles and Social Differentiation.*

23. For details see Bowen, "Peasant Agriculture in Mozambique," 362–63.

24. Geffray and Pedersen, "Sobre a guerra."

25. Geffray, *La cause des armes.*

26. Vines, *Renamo;* Finnegan, *Complicated War.*

27. Borges Coelho, "Protected Villages and Communal Villages."

28. Minter, *Apartheid's Contras.*

29. Roesch, "Renamo and Peasantry," 466.

30. For Manica Province see Alexander, "Local State in Post-War Mozambique."

31. Michel Cahen, "Is Renamo a Popular Movement in Mozambique?," *SARB* 3.2 (1989–1990): 20–21; Cahen, "Mozambique: The Debate Continues. Michel Cahen Writes," *SAR* 5.5 (1990): 26; Gervase Clarence-Smith, "The Roots of the Mozambican Counter-Revolution," *SARB* 2.4 (1989): 7–10; William Minter, "Clarence-Smith on Mozambique," *SARB* 2.6 (1989): 26; Paul Fauvet, "Clarence-Smith on Mozambique," *SARB* 2.6 (1989): 26–27; Fauvet, "Clarence-Smith on Mozambique," *SARB*

3.5 (1990): 21; Otto Roesch, "Is Renamo a Popular Movement in Mozambique?" *SARB* 3.2 (1990): 20–22; Roesch, "Mozambique: The Debate Continues. Otto Roesch Replies," *SAR* 5.5 (1990): 28–29; Roesch, "Renamo and Peasantry."

32. Cahen, *Mozambique*; Cahen, "Clarence-Smith on Mozambique," *SARB* 2.6 (1989): 26–27; Cahen, "Is Renamo a Popular Movement?"; Clarence-Smith, "Roots of the Mozambican Counter-Revolution."

33. Fauvet, "Clarence-Smith on Mozambique"; Minter, *Mozambican National Resistance*; Minter, "Clarence-Smith on Mozambique"; Darch, "Are There Warlords in Mozambique?"; Roesch, "Nampula"; Roesch, "Is Renamo a Popular Movement?"; Roesch, "Mozambique: The Debate Continues"; Roesch, "Renamo and Peasantry."

34. Myers, "Competitive Rights, Competitive Claims"; West and Myers, "A Piece of Land?"; Alexander, "Land and Political Authority"; Negrão, *African Rural Family Economy*; Pitcher, "Conflict and Cooperation." Recent doctoral theses include Borges Coelho, "Protected Villages and Communal Villages"; Chilundo, "Rail and Road Transportation Systems"; Juergensen, "Peasants on the Periphery"; West, "Sorcery of Construction and Sorcery of Ruin."

35. I learned Shangaan sufficiently well to be comfortable in casual conversation, but most interviews were conducted with the assistance of an interpreter. Over the course of the research, I employed three interpreters. In Ilha Josina Machel, an elder and a youth, both males, always worked with me. These individuals assisted in a variety of ways to introduce me to the community (and it to me), to discuss and refine questions and concepts, and to teach me the language. In Chokwe, I worked closely with a woman agronomist who was a well-liked resident of the area. She greatly facilitated my work as both women and men interviewees felt comfortable with her—women tended to be more relaxed and prepared to discuss a wide range of issues, while men respected her agricultural technical knowledge. I conducted all the interviews in Portuguese myself.

## 1. Portuguese Colonialism and the Early Postindependence Years

1. Wuyts, "Economia política"; Brito, "Dependencia colonial."

2. Adam, Davies, and Head, "Mão-de-obra moçambicana," 70.

3. First, *Black Gold*, 33.

4. Wuyts, *Money and Planning*, 25.

5. Missão de Inquérito, *Estatísticas agrícolas*, 7–8.

6. Clarence-Smith, *Third Portuguese Empire*; Pitcher, *Politics in the Portuguese Empire*; Hedges et al., *História de Moçambique*; Newitt, *History of Mozambique*.

7. Mackintosh, "Agricultural Marketing and Socialist Accumulation"; Hermele, *Contemporary Land Struggles*; Bowen, "Peasant Agriculture"; Alexander, "Land and Political Authority."

8. Adam and Gentili, "O movimento dos Liguilanilu"; Adam, "Cooperativização agrícola"; Hedges et al., *História de Moçambique*, 188; Pitcher, "Coercion to Incentives."

9. The Gini coefficient takes values between 0, representing perfect equality, and 1, representing perfect inequality. Thus the higher the value of the coefficient, the greater the degree of inequality. I am grateful to Ian Parker for this calculation, which is accurate within 1 percent (correspondence with Ian Parker, 17 June 1992).

10. Wolpe, "Capitalism and Cheap Labour Power"; Legassick, "South Africa"; Arrighi, "Labour Supplies"; Murray, *Families Divided;* Harries, *Work, Culture, and Identity.*

11. CEA, *Mozambican Miners,* 17 and 20.

12. Bundy, *Rise and Fall of South African Peasantry;* Beinart and Bundy, *Hidden Struggles;* Arrighi, "Labour Supplies"; Phimister, "Commodity Relations and Class Formation"; Vail and White, *Capitalism and Colonialism.*

13. Hermele, *Contemporary Land Struggles,* 18.

14. Roesch, "Migrant Labour and Forced Rice Production," 260–64.

15. For more information on these companies see Vail, "Mozambique's Chartered Companies"; Vail and White, *Colonialism and Capitalism;* Neil-Thomlinson, "Niassa Chartered Company"; Serra, "O capitalismo colonial"; Ishemo, *Lower Zambezi Basin,* 246–69.

16. Wuyts, *Money and Planning,* 33; CEA, *Plantações de chá,* 24–43; Mackintosh, "Agricultural Marketing and Socialist Accumulation," 247–52.

17. Ibid., 246.

18. For examples see Habermeier, "Algodão," 41–42; CEA, *Cotton Production in Mozambique,* 15–21; CEA, *Famílias camponesas da Angonia,* 14; Borges Coelho, "Protected Villages and Communal Villages"; Alexander, "Land and Political Authority," 6.

19. Bravo, *A cultura algodoeira;* CEA, *Cotton Production in Mozambique;* Isaacman, *Cotton Is the Mother of Poverty;* Pitcher, *Politics in the Portuguese Empire;* Pitcher, "Coercion to Incentives"; Lemos, "Fontes para o estudo do algodão."

20. Pitcher, "Coercion to Incentives," 125–31.

21. CEA, *Cotton Production in Mozambique,* 15.

22. For migrant laborers in Malawi see Chirwa, "Alomwe and Mozambican Immigrant Labor."

23. CEA, *Mozambican Miner,* 106–12; Wuyts, *Money and Planning,* 31–32.

24. Vail and White, *Capitalism and Colonialism;* Newitt, *History of Mozambique.*

25. Wuyts, *Peasants,* 30.

26. Vail and White, *Capitalism and Colonialism.*

27. Dolny, "Challenge of Agriculture," 225.

28. Frelimo, *Documento da 8a sessão do Comité Central,* 82, 98, and 93.

29. Bowen, "Let's Build Agricultural Producer Cooperatives"; Harris, "Agricultural Cooperatives"; Roesch, "Socialism and Rural Development."

30. For an analysis of the Tanzanian experience see von Freyhold, *Ujamaa Villages;* Coulson, *Tanzania;* Raikes, "Ujamaa and Rural Socialism."

31. DNH, *Aldeias comunais,* n.p.

32. For Mozambique see de Araújo, "Communal Villages." For Tanzania see Coulson, *Tanzania;* von Freyhold, *Ujamaa Villages.*

33. Land appropriations also took place in other areas where state farms were created, including Angonia, Moamba, Lioma, and the Lower Limpopo Valley, as well as in Chokwe. Hermele, *Land Struggles and Social Differentiation*, 28, 47, and 48.

## 2. Frelimo

1. Wield, "Mozambique—Late Colonialism," 85.

2. Hanlon, *Mozambique: Revolution under Fire*, 48.

3. Saul, *Difficult Road*; Hanlon, *Mozambique: Revolution under Fire*; Darch, "Are There Warlords in Mozambique?"

4. Geffray, *La cause des armes*; Geffray and Pedersen, "Sobre a guerra"; Cahen, "Check on Socialism in Mozambique"; Casal, "Discurso socialista e camponeses africanos."

5. O'Laughlin, "Through a Divided Glass"; Hanlon, *Mozambique: Revolution under Fire*; Mackintosh, "Economic Policy Context"; Mackintosh and Wuyts, "Accumulation, Social Services."

6. Dolny, "Challenge of Agriculture"; Harris, "Agricultural Cooperatives"; Wardman, "Co-operative Movement"; Bowen, "Let's Build Agricultural Producer Cooperatives"; Roesch, "Socialism and Rural Development."

7. Borges Coelho, "Protected Villages and Communal Villages," 363.

8. O'Laughlin, "Interpretations Matter," 28.

9. O'Laughlin, "Past and Present Options."

10. Alexander, "Land and Political Authority."

11. Mamdani, *Citizen and Subject*.

12. Kruks and Wisner, "State, Party, and Female Peasantry," 110.

13. Bernstein, "Agricultural 'Modernisation' and Structural Adjustment."

14. Gilbert, *Sandinistas*; Galli, "On Peasant Productivity"; Kriger, *Zimbabwe's Guerrilla War*; Sylvester, *Zimbabwe*.

15. These parties included the União Democrática Nacional de Moçambique (UDENAMO), the União Africana de Moçambique Independente (UNAMI), and the Makonde African National Union (MANU). Mondlane, *Struggle for Mozambique*.

16. Munslow, *Mozambique*; Isaacman and Isaacman, *Mozambique*; Hanlon, *Mozambique: Revolution under Fire*; Saul, *State and Revolution*.

17. Newitt, *History of Mozambique*.

18. For debates within Frelimo see Isaacman and Isaacman, *Mozambique*, 79–100; Munslow, *Mozambique*, 79–86 and 102–13. Reference to the "two lines" first appeared in a 1969 document by Frelimo, "Os graves acontecimentos de 1968."

19. For Samora Machel see Christie, *Machel of Mozambique*; Newitt, *History of Mozambique*, 545–46. For Lazaro Nkavandame see Henriksen, *Mozambique*, 179–81; Vail and White, *Capitalism and Colonialism*, 394–98; and for a Frelimo view of Nkavandame see Isaacman and Isaacman, *Mozambique*, 96–99.

20. Hyden, *Beyond Ujamaa*.

21. Munslow, *Mozambique,* 142–43; Negrão, "A produção e o comércio nas zonas libertadas."

22. Dolny, "Challenge of Agriculture"; Isaacman and Isaacman, *Mozambique;* Wield, "Mozambique — Late Colonialism," 75–113.

23. Simpson, "Foreign and Domestic Factors."

24. Frelimo, *Report to the Third Congress.*

25. Simpson, "Foreign and Domestic Factors," 323.

26. Frelimo, *Fourth Congress: Committee Report,* 28; Mackintosh and Wuyts, "Accumulation, Social Services," 145.

27. Barker, "Gaps in the Debates," 70.

28. MONAP was funded by the five Nordic countries, which contributed the following percentages: Denmark, 22 percent; Finland, 16 percent; Iceland, 1 percent; Norway, 16 percent; and Sweden, 45 percent. Under MONAP I, the Nordic countries contributed a total of U.S. $50 million. MONAP, *MONAP II — Second Phase,* 1:11.

29. Macintosh and Wuyts, "Accumulation, Social Services," 142–43.

30. Hirschmann, "Rise and Decline of Development Economics."

31. See the studies conducted by the CEA, especially *Mozambican Miner.*

32. Peasant autonomy springs from the fact that land was defined as a "customary" possession by colonial powers, including the Portuguese. The problem is that scholars like Hyden have long equated this fact with an "exit option." But as Mamdani has argued, so long as the land is not subject to market calculations and is a "customary" possession, the only way that customary can be breached is by direct force. And that is how it was breached: the peasant was subject to both force and compulsion. Mamdani, "Extreme but Not Exceptional."

33. Hanlon, *Mozambique: Who Calls the Shots?,* 18–26; Finnegan, *Complicated War;* Vines, *Renamo.*

34. NPC, *Mozambique,* 34.

35. Minter, *Mozambican National Resistance,* 22; Roesch, "Mozambique: The Debate Continues"; Borges Coelho, "Protected Villages and Communal Villages," 428–30.

36. Geffray, *La cause des armes;* Roesch, "Mozambique Unravels?"; Alexander, "Land and Political Authority."

37. Frelimo, *Fourth Congress: Committee Report,* 58–59.

38. Wuyts, *Money and Planning,* 69–70.

39. Bates, *Markets and States in Tropical Africa.*

## 3. Agricultural Change on Ilha Josina Machel

1. Unemployment and migration: O'Laughlin, "Through a Divided Glass," 9; imported food and payments: Mackintosh, "Agricultural Marketing and Socialist Accumulation"; colonial cotton: CEA, *Cotton Production in Mozambique;* Pitcher, *Politics in the Portuguese Empire;* Pitcher, "Coercion to Incentives."

2. Hermele, *Contemporary Land Struggles;* Bowen, "Peasant Agriculture"; Alexander, "Land and Political Authority."

3. Adam and Gentili, "O movimento dos Liguilanilu"; Adam, "Cooperativização agrícola."

4. Bernstein, "Agricultural 'Modernisation' and Structural Adjustment," 8–9.

5. The other localities include Xinavane, 3 de Fevereiro, Nwamatibjana (Palmeira), Calanga, and the town of Manhiça.

6. Republic Popular de Moçambique, *Primeiro recenseamento geral da população,* 6 and 38.

7. *Mozambique: Preliminary Study,* 1.

8. Isaacman, "Chiefs, Rural Differentiation and Peasant Protest."

9. Eduardo Timana, interview, 29 Sept. 1982.

10. Secretaria Distrital de Administração Civil, Distrito de Lourenço Marques, "Assunto."

11. Ibid.

12. Timana, interview.

13. Interviews with: Josef Tlemo, 15 June 1982; Ernesto Cossa, 16 June 1982; José Tlemo, 29 June 1982; and Sebastião Sitoe, 27 Aug. 1983.

14. Interviews with: Moses Baimbai Muchave, 15 Sept. 1982; Sitoe, 21 Oct. 1983; and Fernando Cossa, 20 July 1983.

15. Alexander, "Land and Political Authority," 32.

16. Timana, interview.

17. Vasco Juma Sumbana, interview, 27 Aug. 1983. Their status as evolved farmers exempted them from wheat cultivation and *chibalo.* Josef Tlemo, interview, 1 Oct. 1982.

18. First, *Black Gold,* 32–33.

19. Young, "Fertility and Famine," 73.

20. In my 1982 survey of forty-five families of miners and ex-miners in one neighborhood on Ilha Josina Machel, I found that twenty-seven families bought plows with their wages. Twenty-five of these miners assisted family farming between contracts, while the two who did not were employed at the Incomati Sugar Estates. Of the eighteen men who did not purchase ox-plows with their earnings, seventeen did not assist family farming during their seven-month period in Mozambique. The CEA study found a similar relation between mine workers who did not purchase means of production with their earnings and their nonparticipation in family farming (CEA, *Mozambican Miners,* 21).

21. Josef Tlemo, interview, 15 June 1982.

22. CEA, *Mozambican Miners,* 5–6.

23. First, *Black Gold,* 184.

24. Roesch, "Migrant Labour and Forced Rice Production."

25. Fernando Chavango, interview, 17 July 1982.

26. *Código do trabalho dos indígenas nas colónias portuguêsas de Africa.*

27. *Regulamento do trabalho dos indígenas.*

28. Moses Baimbai Muchave, eighty-two years old at the time of the interview, recalled that he was prevented from returning to South Africa by the Portuguese authorities because they needed him to work with the boilers at the Incomati sugar factory. Muchave, interview, 15 July 1982.

29. Timana, interview.

30. Administrator of Xinavane Post to the district administrator of Gaza, 25 Nov. 1958.

31. "Mapa de mão de obra indígena."

32. Muchave and Petasse Simbine, interview, 15 Sept. 1982.

33. Ibid.

34. António Correira Lopes, interview, 17 Nov. 1982.

35. My 1982 survey of fifteen former migrant mine workers who started work at the Incomati Sugar Estates in the mid-1960s showed that ten managed the irrigation equipment in the fields, one was a tractor driver, two worked inside the factory, and two were guards at the factory.

36. JEC, "Mapa da produção de trigo. Campanha 1959," n.p.

37. Mapa resumo do recenseamento da população e do lancamento do imposto domicíliario.

38. The best-documented cooperatives in the colonial period are those of Chibuto in Gaza, Zavala in Inhambane, and the cooperatives of Ligualanilu of the Mueda Plateau in Cabo Delgado. See CEA, *O papel do estado colonial;* CEA, "As Cooperatives Ligualanilu no planalto de Mueda"; "Documentário fotográfico," *Gazeta do agricultor,* Sept. 1954, 272–73; "Agricultores indígenas," *BGU,* Mar. 1953, 78–82; "Moçambique: Cooperativas indígenas," *BGU,* Jan. 1957, 250–55; "Cooperativa de agricultores indígenas da Manhiça," *BGU,* Aug 1953, 158–61; "Cultura do trigo no Sul do Save," *BGU,* Jan. 1955, 337–41; Lereno A. Barradas, "Trigo no Baixo Limpopo," *Gazeta do agricultor,* June 1958, 161; Missão de estudo do rendimento nacional do Ultramar, "Cooperativas de Moçambique 1958–1959," *Revista Garçia de Orta* 14.2 (1966): 161–80.

39. Rita-Ferreira, *O movimento migratório de trabalhadores,* 169–76.

40. CEA, *O papel do estado colonial,* 11.

41. Ferreira, "Campanha do trigo," 66; Silva, "Alguns aspectos do panorama," 41–45. For Tanzania see von Freyhold, *Ujamaa Villages;* Raikes, "Wheat Production and Capitalism."

42. Mota, "A produção e a industrialização," 21.

43. In this community, *machambeiros* referred to a middle peasantry whose resources included at minimum a plow and several draft animals, as well as other agricultural equipment, and who cultivated three to twenty hectares, relying primarily on household labor. Most significantly, they were commercial agricultural producers. Josef Tlemo, interview, 1 Oct. 1982.

44. For the economic and theoretical reasons behind the price differences for crops produced by Africans and by Europeans see Arrighi, "Labour Supplies."

45. Chavango, interview, 12 Apr. 1983.

46. Josef Tlemo, interview, 9 Apr. 1983; group interview with: Josef Tlemo, Chavango, and Sitoe, 16 Sept. 1982.

47. Josef Tlemo, interview, 1 Oct. 1982.

48. Ibid., 9 Apr. 1983.

49. Ibid.

50. Chavango, interview, 12 Apr. 1983.

51. Josef Tlemo, interview, 9 Apr. 1983.

52. JEC, "Mapa da produção de trigo. Campanha 1961"; *Boletim Oficial* 3.39 (1963): 938.

53. JEC, "Mapa da produção de trigo." Campanha 1959 and 1961; ICM, "Mapa de produção de trigo." Campanha 1963, 1968, and 1969.

54. Josef Tlemo, interview, 12 Apr. 1983; Sitoe, interview, 16 Sept. 1982; Chavango, interview, 30 Sept. 1982; Martins Tivana, interview, 16 Sept. 1982.

55. Administrator of post, Gestão Lopes Pires Ferreira, "Relatório."

56. ICM-Brigada da Palmeira, "Relação dos agricultores da zona da Manhiça."

57. For examples from Gaza, Manica, Tete, and Zambézia see Roesch, "Migrant Labour and Forced Rice Production"; Alexander, "Land and Political Authority"; Borges Coelho, "Protected Villages and Communal Villages"; Mackintosh, "Agricultural Marketing and Socialist Accumulation."

58. Sumbana, interviews, 21 July 1983 and 27 Aug. 1983.

59. Albino Bila, interview, 26 Aug. 1983.

60. Josef Tlemo, interview, 1 Oct. 1982.

61. Sumbana, interview, 21 July 1983.

62. Chavango, interview, 14 Nov. 1982.

63. Ibid.

## 4. Markets and Power

1. In Tete, for example, the Unidade de Produção da Angónia was the only state farm of the entire province and, thus, more peasants were cooperative members than agricultural workers.

2. Geffray and Pedersen, "Sobre a guerra"; Geffray, *La cause des armes;* Gervase Clarence-Smith, "The Roots of the Mozambican Counter-Revolution," *SARB* 2.4 (1989): 7–10; Michel Cahen "Is Renamo a Popular Movement in Mozambique?," *SARB* 3.2 (1989–1990): 20–21.

3. The districts of Maputo Province include Matutuine, Namaacha, Boane, Marracuene, Manhiça, Magude, and Moamba. The capital, Maputo, has provincial status in the 1980 census.

4. Eduardo Moses Timana, interview, 29 Sept. 1982.

5. Gersony, *Summary of Mozambican Refugee Accounts;* Minter, *Mozambican National Resistance;* Nilsson, *Unmasking the Bandits.*

6. Minter, *Mozambican National Resistance;* Minter, *Apartheid's Contras.*

7. Roesch, "Mozambique Unravels?"

8. Ibid.; Alexander, "Land and Political Authority."

9. Ibid., 51.

10. Wilson, "Cults of Violence."

11. Roesch, "Renamo and Peasantry."

12. Magaia, *Dumba Nengue.*

13. Borges Coelho, "Protected Villages and Communal Villages," 428–29.

14. Egerö, *Mozambique,* 110.

15. Republic Popular de Moçambique, "Relatório do conselho executivo a XI sessão da Assembleia da Localidade."

16. Secretary Chauque, "Relatório." The only exception was José Farias, a Portuguese shopkeeper who remained with his family on the island until he died in 1980.

17. Albino Bila, interview, 26 Aug. 1983.

18. Tickner, "Government and Food Distribution," 2.

19. Bila, interviews, 14 Sept. 1982 and 26 Aug. 1983.

20. Fernando Langa, assistant to the director of Hortifruta, interview, 20 Oct. 1982.

21. Group interview with: Johanne Chauque, Josef Tlemo, and Jacinto Cossa, 30 Mar. 1983; Administrator Simba, interview, 30 Mar. 1983.

22. File from Agricom, Ministry of Internal Commerce, Maputo Province.

23. Sebastião Sitoe, interview, 29 May 1982; Moses Baimbai Muchave, interview, 15 Sept. 1982; group interview with: Josef Tlemo, Fernando Chavango, Martins Tivane, and Joaquim Timbe, 16 Sept. 1982.

24. Mr. Sergio, Manhiça warehouse director, interview, 29 June 1983.

25. Fernando Xerindza Majonane, interview, 24 May 1983.

26. Wuyts, *Money and Planning,* 133, 121–22.

27. Chavango, interview, 17 July 1982.

28. José Binto, interview, 27 Aug. 1983.

29. From 1950 to 1969, wheat production on the colonial cooperative varied from 231.7 to 931.1 kilograms per hectare, with an average of 445.1 kilograms/hectare for these eleven years. JEC, "Mapa da produção de trigo." Campanha 1959 and 1961; ICM, "Mapa de produção de trigo." Campanha 1963, 1968, and 1969.

30. Letter ref. no. 317/D/2, 15 Nov. 1976, administration office of Xinavane, Maputo Province.

31. Fernando Cossa, interview, 20 July 1983.

32. In December 1982, Cooperative 1 de Maio merged with Vista Alegre to form one cooperative, making eleven collective production units on the island.

33. Frelimo, decreto no. 4/80, 1980.

34. Binto, interview, 23 Aug. 1983; Majonane, interview.

35. Chavango, interview, 10 Aug. 1982; Josef Tlemo, interviews, 15 June 1982 and 9 Apr. 1983.

36. Vasco Juma Sumbana, interview, 27 Aug. 1983.

## 5. Cooperative Agriculture

1. Dolny, "Challenge of Agriculture."

2. MONAP, *Annual Report—1982*, 47.

3. In the ministry's 1978–1979 capital budget, MONAP accounted for about 90 percent (U.S. $15 million) of its foreign exchange resources; in 1979–1980, the Nordic contribution of U.S. $15 million accounted for over half of the ministry's total funds of hard currency; and in 1980, MONAP projects represented about 35 percent of the ministry's total planned investments and 82 percent (U.S. $20 million) of its total foreign exchange. MONAP, *MONAP II—Second Phase*, 1:11, 13, and 16.

4. In 1982, it was decided to extend the program for one more year. Campbell et al., "MONAP Mid-Term Evaluation of MONAP II," 135.

5. MONAP, *MONAP II—Second Phase*, 2:iii.

6. Projecto-CO1, "Relatório anual de actividades," 15.

7. See Harris, "Agricultural Cooperatives"; Wardman, "Co-operative Movement"; CEA, *Problemas de transformação;* Roesch, "Socialism and Rural Development."

8. Agapito Salamander, interview, 29 Mar. 1983.

9. Alberto Chavango, interview, 18 Aug. 1983.

10. Interviews with: Adão Mombasso, Fernando Chavango, and Josef Tlemo, 12 Aug. 1983. Given the scarcity of consumer goods, especially clothing in the countryside, the state calculated that farmers would barter double the quantity of sweet potato vine in exchange for a capulana.

11. Alberto Chavango, interview.

12. Elias Mula, interview, 29 Mar. 1983.

13. Fernando Chavango, interview, 8 Apr. 1983.

14. Interviews with: Pedro Novela and Fernando Chavango, 31 Mar. 1983.

15. Jacinto Alexandre Cossa, interview, 8 Mar. 1983.

16. Josef Tlemo, general assembly meeting, Cooperative 25 de Setembro, Ilha Josina Machel, 3 June 1983.

17. Notes from author's personal daily journal, entry of 21 July 1983.

18. Mula, interview.

19. Lucia Nuvunga, a member of Cooperative Arma da Frelimo, at a meeting held on Ilha Josina Machel, 19 May 1982.

20. Bowen, "Let's Build Agricultural Producer Cooperatives," 484.

21. Marshall, "Reflexões sobre uma experiência da alfabetização," 6.

22. Fernando Chavango, interview, 28 Nov. 1982.

23. Marshall, "Reflexões sobre uma experiência da alfabetização," 10.

24. MONAP, *Annual Report—1983*, 64.

25. Mecanagro tractors plowed 789.5 hectares and harrowed 571.5 hectares in the 1982–1983 season, compared to 519 and 131.5 hectares, respectively, in 1981–1982. Data collected from the Office of Mecanagro, Palmeira, District of Manhiça, in Aug. 1983.

26. Brigada A—Namaacha, "Relatório sobre o mês de novembro," n.p.

27. Private communication with CO-1 technician, 29 July 1983.

## 6. Peasant Farmers and Household Survival Strategies

1. Saith, "Primitive Accumulation, Agrarian Reform and Socialist Transitions"; Littlejohn, "Agrarian Marxist Research."

2. World Bank, *Accelerated Development in Sub-Saharan Africa;* World Bank, *Sub-Saharan Africa;* Bates, *Markets and States;* Lofchie and Commins, "Food Deficits and Agricultural Policies"; Williams, "World Bank and Peasant Problem"; Lofchie, *The Policy Factor.*

3. There is no breakdown between adults and children in the 1980 census. This figure corresponds to a total of 1,362 families.

4. In Mozambique, family refers to a broader unit including all matrilineal and patrilineal connections.

5. The details of this case study are from Olinda Fulana, interviews, 23 June 1982, 13 and 26 Apr. 1983.

6. Unless otherwise noted, the details of this case study are from Josef Tlemo, interviews, 15 June 1982 and 9 Apr. 1983.

7. Interviews with miners in First, *Black Gold,* 96–101.

8. Unless otherwise noted, the details of this case study are from Fernando Chavango, interview, 17 July 1982 and 20 Apr. 1983.

9. Fernando Cossa, interview, 20 July 1983.

10. The details of this case study are from Talita Mucavete, interviews, 4 June and 14 July 1982.

11. The details of this case study are from Maria Macamo, interviews, 14 July 1982 and 26 Apr. 1983.

12. The details of this case study are from Petasse Matsolo Hobjana, interviews, 14 July 1982 and 26 May 1983.

13. The details of this case study are from Ernesto Cossa, interviews, 16 June 1982 and 26 Apr. 1983.

14. White and Manghezi, "Role of Cooperative Agriculture"; Harris, "Agricultural Cooperatives"; CEA, *Problemas de transformação rural;* Roesch, "Socialism and Rural Development."

15. Pedro Novela, interview, 13 Apr. 1983.

16. Marta Tivana, interview, 6 Apr. 1983.

17. João Muiambo, interview, 14 Apr. 1983.

18. Ibid.

19. Novela, interview, 14 Apr. 1983.

20. Jacinto Cossa, interview, 6 Apr. 1983.

21. Elias Mula, interview, 29 Mar. 1983.

22. Chavango, interview, 20 Apr. 1983.

23. Mula, interview.

24. Group interview with: Novela and Chavango, 13 Apr. 1983.

25. Popkin is a main proponent of the profit-maximizing thesis. See Popkin, *Rational Peasant*. His work challenges Scott's thesis that all peasants are essentially "risk minimizing." See Scott, *Moral Economy of the Peasant*.

## 7. Postsocialist Mozambique and Land Reform

1. Bowen, "Beyond Reform"; Tanner, Myers, and Oad, "State Farm Divestiture"; Tanner et al., "Land Disputes and Ecological Degradation"; Myers, "Competitive Rights, Competitive Claims."

2. Hermele, *Mozambican Crossroads*; Hanlon, *Mozambique: Who Calls the Shots?*; Hanlon, *Peace without Profit*; Plank, "Aid, Debt, and the End of Sovereignty"; Saul, *Recolonization and Resistance*; Simpson, "Foreign and Domestic Factors."

3. Saul, *Recolonization and Resistance*, 61.

4. Hanlon, *Mozambique: Who Calls the Shots?*, 7.

5. Plank, "Aid, Debt, and the End of Sovereignty," 429–30.

6. Bowen, "Beyond Reform."

7. Myers, Eliseu, and Nhachungue, "Security, Conflict, and Reintegration," 32.

8. Ibid.; Myers, "Competitive Rights, Competitive Claims"; West and Myers, "A Piece of Land in a Land of Peace?"; Marshall and Roesch, "'Green Zones' Agricultural Cooperatives."

9. O'Laughlin, "Past and Present Options," 100–101.

10. "Prime Minister's Report on Economic Recovery," *Mozambique Information Office*, 24 Sept. 1987, 5.

11. Hermele, *Mozambican Crossroads*, 12–18.

12. Government of Mozambique, "Policy Framework Paper 1992–94," 2.

13. Gibbon, Havnevik, and Hermele, *Blighted Harvest*, 49.

14. Carrilho et al., *An Alternative Strategy for Agricultural Development*, 26.

15. "Machungo Paints Grim Economic Picture," *Mozambiquefile* 164 (1990): 15–17.

16. "Budget and Plan for 1991," *Mozambiquefile* 174 (1991): 10–11.

17. Abrahamsson and Nilsson, *Mozambique*, 117.

18. Roberto Uaene, "Ilha Josina Machel: Excedentes agrícolas sem comercialização," *Tempo*, 1 Nov. 1987, 16–23; António Muiambo, "Cooperativa '25 de Setembro' constitui exemplo," *Notícias*, 31 Jan. 1985, 3; Teodósio Ângelo, "Ilha Josina Machel obteve bons resultados," *Notícias*, 3 Mar. 1985, 2.

19. Uaene, "Ilha Josina Machel," 22, 23, 19.

20. Marshall, *War, Debt and Structural Adjustment*, 25.

21. Ministério da Agricultura, "Analise económica dos sistemas de produção de cereais"; Ministério da Agricultura, "Impacto do PRE no sector camponês"; Adam and Cruz e Silva, *Mercados e preços nas zonas rurais*; Stockholm Group for Development Studies, "Market Intervention and Price Policies."

22. Uaene, "Ilha Josina Machel," 23.

23. "Food Aid Policies Distort Local Markets," *Mozambique News Agency* 21 (15 Nov. 1993): 4.

24. Mamdani, "Disaster Prevention"; Newbury, "State, Peasantry, and Agrarian Crisis in Zaire."

25. "Production Facilities," *AIM,* 6 and 13 Feb. 1989, n.p.

26. Mozambique: Increased MNR Activity in Josina Machel Island," *Facts and Reports* 22, E (1992): n.p.; "Xinavane: A desolação continua," *Mediafax,* 14 July 1992, 3; "Land Mines Prevent Agriculture," *AIM Reports* 91 (1996): 3.

27. Fernando Chavango, interview, 28 June 1993.

28. Adam and Cruz e Silva, *Mercados e preços nas zonas rurais.*

29. For a comparative study of Kenya, Mozambique, Tanzania, Ghana, Zambia, and Uganda see Gibbon, Havnevik, and Hermele, *Blighted Harvest.*

30. World Bank, *Mozambique: Restoring Rural Production and Trade.*

31. People's Republic of Mozambique, *Strategy and Program for Economic Rehabiliations,* 15.

32. World Bank, *Mozambique Food Security Study;* World Bank, *Mozambique Population, Health and Nutrition Sector Report.*

33. Quoted in Marshall, *War, Debt and Structural Adjustment,* 22.

34. Dinerman, *Mozambique,* 45.

35. "Reaching the 'Riot Threshold,'" *Mozambiquefile* 182 (1991): 3.

36. Roesch, "Economic Reforms in Mozambique," 123.

37. Marshall, *War, Debt and Structural Adjustment,* 53.

38. "Budget and Plan," 11.

39. Cliff, Kanji, and Muller, "Mozambique Health Holding the Line," 18.

40. *Review of African Political Economy,* "NGOs and the Development Industry."

41. Dani Wadada Nabudere, "A Changing Eastern Europe: The Chance for Africa," *Southern African Political and Economic Monthly* 3.4 (1990): 4; Tajudeen Abdul-Raheem, "Is Africa Being Recolonised?" *SAPEM* 10.8 (1997), 5–7.

42. Hanlon, *Mozambique: Who Calls the Shots?,* 83.

43. Bratton, "The Politics of Government-NGO Relations in Africa"; Hyden, *No Shortcuts to Progress.*

44. Marshall, *War, Debt and Structural Adjustment;* Head, "Review Article."

45. Marshall and Roesch, "'Green Zones' Agricultural Cooperatives."

46. See Isaacman and Isaacman, *Mozambique;* Saul, *Difficult Road.*

47. Bernstein, "Agricultural 'Modernisation' and Structural Adjustment," 19.

48. Hermele, "Stick and Carrot," 184.

49. See "Corruption and Poverty Debated at People's Assembly," *Mozambiquefile* 162 (1990): 5.

50. Quoted in Pitcher, "Recreating Colonialism or Reconstructing the State," 50.

51. "Party Leader Interviewed on Frelimo's Perspectives," *Mozambique Information Office* 200 (1991): 3.

52. Saul, "Mozambique: The Failure of Socialism?," 20.

53. Hermele, *Mozambican Crossroads,* 31.

54. Rachel Waterhouse, "Economists Bemoan Lost Industrial Opportunities," *African Business,* Nov. 1991, 35.

## Conclusion

1. Atieno-Odhiambo, "The Rise and Decline of the Kenyan Peasant"; Brett, *Colonialism and Underdevelopment in East Africa;* Arrighi, "Labor Supplies in Historical Perspective"; Phimister, "Peasant Production and Underdevelopment in Southern Rhodesia."

2. O'Laughlin, "Through a Divided Glass," 9; Mackintosh, "Agricultural Marketing and Socialist Accumulation."

3. CEA, *Cotton Production in Mozambique;* Pitcher, *Politics in the Portuguese Empire;* Pitcher, "From Coercion to Incentives."

4. O'Laughlin, "Through a Divided Glass," 10–15.

5. Ibid., 25.

6. Geffray, *La cause des armes.*

7. Mamdani, "Disaster Prevention," 94.

8. Myers, West, and Eliseu, "Land Tenure Security"; Myers, Eliseu, and Nhachungue, "Security Conflict, and Reintegration in Mozambique"; Rose et al., "Residential and Agricultural Land Disputes"; Tanner et al., "State Farm Divestiture"; Tanner, Myers, and Oad, "Land Disputes and Ecological Degradation."

9. O'Laughlin, "Through a Divided Glass," 2; Myers and Weiss, "Second National Land Conference."

10. Pitcher, "Politics of the Countryside," 11.

11. Vasco Juma Sumbana, interview, 28 June 1993.

12. Fernando Chavango, interview, 28 June 1993.

13. Issa Shivji, "Land, the Terrain of Democratic Struggles in Africa," *CODESRIA Bulletin* 4 (1996): 23–26.

# Bibliography

## Oral Sources

In the course of this work, I conducted multiple interviews with cooperative members, peasant and private farmers, government and party officials, as well as foreign technicians and aid personnel. I also participated in party, government, and cooperative meetings. Material from these meetings is included in this study. A set of English- and Portuguese-language notes of the interviews and tape recordings is in my possession; another set in the library at the Ministry of Agriculture and Fisheries in Maputo, Mozambique.

## Government and Party Documents

Administrator of Xinavane post to the district administrator of Gaza, 25 Nov. 1958. Ref. no. 4/1958, Administration Office of Xinavane, Maputo Province.

Administrator of Xinavane post, Gestão Lopes Pires Ferreira. "Relatório: Cheias do Rio Incomati 1972." 5 Apr. 1972, Administration Office of Xinavane, Maputo Province.

Brigada A—Namaacha. "Relatório sobre o mês de novembro, 1982." Mimeo.

Chauque, Filipe Mitine. "Relatório. Relação das cantinas existentes e abandonadas." 19 Jan. 1978, Administration Office of Xinavane, Maputo Province.

*Código do trabalho dos indígenas nas colónias portuguêsas de Africa.* Lisbon: Imprensa Nacional, 1929.

Direcção Nacional de Habitação. *Aldeias comunais: Relatório da situação ao nivel nacional.* Maputo: DNH, 1977.

Frelimo. "Os graves acontecimentos de 1968 e as divergências ideológicas." Dar es Salaam: Mimeo, 1969.

———. *Documento da 8a sessão do Comité Central da Frelimo.* Maputo: Frelimo, 1976.

———. *Central Committee Report to the Third Congress.* London: Mozambique, Angola and Guinea-Bissau Information Center, 1977.

————. *Fourth Congress: Central Committee Report. Out of Underdevelopment to Socialism*. Maputo: INLD, 1983.

Government of Mozambique. "Policy Framework Paper, 1992–94." Maputo: Government of Mozambique, 1992.

ICM. "Mapa de produção de trigo. Campanha 1963." Lourenço Marques: ICM, 1964.

————. "Mapa de produção de trigo. Campanha 1968." Lourenço Marques: ICM, 1968.

————. "Mapa de produção de trigo. Campanha 1969." Lourenço Marques: ICM, 1970.

ICM-Brigada da Palmeira. "Relação dos agricultores da zona da Manhiça e Marracuene que se dedicaram a cultura do milho no campanha de 1971/72." Palmeira, Maputo Province: ICM, n.d.

JEC. "Mapa da produção de trigo. Campanha 1959." Lourenço Marques: JEC, 1960.

————. "Mapa da produção de trigo. Campanha 1961." Lourenço Marques: JEC, 1962.

"Mapa de mão do obra indígena. Sociedade Agrícola do Incomati." Administration Office of Xinavane, Maputo Province, 1959.

"Mapa resumo do recenseamento da população e do lancamento do imposto domicíliario." Administration Office of Xinavane, Maputo Province, 1959.

Ministério da Agricultura. "Analise económica dos sistemas de produção de cereais no contexto do PRE." Maputo: Direcção Nacional de Agricultura, 1988.

————. "Impacto do PRE no sector camponês. Analise dos termos de troca." Maputo: Direcção de Economia Agrária, 1988.

Ministério da Educação e Cultura. *Atlas geografico*. Sweden: Stockholm, 1980.

Missão de Inquérito Agrícola de Moçambique. *Estatísticas agrícolas de Moçambique 1970*. Lourenço Marques: Ministério do Ultramar, 1973.

MONAP. *MONAP II—Second Phase*. 2 vols. Maputo: MONAP, 1980.

————. *Annual Report—1982*. Maputo: MONAP, 1983.

————. *Annual Report—1983*. Maputo: MONAP, 1984.

NPC. *Mozambique Economic Report*. Maputo: National Planning Commission, 1984.

People's Republic of Mozambique. *Strategy and Program for Economic Rehabilitations, 1989–92*. Maputo: Government of Mozambique, 1989.

Projecto-CO1. "Relatório anual das actividades." 1982. Photocopy.

*Regulamento do trabalho dos indígenas*. Lisbon: Imprensa Nacional, 1930.

Republic Popular de Moçambique. Província de Maputo, Distrito de Manhiça, localidade de Ilha Josina Machel. "Relatório do conselho executivo a XI sessão da Assembleia de Localidade." 20 June 1982.

————. *Primeiro recenseamento geral da população*. Maputo: Conselho Coordenador de Recenseamento, 1983.

Secretaria distrital de administração civil, Distrito de Lourenço Marques,
Província de Moçambique. "Assunto: Sucessão de regedores indígenas.
Aditamento ás instruções de serviço no 18/1961, de 2–3 1961," 17 Mar. 1961,
Lourenço Marques, Moçambique.

## Newspapers, Bulletins, and Periodicals

*Africa Confidential*
*AIM Information Bulletin*
*Boletim de Agência Geral do Ultramar*
*Boletim informativo da oficina de história*
*Boletim oficial*
*CODESRIA Bulletin*
*Gazeta do agricultor*
*Mediafax*
*Mozambiquefile*
*Mozambique Information Office News Review*
*Notícias*
*Revista Garçia de Orta*
*Southern African Review of Books*
*Southern Africa Political and Economic Monthly*
*Tempo*
*Weekly Mail and Guardian*

## Books and Articles

Abrahamsson, Hans, and Anders Nilsson. *Mozambique: The Troubled Transition.*
     London: Zed Books, 1995.
Adam, Yussuf, and Teresa Cruz e Silva. *Mercados e preços nas zonas rurais.*
     Maputo: CEA, 1989.
Adam, Yussuf, Robert Davies, and Judith Head. "Mão-de-obra moçambicana
     na Rodésia do Sul." *Estudos moçambicanos* 2 (1981): 59–72.
Adam, Yussuf, and A. M. Gentili. "O movimento dos Liguilanilu no planalto de
     Mueda." *Estudos moçambicanos* 4 (1983): 41–75.
Araújo, Manuel G. M. de. "Communal Villages and the Distribution of the
     Rural Population in the People's Republic of Mozambique." In *Population
     and Development Projects in Africa,* ed. John I. Clarke, Mustafa Khogali, and
     Leszeke A. Kosínski, 153–62. Cambridge: Cambridge Univ. Press, 1985.
Arrighi, Giovanni. "Labour Supplies in Historical Perspective: A Study of the
     Proletarianisation of the African Peasantry in Rhodesia." In *Essays on the
     Political Economy of Africa,* ed. Giovanni Arrighi and John S. Saul, 180–234.
     New York: Monthly Review Press, 1973.
Atieno-Odhiambo, E. S. "The Rise and Decline of the Kenyan Peasant,
     1880–1992." *East African Journal* 9 (1972): 11–15.

Barker, Jonathan. "Gaps in the Debates about Agriculture in Senegal, Tanzania and Mozambique." *World Development* 13 (1985): 59–76.

Bates, Robert. *Markets and States in Tropical Africa: The Political Basis of Agricultural Policies.* Berkeley and Los Angeles: Univ. of California Press, 1981.

Beinart, William, and Colin Bundy. *Hidden Struggles in Rural South Africa.* Berkeley: Univ. of California Press, 1987.

Bernstein, Henry. "Agricultural 'Modernisation' and the Era of Structural Adjustment: Observations on Sub-Saharan Africa." *Journal of Peasant Studies* 18 (1990): 3–35.

Bowen, Merle L. "Peasant Agriculture in Mozambique: The Case of Chokwe, Gaza Province." *Canadian Journal of African Studies* 23 (1989): 355–79.

———. "Beyond Reform: Adjustment and Political Power in Contemporary Mozambique." *Journal of Modern African Studies* 30 (1992): 255–79.

Bratton, Michael. "The Politics of Government-NGO Relations in Africa." *World Development* 17 (1989): 569–87.

Bravo, Nelson Saraiva. *A cultura algodoeira na economia do norte de Moçambique.* Lisbon: Junta de Investigações do Ultramar, 1963.

Brett, E. A. *Colonialism and Underdevelopment in East Africa.* London: Heinemann, 1973.

Brito, Luis de. "Dependencia colonial e integração regional." *Estudos moçambicanos* 1 (1980): 23–32.

Bundy, Colin. *The Rise and Fall of the South African Peasantry.* Berkeley: Univ. of California Press, 1979.

Cabral, Amilcar. "Brief Analysis of the Social Structure in Guinea." In *Revolution in Guinea,* 56–75. New York: Monthly Review Press, 1972.

Cahen, Michel. *Mozambique: La révolution implosée.* Paris: L'Harmattan, 1987.

———. "Check on Socialism in Mozambique. What Check? What Socialism?" *Review of African Political Economy* 57 (1993): 46–59.

Carrilho, João, et al. *An Alternative Strategy for Agricultural Development.* Maputo: Ministry of Agriculture, 1990.

Casal, Adolfo. "Discurso socialista e camponeses africanos: Legitimação política-ideológica da socialização rural em Moçambique (FRELIMO, 1965–1984)." *Revista internacional de estudos africanos* 14–15 (1991): 35–75.

CEA. *The Mozambican Miner: A Study in the Export of Labour.* Maputo: CEA, 1977.

———. *Mozambican Miners in South Africa.* Maputo: CEA, 1979.

———. *Problemas de transformação rural na província de Gaza.* Maputo: CEA, 1979.

———. *Cotton Production in Mozambique: A Survey, 1936–1979.* Maputo: CEA, 1981.

———. *O papel do estado colonial: Apoio a produção agrária.* Maputo: CEA, 1982.

———. *Plantações de chá e economia camponesa.* Maputo: CEA, 1982.

———. "As cooperatives Ligualanilu no planalto de Mueda 1957–1963." *Boletim informativo da oficina de história.* Feb. 1983, 7–19.

———. *Famílias camponesas da Angonia no processo de socialização do campo.* Maputo: CEA, 1983.

Chirwa, Wiseman Chijere. "Alomwe and Mozambican Immigrant Labor in Colonial Malawi, 1890–1945." *International Journal of African Historical Studies* 27 (1994): 525–50.

Christie, Ian. *Machel of Mozambique.* Harare: Zimbabwe Publishing House, 1988.

Clarence-Smith, Gervase. *The Third Portuguese Empire, 1925–1975.* Manchester: Manchester Univ. Press, 1985.

Cliff, Julie, Najmi Kanji, and Mike Muller. "Mozambique Health Holding the Line." *Review of African Political Economy* 36 (1986): 7–23.

Coulson, Andrew. *Tanzania: A Political Economy.* New York: Oxford Univ. Press, 1982.

Cross, Michael. "O capitalism colonial e a força de trabalho: A economia política nas plantações de chá do norte de Moçambique 1930–1975." *Revista internacional de estudos africanos* 16–17 (1992–1994): 131–54.

Darch, Colin. "Are There Warlords in Mozambique?" *Review of African Political Economy* 45–46 (1989): 34–49.

Davidson, Basil. "The Politics of Armed Struggle: National Liberation in the African Colonies of Portugal." In *Southern Africa: The New Politics of Revolution,* ed. Basil Davidson et al., 17–102. Harmondsworth: Penguin, 1975.

———. *The People's Cause: A History of Guerrillas in Africa.* London: Longman, 1981.

Dinerman, Alice. *Mozambique: An Elusive Peace.* New York: National Council of Churches, 1991.

Dolny, Helena. "The Challenge of Agriculture." In *A Difficult Road: The Transition to Socialism in Mozambique,* ed. John S. Saul, 211–52. New York: Monthly Review Press, 1985.

Egerö, Bertil. *Mozambique: A Dream Undone. The Political Economy of Democracy, 1975–84.* Uppsala: Scandinavian Institute of African Studies, 1987.

Egerö, Bertil, and Jens Erik Torp. *Country Case Study on Mozambique.* Uppsala: Scandinavian Institute of African Studies, 1982.

Ferreira, Anibal do Nascimento. "Manhiça-campanha do trigo de 1953," *Gazeta do agricultor.* Mar. 1954, 65–69.

Finnegan, William. *A Complicated War: The Harrowing of Mozambique.* Berkeley and Los Angeles: Univ. of California Press, 1992.

First, Ruth. *Black Gold: The Mozambican Miner, Proletarian and Peasant.* Brighton: Harvester, 1983.

Galli, Rosemary. "On Peasant Productivity: The Case of Guinea-Bissau." *Development and Change* 18 (1987): 69–98.

Geffray, Christian. *La cause des armes au Mozambique: Anthropologie d'une guerre civile.* Paris: CREDU-Karthala, 1990.

Geffray, Christian, and Mögens Pedersen. "Sobre a guerra na província de Nampula. Elementos de análise e hipóteses sobre as determinações e consequências socio-económicas locais." *Revista internacional de estudos africanos* 4–5 (1986): 303–18.

Gersony, Robert. *Summary of Mozambican Refugee Accounts of Principally Conflict-Related Experience in Mozambique.* Washington, D.C.: Bureau for Refugee Program, 1988.

Gibbon, Peter, Kjell J. Havnevik, and Kenneth Hermele. *A Blighted Harvest: The World Bank and African Agriculture in the 1980s.* Trenton: Africa World Press, 1993.

Gilbert, Dennis. *Sandinistas. The Party and the Revolution.* Cambridge, Mass.: Basil Blackwell, 1988.

Habermeier, Kurt. "Algodão: Das concentrações a produção colectiva." *Estudos moçambicanos* 2 (1981): 37–58.

Hanlon, Joseph. *Mozambique: The Revolution under Fire.* London: Zed Press, 1984.

———. *Mozambique: Who Calls the Shots?* Bloomington: Indiana Univ. Press, 1991.

———. *Peace without Profit. How the IMF Blocks Rebuilding in Mozambique.* Oxford: James Currey, 1996.

Harries, Patrick. *Work, Culture, and Identity: Migrant Laborers in Mozambique and South Africa, c. 1860–1910.* Portsmouth: Heinemann, 1994.

Harris, Laurence. "Agricultural Cooperatives and Development Policy in Mozambique," *Journal of Peasant Studies* 7 (1980): 338–52.

Head, Judith. "Review Article: Paying the Piper." *Journal of Southern African Studies* 18 (1992): 430–38.

Hedges, David, et al. *História de Moçambique*, vol. 3. Maputo: Universidade Eduardo Mondlane, 1993.

Henriksen, Thomas. *Mozambique: A History.* London: Rex Collings, 1978.

———. *Revolution and Counterrevolution. Mozambique's War of Independence, 1964–1974.* Westport: Greenwood Press, 1983.

Hermele, Kenneth. *Contemporary Land Struggles on the Limpopo: A Case Study of Chokwe, Mozambique, 1950–1985.* Uppsala: AKUT, 1986.

———. *Land Struggles and Social Differentiation in Southern Mozambique. A Case Study of Chokwe, Limpopo, 1950–1987.* Uppsala: Scandinavian Institute of African Studies, 1988.

———. *Mozambican Crossroads.* Bergen: Chr. Michelsen Institute, 1990.

———. "Stick and Carrot: Political Alliances and Nascent Capitalism in Mozambique." In *Authoritarianism, Democracy, and Adjustment: The Politics of Economic Reform in Africa*, ed. Peter Gibbon, Yusuf Bangura, and Arve Ofstad, 169–87. Uppsala: Scandinavian Institute of African Studies, 1992.

Hirschmann, Albert O. "The Rise and Decline of Development Economics." In *Essays in Trespassing: Economics to Politics and Beyond*, 1–24. Cambridge: Cambridge Univ. Press, 1981.

Hyden, Goran. *Beyond Ujamaa in Tanzania: Underdevelopment and an Uncaptured Peasantry*. Berkeley: Univ. of California Press, 1980.

———. *No Shortcuts to Progress: African Development Management in Perspective*. Berkeley: Univ. of California Press, 1983.

Isaacman, Allen. *A Luta Continua: Creating a New Society in Mozambique*. Binghamton: State Univ. of New York, 1978.

———. "Chiefs, Rural Differentiation and Peasant Protest: The Mozambican Forced Cotton Regime, 1938–1961." *African Economic History* 14 (1985): 15–59.

———. *Cotton Is the Mother of Poverty: Peasants, Work, and Rural Struggle in Colonial Mozambique, 1938–1961*. Portsmouth: Heinemann, 1996.

Isaacman, Allen, and Barbara Isaacman. *Mozambique: From Colonialism to Revolution, 1900–1982*. Boulder: Westview Press, 1983.

Ishemo, Shubi Lugemalila. *The Lower Zambezi Basin in Mozambique. A Study in Economy and Society, 1850–1920*. Aldershot: Avebury, 1995.

Kriger, Norma J. *Zimbabwe's Guerrilla War: Peasant Voices*. Cambridge: Cambridge Univ. Press, 1992.

Kruks, Sonia, and Ben Wisner. "The State, the Party, and the Female Peasantry in Mozambique." *Journal of Southern African Studies* 11 (1984): 105–27.

Legassick, Martin. "South Africa: Capital Accumulation and Violence." *Economy and Society* 3 (1974): 253–91.

Littlejohn, Gary. "The Agrarian Marxist Research in Its Political Context: State Policy and the Development of the Soviet Rural Class Structure in the 1920s." In *Kritsman and the Agrarian Marxists*, ed. Terry Cox and Gary Littlejohn, 61–84. London: Frank Cass, 1984.

Lofchie, Michael F. *The Policy Factor: Agricultural Performance in Kenya and Tanzania*. Boulder: Lynne Rienner, 1989.

Lofchie, Michael F., and Stephen K. Commins. "Food Deficits and Agricultural Policies in Tropical Africa." *Journal of Modern African Studies* 20 (1982): 1–25.

Mackintosh, Maureen. "Economic Policy Context and Adjustment Options in Mozambique." *Development and Change* 17 (1986): 557–81.

———. "Agricultural Marketing and Socialist Accumulation: A Case Study of Maize Marketing in Mozambique." *Journal of Peasant Studies* 14 (1987): 243–67.

Mackintosh, Maureen, and Marc Wuyts. "Accumulation, Social Services and Socialist Transition in the Third World: Reflections on Decentralized Planning Based on the Mozambican Experience." *Journal of Development Studies* 24 (1988): 136–79.

Magaia, Lina. *Dumba Nengue: Run for Your Life: Peasant Tales of Tragedy in Mozambique*. Trenton: Africa World Press, 1988.

Mamdani, Mahmood. "Disaster Prevention: Defining the Problem." *Review of African Political Economy* 33 (1985): 92–96.

———. "Extreme but Not Exceptional: Towards an Analysis of the Agrarian Question in Uganda." *Journal of Peasant Studies* 14 (1987): 191–225.

———. *Citizen and Subject. Contemporary Africa and the Legacy of Late Colonialism.* Princeton: Princeton Univ. Press, 1996.

Marshall, Judith. *War, Debt and Structural Adjustment in Mozambique: The Social Impact.* Ottawa: North South Institute, 1992.

Marshall, Judith, and Otto Roesch. "The 'Green Zones' Agricultural Cooperatives of Nampula City: A New Phase in the Mozambican Cooperative Movement." *Journal of Southern African Studies* 19 (1993): 240–72.

Minter, William. *The Mozambican National Resistance (Renamo) as Described by Ex-Participants.* Washington, D.C.: Ford Foundation and the Swedish International Development Agency, 1989.

———. *Apartheid's Contras. An Inquiry into the Roots of War in Angola and Mozambique.* London: Zed Books, 1994.

Mondlane, Eduardo. *The Struggle for Mozambique.* Harmondsworth: Penguin Books, 1969.

Mota, Teresa P. "A produção e a industrialização do trigo em Moçambique. Panorama actual." *Agronomia moçambicana* 5.1 (1971): 11–28.

*Mozambique: Preliminary Study.* Uppsala: Swedish Univ. of Agriculture, Forestry and Veterinary Medicine, 1976.

Munslow, Barry. *Mozambique: The Revolution and Its Origins.* London: Longman, 1983.

Murray, Colin. *Families Divided.* Johannesburg: Ravan Press, 1981.

Myers, Gregory. "Competitive Rights, Competitive Claims: Land Access in Post-War Mozambique." *Journal of Southern African Studies* 20 (1994): 603–32.

Negrão, José. *One Hundred Years of African Rural Family Economy: The Zambezi Delta in Retrospective Analysis.* Lund: Univ. of Lund, 1995.

Neil-Thomlinson, Barry. "The Niassa Chartered Company 1891–1929." *Journal of African History* 18 (1977): 109–28.

Neocosmos, Michael. *The Agrarian Question in Southern Africa and "Accumulation from Below."* Uppsala: Scandinavian Institute of African Studies, 1993.

Newbury, Catharine. "State, Peasantry, and Agrarian Crisis in Zaire: Does Gender Make a Difference?" In *Women and the State in Africa,* ed. Jane L. Parpart and Kathleen A. Staudt, 91–110. Boulder: Lynne Rienner, 1989.

Newitt, Malyn. *A History of Mozambique.* Indianapolis: Indiana Univ. Press, 1995.

"NGOs and the Development Industry." *Review of African Political Economy* 71 (1997).

Nilsson, Anders. *Unmasking the Bandits: The True Face of the M.N.R.* London: European Campaign Against South African Aggression Against Mozambique and Angola, 1990.

O'Laughlin, Bridget. "Interpretations Matter: Evaluating the War in Mozambique." *SAR* 7.3 (1991): 23–33.

————. "Past and Present Options: Land Reform in Mozambique." *Review of African Political Economy* 63 (1995): 99–106.

————. "Through a Divided Glass: Dualism, Class and the Agrarian Question in Mozambique." *Journal of Peasant Studies* 23 (1996): 1–39.

O'Meara, Dan. "The Collapse of Mozambican Socialism." *Transformation* 14 (1991): 82–103.

Penvenne, Jeanne Marie. *African Workers and Colonial Racism. Mozambican Strategies and Struggles in Lourenço Marques, 1877–1962.* Portsmouth: Heinemann, 1995.

Phimister, Ian. "Peasant Production and Underdevelopment in Southern Rhodesia, 1890–1914." *African Affairs* 73 (1974): 217–28.

————. "Commodity Relations and Class Formation in the Zimbabwean Countryside, 1898–1920." *Journal of Peasant Studies* 13 (1986): 240–57.

Pitcher, M. Anne. *Politics in the Portuguese Empire.* Oxford: Clarendon Press, 1993.

————. "From Coercion to Incentives: The Portuguese Colonial Cotton Regime in Angola and Mozambique, 1946–1974." In *Cotton, Colonialism, and Social History in Sub-Saharan Africa*, eds. Allen Isaacman and Richard Roberts, 119–43. Portsmouth: Heinemann, 1995.

————. "Conflict and Cooperation: Gendered Roles and Responsibilities within Cotton Households in Northern Mozambique." *African Studies Review* 39.3 (1996): 81–112.

————. "Recreating Colonialism or Reconstructing the State: Privatisation and Politics in Mozambique." *Journal of Southern African Studies* 22 (1996): 49–74.

Plank, David N. "Aid, Debt, and the End of Sovereignty: Mozambique and Its Donors." *Journal of Modern African Studies* 31 (1993): 407–30.

Popkin, Samuel L. *The Rational Peasant: The Political Economy of Rural Society in Vietnam.* Berkeley: Univ. of California Press, 1979.

Raikes, Philip. "Ujamaa and Rural Socialism." *Review of African Political Economy* 3 (1975): 33–52.

————. "Wheat Production and the Development of Capitalism in North Iraqw, Tanzania." In *Rural Cooperation in Tanzania*, ed. Lionel Cliffe et al., 79–102. Dar es Salaam: Tanzanian Publishing House, 1975.

Rita-Ferreira, António. *O movimento migratório de trabalhadores entre Moçambique e a Africa do Sul.* Lisbon: Junta de Investigações do Ultramar, 1963.

Roesch, Otto, "Peasants and Collective Agriculture in Mozambique." In *The Politics of Agriculture in Tropical Africa*, ed. Jonathan Barker, 291–316. Beverly Hills: Sage Publications, 1984.

————. "Rural Mozambique and FRELIMO's Fourth Congress Policies: The Situation in the Baixo Limpopo." *Review of African Political Economy* 41 (1988): 73–91.

————. "Nampula: What's Left?" *SAR* 5.2 (1989), 9–13.

————. "Economic Reform in Mozambique: Notes on Stabilization, War and Class Formation." *Taamuli* 1 (1990): 116–37.

————. "Mozambique: The Debate Continues. Otto Roesch Replies." *SAR* 5.5 (1990): 28–29.

————. "Migrant Labour and Forced Rice Production in Southern Mozambique: The Colonial Peasantry of the Lower Limpopo Valley." *Journal of Southern African Studies* 17 (1991): 239–70.

————. "Mozambique Unravels? The Retreat to Tradition." *SAR* 7.5 (1992): 27–30.

————. "Renamo and the Peasantry in Southern Mozambique: A View from Gaza Province." *Canadian Journal of African Studies* 26 (1992): 462–84.

Saith, Ashwani. "Primitive Accumulation, Agrarian Reform and Socialist Transitions: An Argument." *Journal of Development Studies* 22 (1985): 1–48.

Saul, John S. *The State and Revolution in Eastern Africa.* New York: Monthly Review Press, 1979.

————. "Mozambique: The Failure of Socialism?" *SAR* 6.2 (1990), 20–24.

————. *Recolonization and Resistance in Southern Africa in the 1990s.* Trenton: Africa World Press, 1993.

————. "Rethinking the Frelimo State." In *Socialist Register 1993.* London: Merlin Press, 1993.

————, ed. *A Difficult Road: The Transition to Socialism in Mozambique.* New York: Monthly Review Press, 1985.

Scott, James C. *The Moral Economy of the Peasant: Rebellion and Subsistence in Southeast Asia.* New Haven: Yale Univ. Press, 1976.

Serra, Carlos. "O capitalismo colonial na Zambézia 1855–1930." *Estudos moçambicanos* 1 (1980): 33–52.

Silva, Manuel dias de. "Alguns aspectos do panorama económico-social de cultura de trigo em Moçambique." *Boletim da Sociedade de Estudos de Moçambique* 131 (1962): 41–45.

Simpson, Mark. "Foreign and Domestic Factors in the Transformation of Frelimo." *Journal of Modern African Studies* 31 (1993): 309–37.

Sylvester, Christine. *Zimbabwe: The Terrain of Contradictory Development.* Boulder: Westview Press, 1991.

Vail, Leroy. "Mozambique's Chartered Companies: The Rule of the Feeble." *Journal of African History* 17 (1976): 389–419.

Vail, Leroy, and Landeg White. *Capitalism and Colonialism in Mozambique: A Study of Quelimane District.* Minneapolis: Univ. of Minnesota Press, 1980.

Vines, Alex. *Renamo: Terrorism in Mozambique.* York: Univ. of York, 1991.

von Freyhold, Michaela. *Ujamaa Villages in Tanzania.* New York: Monthly Review, 1979.

Wardman, Ann. "The Co-operative Movement in Chokwe, Mozambique." *Journal of Southern African Studies* 11 (1985): 295–304.

West, Harry, and Gregory Myers. "A Piece of Land in a Land of Peace? State Farm Divestiture in Mozambique." *Journal of Modern African Studies* 34 (1996): 27–51.

Wield, David. "Mozambique—Late Colonialism and Early Problems of Transition." In *Revolutionary Socialist Development in the Third World,* ed. Gordon White, Robin Murray, and Christine White, 75–113. Brighton: Univ. of Sussex, 1983.

Williams, Gavin. "The World Bank and the Peasant Problem." In *Rural Development in Tropical Africa,* ed. Judith Heyer, Pepe Roberts, and Gavin Williams, 16–51. New York: St. Martin's Press, 1981.

Wilson, Kenneth B. "Cults of Violence and Counter–Violence in Mozambique." *Journal of Southern African Studies* 18 (1992): 527–83.

Wolpe, Harold. "Capitalism and Cheap Labour Power in South Africa: From Segregation to Apartheid." *Economy and Society* 1 (1972): 425–56.

World Bank. *Accelerated Development in Sub-Saharan Africa.* Washington, D.C.: World Bank, 1981.

———. *Sub-Saharan Africa: From Crisis to Sustainable Growth.* Washington, D.C.: World Bank, 1989.

———. *Mozambique: Restoring Rural Production and Trade.* Washington, D.C.: World Bank, 1990.

———. *Mozambique Food Security Study.* Washington, D.C.: World Bank, 1990.

———. *Mozambique Population, Health and Nutrition Sector Report.* Washington, D.C.: World Bank, 1990.

Wuyts, Marc. *Peasants and the Rural Economy in Mozambique.* Maputo: CEA, 1978.

———. "Economia política do colonialism em moçambique." *Estudos moçambicanos* 1 (1980): 9–22.

———. *Money and Planning for Socialist Transition: The Mozambican Experience.* Brookfield, Vt.: Gower, 1989.

Young, Sherilynn. "Fertility and Famine: Women's Agricultural History in Southern Mozambique." In *The Roots of Rural Poverty in Central and Southern Africa,* ed. Robin Palmer and Neil Parsons, 66–81. London: Heinemann, 1977.

**Dissertations and Unpublished Papers**

Adam, Yussuf. "Cooperativização agrícola e modificações das relações de produção no período colonial em Moçambique." M.A. thesis, Universidade Eduardo Mondlane, 1986.

Alexander, Jocelyn. "Land and Political Authority in Post-War Mozambique: A View from Manica Province." Madison: Land Tenure Center, University of Wisconsin–Madison/MOA, 1994.

————. "The Local State in Post-War Mozambique: Political Practice and Ideas about Authority." Paper presented at the African Studies Association Meeting, San Francisco, 24 Nov. 1996.

Borges Coelho, João Paulo Constantino. "Protected Villages and Communal Villages in the Mozambican Province of Tete (1968–1982). A History of State Resettlement Policies, Development and War." Ph.D. diss., University of Bradford, 1993.

Bowen, Merle L. "'Let's Build Agricultural Producer Cooperatives': Socialist Agricultural Development Strategy in Mozambique 1975–1983." Ph.D. diss., University of Toronto, 1986.

Campbell, Guillermo, et al. "MONAP Mid-Term Evaluation of MONAP II." 1982. Photocopy.

Chilundo, Arlindo Gonçalo. "The Economic and Social Impact of the Rail and Road Transportation Systems in the Colonial District of Moçambique (1900–1961)." Ph.D. diss., University of Minnesota, 1995.

Head, Judith. "State, Capital and Migrant Labour in Zambezia, Mozambique: A Study of the Labour Force of Sena Sugar Estates Limited." Ph.D. diss., University of Durham, 1980.

Juergensen, Olaf Henry Tataryn. "Peasants on the Periphery: A Geohistory of Rural Change in Mozambique, c. 1960–1992." Ph.D. diss., Queen's University, 1996.

Lemos, Manuel Jorge Correia de. "Fontes para o estudo do algodão em Moçambique: Documentos de arquivo, 1938–1974." M.A. thesis, Universidade Eduardo Mondlane, 1984.

Marshall, Judith. "Reflexões sobre uma experiência da alfabetização no campo Ilha Josina Machel 1983." 1984. Photocopy.

Myers, Gregory, Julieta Eliseu, and Erasmo Nhachungue. "Security, Conflict, and Reintegration in Mozambique: Case Studies of Land Access in the Postwar Period." LTC Research Paper no. 119. Madison: Land Tenure Center, University of Wisconsin–Madison/MOA, 1993.

Myers, Gregory, and Ricky Weiss, eds. "Second National Land Conference in Mozambique: Briefing Book." Madison: Land Tenure Center, University of Wisconsin–Madison/MOA, 1994.

Myers, Gregory, Harry G. West, and Julieta Eliseu. "Land Tenure Security and State Farm Divestiture in Mozambique: Case Studies in Nhamatanda, Manica, and Montepuez Districts." LTC Research Paper no. 110. Madison: Land Tenure Center, University of Wisconsin–Madison/MOA, 1993.

Negrão, José. "A produção e o comércio nas zonas libertadas." Maputo: Arquivo Historico de Moçambique, 1984.

Pitcher, M. Anne. "The Politics of the Countryside: Democracy and Economic Liberalization in Northern Mozambique." Paper presented at the African Studies Association Meeting, San Francisco, 24 Nov. 1996.

Roesch, Otto. "Socialism and Rural Development in Mozambique." Ph.D. diss., University of Toronto, 1986.

Rose, Laurel, et al. "Residential and Agricultural Land Disputes in Maputo." Madison: Land Tenure Center, University Wisconsin–Madison, 1992.

Stockholm Group for Development Studies. "Market Intervention and Price Policies for Agricultural Marketing in Mozambique." Mimeo. 1990.

Tanner, Christopher, et al. "State Farm Divestiture in Mozambique: Property Disputes and Issues Affecting New Land Access Policy—The Case of Chokwe, Gaza Province." A report by the University of Wisconsin–Madison, Land Tenure Center for USAID-Maputo and the Government of the Republic of Mozambique. Madison: Land Tenure Center, University of Wisconsin–Madison, 1992.

Tanner, Christopher, Gregory Myers, and Ramchand Oad. "Land Disputes and Ecological Degradation in an Irrigation Scheme: A Case Study of State Farm Divestiture in Chokwe, Mozambique." LTC Research Paper no. 111. Madison: Land Tenure Center, University of Wisconsin–Madison/MOA, 1993.

Tickner, Vincent. "Government and Food Distribution in Mozambique." Discussion Paper. 13 Mar. 1979. Photocopy.

West, Harry G. "Sorcery of Construction and Sorcery of Ruin: Power and Ambivalence on the Mueda Plateau, Mozambique (1882–1994)." Ph.D diss., University of Wisconsin–Madison, 1997.

White, Christine Pelzer, and Alpheus Manghezi. "The Role of Cooperative Agriculture in Transforming Labour Relations and Gender Relations: Experiences from the Green Zones, Maputo, Mozambique." Maputo: CEA, 1985.

# Index

*Page references in italic indicate maps, tables, and figures.*